FROM EGYPT TO MÉXICO

A GAY MAN'S JOURNEY IN ADDICTION AND FAITH

David McClanahan

Glue Pot Press
New Orleans, Louisiana

Copyright © 2025 David McClanahan All Rights Reserved

No part of this publication may be reproduced, distributed, or transmitted in any form or by any means, including photocopying, recording, or other electronic or mechanical methods, without the prior written permission of the author, except in the case of brief quotations embodied in critical reviews and certain other noncommercial uses permitted by copyright law.

ISBN: 978-1-7379423-8-2

davidmcclan@icloud.com

"Be yourself; everyone else is already taken."

— Oscar Wilde

EGYPT, THE EARLY YEARS

My parents, Paul and Ruth, shipped out from New York to create a new life of service as missionaries for the United Presbyterian Church. My father was returning to Egypt, the land of his birth, where his parents had lived as missionaries for forty years. Gazing into the deep blue of the Mediterranean, my father assured his uncertain wife,

"Ruth, you're going to love it. I am so happy. We will make a fine home together in Assiut."

"I'm a little afraid, Paul, I know so little, but do love you and want the best for us."

My mother, originally from Pittsburgh, had embarked on a journey for which she had no experience or understanding. The family of five, soon to be six, took the ocean voyage across the Atlantic through the Straits of Gibraltar to the port of Alexandria. From there, it was an eight-hour dusty train ride to their new home in Assiut.

Thick climbing vines rose two floors and shaded a part of the wide veranda. A grand stone staircase welcomed guests to the second floor of their new home. *Fellaheen* (peasant) laundry women climbed a circular staircase at the back of the house to the roof. From the veranda, a verdant view ran through the gardens, over the six-foot stone wall, across the narrow road, and into the brown flowing waters of the Nile. Short shepherd boys armed with thick sticks ran herds of sheep and goats along the path.

By Thanksgiving, members of the Egyptian Presbyterian Mission were taking bets on when my mother would go into labor. Her labor was long but not complicated. Her doctor had advised her not to have another child, but she consulted with a mission nurse and together in prayer, she decided to risk it.

When I was little she told me, "David, I felt guided and knew you would be a special boy."

She was proud of her mothering skills. When another mission wife gave birth and couldn't breastfeed, my mother gladly took up the task. From the start, there was already less of my mother for me.

My father was a dignified, erudite, and humble man. Born in Fayum, Egypt, he was fluent in Arabic. He went into the Christian villages outside of Assiut and served the people, giving sermons, conducting funerals, and presiding at weddings. He was president of Assiut College, a boys' preparatory school where he taught English. The mission compound was part of Assiut College.

At nine months, I reached out from a photo, a smiling plump baby on an oriental rug, with hair standing on end. People drew me. Visitors came to our home for tea. My siblings would push me into the salon to break the ice, and I would try to help my mother serve tea. My efforts were not enough. I was the fourth child, and my need to be close was too much for her. A village girl of sixteen, Samiah, was hired to care for me. She, too, left me alone in a bassinet on the veranda for hours. Later, my sister told me that our mother said she fired Samiah because she put me between her legs in a sexual way.

My oldest brother Neal, who was eight years older, tried to help with my education by taking me around different parts of the garden and naming the insects and plants. After two years of silence, one afternoon I spoke my first words to Neal, "The sky is blue."

My first awareness of sexual feelings came at five, getting into a hall closet with an Egyptian boy and playing with his penis. His body was dark and warm. My mother was speaking with Anis, our cook, when we sneaked away. Realizing we were gone, she went looking for us. She came to the closet door and hearing voices, drew it open. "David, what are you doing? You bad boy, you two leave this closet at once." I was chastened, but my interest remained.

One Sunday, my father took my hand, and we met some missionary friends of his. We had tea in the garden and walked a little in the compound. We passed a bed of lovely pansies. In conversation my father referred to a colleague as a pansy and a weak sister. They laughed. I felt ashamed, I somehow knew it applied to me.

Mahmoud, a friendly young Egyptian teacher befriended my brothers. He would sometimes take me for a ride on his bicycle to visit neighboring Egyptian families. I was afraid of sitting on the handlebars yet enjoyed leaning against Mahmoud's chest. When we arrived, I was happy being offered hard candies, *Itfuddal* please have some, *Shukrin, shukrin awee* thank you, thank you very much.

I wanted to be like my brother Paul. He was adventurous, hung out with the servants, and learned Arabic. He was exceptionally clever in negotiating trades with the Egyptian kids and gardeners. Paul became famous for one bold act. There was a bean field between the mission apartments and a small farm. Kids loved to play hide and seek in the bean field. One day, a six-foot cobra was spotted slithering between the bean stalks. All the kids ran screaming, "Cobra, Cobra." Paul, on the other hand, ran to grab a wooden stilt. He returned and struck the serpent with a fatal blow. Paul was a hero. With such a victory, he got to skin the snake and hang the trophy on the back of his bedroom door.

After forty years of serving as missionaries in Egypt, my grandparents had become fluent in Arabic. They made great friends with several wealthy Christian and Muslim landowners, many of whom were educated in England. Naturally, these were their friends because they shared language, education, and cultural backgrounds. My grandfather developed great respect for Islam and its scholars. At one point he wrote that if he had not been born a Christian, he would have chosen to be Muslim.

One of their friends, Alfie Bey, would host a lovely Christmas luncheon with traditional English plum cake. Inside the cakes were two coins dipped in real gold. There was a blessing and then significant posturing by the kids. "I can't wait to get that coin." "Yes, you can. You got it two years ago." "Yes, but that doesn't count." Fortunately, one year, I got the shiny prize, and it remained a treasure.

Alfie Bey kept an elegant houseboat moored on the Nile. He graciously invited our family to tea with wonderful date treats. The Leon Pasha family had a nearby mansion on the Nile. Boats could dock, and guests went up the marble stairs to enter it. To me, it was like a small palace, filled with a sweeping interior staircase, lovely paintings, and rich Persian rugs.

Among the missionary community, there was one woman who I felt was very special, Lillian Trasher. She said she did not know why, but God had called her to Assiut. After several months, one morning she opened her door and found a crying baby on her doorstep. She picked up the baby and looked for the mother. There was no mother. She did her best to care for the baby. Two weeks later, she opened her door and there were two babies laying there. Desperately poor women had heard she would take in children they could not care for. Not only children were left, but bags of food started arriving. She needed to move to make accommodation. As the need increased the donations increased. An orphanage was founded, followed by a school. When we would go to the orphanage to visit, I remember she was a large woman, and the children loved to hide in her skirts and dresses. She became known as Umm Lillian, Mother Lillian. Her children never went without a meal. She became famous for her love, generosity, and compassion.

Although we lived on a missionary's budget, we were able to have a cook and other household help. The cook I remember most was Anis, a short, small, and crabby man. Part of my vivid memory were the terrible bunions on both his feet. Anis cut big holes in his shoes to accommodate them so the bunions stuck out. His temper especially tempted Paul who would sneak into the kitchen and tease him. Anis would explode, grab a knife, and give chase to Paul. Paul would fly under a bed and Anis would lean over, panting and crying out, "*Inta ouze Zakina*"? "*Ouze Zakina*", You want the knife? Want the knife?

One day I heard extra noise in the kitchen and ventured in. There in the corner was a wooden box with cries and flapping emanating from it. Anis, turned a crooked eye on me and said, "*Inta auz eh*"? What do you want? I said nothing but went over to the box. "*Dijaj*" chickens, Anis said. Fascinated, I got down on my knees and peered in. How funny they were, stomping around, sticking their beaks through the sides of the box. I wondered what kind of pet they would make.

Anis finished what he was doing and said to me, "*Taaila henna,* come here." He picked up the box and a knife and headed down the back wooden staircase. I followed at a distance wondering why Anis was taking a knife out of the kitchen. He would never allow kids near his knives. When we got outside, I followed him to a large grassy area where some boys were playing soccer.

Anis sat on an old green wooden bench, lifted the box lid, and took out a chicken by its legs. It was flapping like crazy. He let the lid drop. Anis held the chicken between his knees, grabbed its head, and drew the knife across its throat.

I screamed in horror as the chicken was released and danced through the grass. Its head hanging by a thread, crimson sprayed in all directions. The second chicken was snatched out, this time the execution was done poorly. Blood splattered over Anis's right hand. Anis rose and wiped his hand on his *gelibia* robe. Bright, red-colored fingerprints embedded in the cloth. To my child's mind, he was a murderer. After that, when chicken was served for dinner, I would pet it and say, "poor chicken."

Each summer, we would move to *Sidi Bishr*, a mission camp built near a railroad line on the desert sands at the edge of Alexandria. Our woven straw cabins had no electricity. We used oil lanterns at night and butane for cooking. With his donkey, an older gentleman brought us butane supplies and big blocks of ice for the ice box. In this setting, my father would show his whistling agility. He could whistle any hymn, folk song, or Egyptian lullaby. But the most important whistle to me was his unique family call. It was gentle yet rang out over the small straw homes and sand, telling us to come, usually for dinner. It also served as a beacon if we got lost.

There was a little round swimming pool in the sand beside one of the cabins. Of course, swimming was one of the mission kids' favorite activities. I was shy to be in the water with the kids splashing everyone. I also felt shame. All the others wore bathing suits appropriate for the early 1950s. My mother had put me in a wool bathing outfit that went from my neck down to my knees. I felt horribly out of place and alone.

Figure 1 Grandma, Grandpa Assuit

Figure 2 Dad, prep school

Figure 3 Mom, senior prom

Figure 4 With Mom Assuit

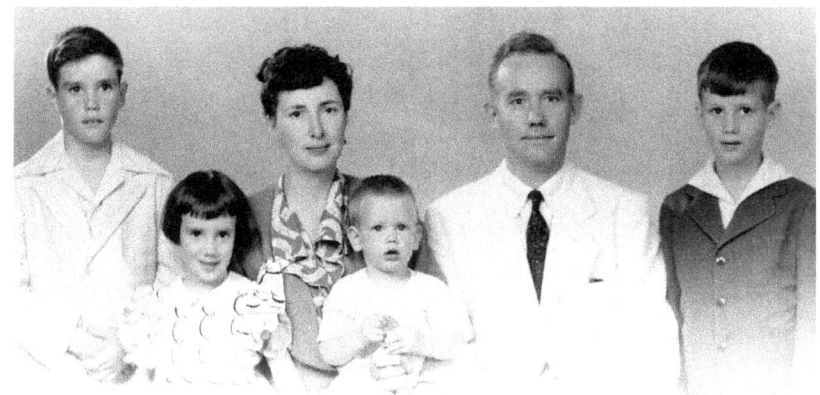

Figure 5 Whole Family

Figure 6 Family Outing

Figure 7 With Dad in Luxor

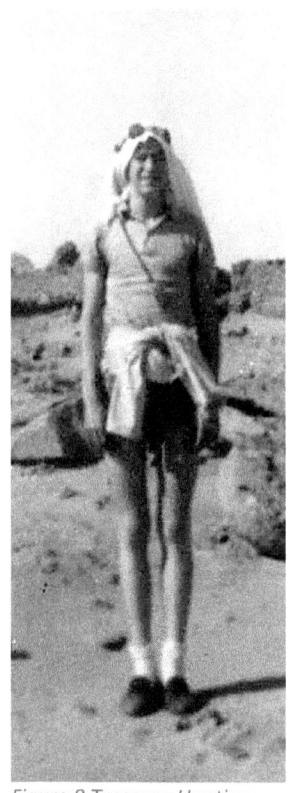
Figure 8 Treasure Hunting

Figure 9 Nile Houseboat

My mother, Ruth, was struggling. In ignorance, she had embraced a foreign life out of love for my father as well as from her adventurous nature. She went from being a free spirit who loved the arts into a strict religious environment that demanded conformity. She also lived directly under the eye of her critical mother-in-law who decades earlier had adjusted well to Egyptian culture. My mother had no gift for languages. Her primary roles were to be a good mother and missionary wife. She lived under continuous stress and suffered emotionally.

My father carried much responsibility within the mission community as the president of Assiut College. This included considerable interaction with the government officials of Assiut. He might show up for dinner whenever possible but was generally either absent or in his home office with the door closed. A couple of times I went with him to a Christian village to hear him preach in Arabic. These journeys together were special memories. He would also try to help my mother. If he were in the house during nap time, he would say, "Quiet, be quiet, your mother is resting."

One Sunday, when I was six, we were preparing for church. My father rushed my mother because she was always late. He called out, "Ruth, Ruth we're going to be late. I must go, please hurry." We started down the wooden back steps. I turned to look at my mother. Surprised, I said, "Mommy, Mommy, aren't you going to wear a dress?" In her confusion, my mother had only put a slip on.

I did love going to church on Sundays. I would try to join in as soon as I recognized the music. My grandfather, grandmother, and father were excellent singers. My mother really couldn't sing. I was especially enthusiastic and loud when it was father's time to lead the worship service. I would throw myself into making a joyful noise unto the Lord! My exuberance got to be too much for my father. One Sunday evening, during a hymn, he came down from the pulpit, took me to the back of the congregation, and scolded me.

My mother took me to an unfamiliar grey building in my sixth year. I heard children's voices but could not understand them very well. We walked into a preschool classroom filled with dark-skinned, dark-eyed children speaking Arabic. I froze, looked down, and began to tremble. She left me. At snack time, there were biscuits and water-buffalo milk. I was set up by my bright green eyes, silver blond hair, pink and white skin. I was poked, pushed, tapped and scrutinized. Day after day, my mother brought me back. She had to break my hold on her to get me through the door.

My fear and rage grew within the walls of the Egyptian preschool. In final desperation, I spread a bowel movement across the cement walls of the classroom. My mother gave in and took me home, briefly ending my exile from her. At home, she would read to me sometimes. I loved it but had trouble reading myself. I would get words backwards and was terrible at spelling.

"But Mommy, I don't want you to go," I said as she pried my hand out of hers. She was dropping me off at Schutz, the mission boarding school in Alexandria. I was seven.

"I have to go now honey,"

"Why Mommy, please don't go,"

"I explained it to you before, you need to go to a real school,"

"I don't want to go to school, I want to be with you Mommy," I begged.

"I told you that you can't, you have to go to school.... Don't worry, Daddy and I will come visit you."

"But why Mommy?"

"Paul," she said to my second brother who was at the school with me, "Take his hand, I'll miss my train"

"But, Mom, I don't want to be responsible for him."

"Paul, take his hand, he's your younger brother!" Hand-taken, not a word passed between the brothers.

I ran as fast as I could up the large cement steps to the dormitory's third floor balcony. Falling on my knees on the tile floor, pressing my face against the wooden slats of the balustrade, I was just in time to see my mother's taxi exit the rusty iron gate and make the right turn through the glass peaked walls.

"Mommy, mommy, "come back, come back," I cried desperately, not caring what the other kids thought. "I'll be good Mommy, don't leave me" ...... and she did.

I lost my first fight to a boy a year older and was then ignored by the other kids. I hated mealtimes, everyone had to stay seated until all were finished. The big kids wolfed down their food and glared at me, "Hurry up, David, hurry up, come on, we want to go." I struggled to swallow my food. With the pressure, I felt like throwing up and fought to keep food down. Finally, the other kids could go, and I remained alone.

I felt safe during the two daily chapel services and church services on Sundays. I continued to love singing and had a strong voice. Hymns were my salvation. The tunes and words elevated me above the circumstances of the school. "I Need Thee Every Hour," was a favorite of my grandmother's and felt true for me. I could close my eyes, forget where I was, and belt out the words.

 My brother Neal had already gone to the United States for prep school. My brother Paul was popular and funny. He excelled at roller skating backward and could spit a wad the furthest. He found little time for a seven-year-old younger brother. My sister Alice, three years older, was busy with her girlfriends.

I often cried myself to sleep but did not dare make a sound. If the boys in the other bunks heard me, I would be teased mercilessly. Paul did let me sleep briefly with him, but then I had to go to my own bed. I went around the walled campus in a daze and had trouble remembering instructions given by the school staff. For several months I was lost.

One day as I was walking out the back door of the dorm, something was flung over the wall. It was making a noise, so I went to see. The flying object was a tiny kitten, unable to breathe from the fall. It was gasping, so I carried it into the building for help. A teacher came, looked, and said, "It is too small, it can't get better," and walked away. I held it for a long time, crying and hoping it could live. I experienced its suffering and death. My spirit was crushed. To this day, the sound of a young cat crying twists my stomach.

I prayed hard to be rescued from boarding school but did not know that it would take a war to free me. After two and a half months, words were whispered throughout the school that a real war was about to begin. Everything changed. Classes were cancelled. Students were told to pack their suitcases and be ready to move. Egyptian mission parents were arriving to get their kids. It meant my mother would be coming. I almost peed in my pants in anticipation.

It was explained to the older kids, who passed it on, that the President of Egypt, Gamal Abdul Nasir, had nationalized the Suez Canal. He had seized it from the French and British companies' control. There was going to be a war on Egypt by England, France, and Israel. Schutz school was eerily quiet. Local kids sent home, and doubt remained about the rest of us.

American nationals would be flown out of Cairo, 140 miles up the Nile from Alexandria. A convoy of cars and buses formed to take the Desert Road to Cairo by night. A line of about fifty vehicles crept through the desert with lights off. The danger of being seen by enemy planes was great.

About two hours into the journey, the convoy stopped for a bathroom break. I really had to go bad and hit the sand. The moon gave faint light, casting ghostly shadows of the other buses and cars. At that moment, overhead came a growing sound like thunder. It was whispered that it was the sound of the engines of bombers heading for Cairo, our destination. I froze and held my breath, fearfully excited.

We arrived in Cairo while it was still dark. Housing was with friendly American and Egyptian families. Halfway through the first day we learned that Cairo Airport had been bombed. There was no means of escape by air. Fear of more bombing made blackout window covers obligatory for all buildings throughout Cairo. I wanted to peek out and see what was happening on the street but was told how dangerous it was. Being forbidden to look made me want to do it more!

The situation lasted for days until word came to form another night convoy and return to Alexandria for evacuation. The U.S. Navy would rescue us. This exit strategy was even better. I had been on ocean liners and loved watching the waves. The mission decided that all male missionaries would stay at their posts, only women and children would leave Egypt. My father would not be with us, which was a great blow to my mother. We headed to the Desert Road for a blackout return convoy to Alexandria.

For a few days we stayed on the school campus. This time I was happy. I was with my mother, but I wasn't sure she was happy. I tried to make her laugh. The day came to head for the harbor and board ship. Our assigned destroyer was at double capacity, so hammocks were strung up in strange places. We got to go up to the deck for a little while before dinner. It was hard to see at first, but there was some activity in the sky. There were two fighters, and one was chasing the other. The one in front flew low above the water, using the American ships as protection. In a flash, they were both gone.

Despite the crowded state of the ship, the meals were fun, better than the usual fare at Schutz. The crew also organized some games and activities for us. The ship headed for Crete, where we moved to an aircraft carrier. In the new setting, the staff wanted to put me in the men's section, a different part of the ship from my mother's. She stood up to them and refused, saying, "He's only seven."

We arrived in Naples in the early evening. We kids were allowed on deck to see the famous Italian city from the bay. After all the blackouts it appeared sparkly. We were put up at a cheap *pension* boarding house in the city. Our room, three flights up, had two beds, one for my mother and sister and the other for Paul and me. How long we would be staying was not clear, so I was sent to the American School in Naples.

I joined a class of first and second graders that had been running a couple of months. It was a new setting, I knew no one. When I entered the classroom, the teacher asked me to introduce myself. I gulped and said, "David." The teacher asked, "And where are you from David?" I answered, "Egypt." The teacher instructed me on the dangers of lying and asked me again angrily, "Where are you from, David?" I was embarrassed and again answered, "Egypt." This time the teacher pointed out to the class that I was a bad example to them and not to be like me. I didn't understand but felt shamed.

Back at the pension, I cried as I told my mother what had happened. The following day, she went to the school and clarified with the teacher. After my mother left, in the hallway the teacher said she was sorry to me. But she didn't say or explain anything to the other pupils when we entered the classroom. I felt ashamed again because the others still thought I was bad. I knew what she had done wasn't right, and I hated being in her classroom.

Because of the circumstances, my mother had little money. She made tomato soup nightly in our room and served it in green plastic bowls. My bowl got a crack in it, and I would get soup on my pants. My birthday happened during the six weeks we were in Naples. My mother managed to get one piece of cake from somewhere and put a candle in it. There was no money for a gift. It was the rainy season. We had to wrap our feet in plastic to stay dry.

At last, word came that it was safe to travel to the U.S. The first leg of the trip was to Copenhagen. All the Christmas decorations were up, and the city was dazzling. As we walked down a busy boulevard, we saw a box with moving images in a showcase window. It was called a television. I was mesmerized. Before we left Copenhagen, we went to see the royal palace. The queen of Denmark came out onto a balcony. She waved at the gathered crowd. I was excited, "Look Mommy, Look. The Queen is waving at me!"

Figure 10 Pittsburg, Dancing with Mom

Arriving in America, we settled where my father was hired as pastor of the Third Presbyterian Church of Pittsburgh. It was Christmas time and Aunt Kay's large house had many lights and a giant Christmas tree. There were so many presents under the tree that I got tired of counting them. The big morning came, and gifts were passed out. I got a box with a toy tank inside. I thought it was great. A little later, I was handed another box. I handed it back saying, "Oh no…. I already have my gift." Everyone laughed. In Egypt there was only one small gift per child.

I was attending third grade in the Brentwood section of Pittsburgh. I was a novelty in the classroom because of my background. In fourth grade, I made a rule I would kiss any classmate who walked by my desk, boy or a girl. The idea had just come to me. The game was short-lived but fun. The teachers found me dubious due to my claims during geography and world history that I was born in Egypt and had visited Italy, Greece, and Denmark. The children of Pittsburgh did not travel much beyond the Pennsylvania Turnpike.

My parents thought it would be good for me to see a clinical psychologist. I would not let my mother out of my sight. I followed her to the laundry, the corner store, every place. My fearful clinging was disturbing to her. They also believed I was having trouble with my sexual identity.

At last, I had a best friend. His name was Ralph. We were in the same class. We played together, and I enjoyed telling him tales I had learned from my father. My father's stories were of thieves, smugglers, and the Desert Patrol in the Sahara. One Halloween, Dad gathered kids of all ages around a tree on the college grounds. He sat them down and began with a new tale. At the point where the Desert Patrol fired on the smugglers, an actual gun went off, and a dummy cascaded down through the branches, landing among the children. They screamed and fled as angry parents admonished my father.

I did not care for any sports activities. Pittsburgh, of course, was dedicated to baseball. I knew nothing about the sport, so when the teacher requested a suggestion for a recess activity I said, "How about the game where we hit a ball with a stick?" When forced to join Little League, I ensured getting lost enough times to be dropped.

THE RETURN-BOARDING SCHOOL

Figure 11 The Return

After three years in the States, my father's parish assignment was over, and we returned to Egypt. I had to go back to boarding school in Alexandria. I re-entered the Schutz world with fear. I was afraid of the other boys my age and school itself was not easy due to my dyslexia. My sixth-grade teacher did not see promise in me and put me in a remedial group. I grew to hate how she spoke to me and turned her back when I had a question.

We continued to have a chapel service every morning with the hymns that brought me some comfort. On Sundays we attended a service at the Anglican church downtown. It was a musty old church with an old organ. We always knew when a hymn was coming. We would hear the hooof hooof as the little Egyptian man, hidden back behind the organ, started pumping the billows.

I became a member of the Coptic Evangelical Church, the Egyptian Presbyterian church. I remembered the church where the ceremony was held. I needed to go to the bathroom and went looking. What I found was not a toilet but a hole in the ground with two porcelain footprints. I crouched as was required. Part of a newspaper was present to be read and used as toilet paper.

My friends were older girls who enjoyed my humor and loud laugh. I was most comfortable with them and felt safe. With the boys, it was the opposite. I never knew when I would be teased for "being a girl." I felt alone and different. I had trouble sleeping. Heights frightened me, but I had ended up on an upper bunk because I didn't stand up for myself.

 One night I felt shivers from a new feeling and sweat trickled down my body. There was no breeze. I had to go to the bathroom. I thought about the room down the hall on the right, and Danny. To reach the bathroom, I had to pass by his room. I shook with the new feeling. I didn't know what it was. Pale moonlight filtering through the thick balcony shutters streaking the room in gray. I tried to pretend I didn't have to pee but that only worked briefly.

Crunching myself in the corner of my bed, I slowly extended my left leg, searching for the top step. I shifted my weight to that leg and made sure of my balance. Then came the right leg over the top. Loud breathing came from two bunks, and I paused. When I was satisfied that I hadn't woken Mike in the lower bunk, I kept going. My bare feet hit the cool tiles, and I inhaled suddenly.

I prayed no one would hear me. Moving down the black-and-white stone hallway, I was suddenly unsure of where I was going. I felt drawn to Danny's room on my right and froze as I imagined going in that direction. I felt pulled relentlessly and forgot about the bathroom. My trembling increased. Fear held me back, but with a pounding heart I reached out. I still had a chance to escape, but my hand moved on its own. It was too late.

Inside the door and there he was, one of four, sleeping in his white undies. His body slightly curved, his bristly hair pointing up, his dark, suntanned skin etched against the white sheets. Frozen, I started to shake. A great feeling of longing came over me. My bladder released and a stream of urine surged down my leg. Running, I left the puddle. I was twelve years old.

The only safe place was the library. Boys didn't like the library, especially on weekends when they played basketball and tennis. I was secure within the bookshelves, loosing myself in the novels and histories. I discovered several anatomy books with drawings of men's bodies including penises. This excited me and brought a lump to my throat. Somehow, I knew the word "homosexual" and looked through the library but could find no material.

Pomegranate bushes lined the back wall of the school. Parallel to the wall, lay a street with a row of houses. One of the houses had different women at times hanging out of the windows. These were large women, some had children with them. One of the older boys told me it was a whore house. I'd collect some pomegranates and gaze, wondering what their life was like. Over a wall we passed during track, occasionally we could see a teenage Egyptian boy. He pulled up his *gelibia* and danced with his penis bouncing around. His surprise appearances motivated me to run.

I came across a writing about Christine Jorgensen, an early American transsexual. It was the only information I could find about sex. I wondered if I would have to become a woman to be able to love. The idea scared me, and I stopped my investigation. I continued being humiliated. I strove to get out of sports activities and hide in the library.

I was desperate to go home. Train travel was difficult. There was no air conditioning, and the windows were open with wooden shutters covering them. The dust came billowing in, it was hard to breathe. Three classes were available: first class, which was too expensive; second class, which we took; and the third class that the *fellaheen* peasants used.

My father told the story of a missionary once having to use third class. It was packed with people, baskets, chickens, goats and more. One large woman was sitting across from him. The conductor came by, and she gave him one ticket. There was a giggle under her *gelibea* dress. Being clever, the conductor told her to bring the child out. She did, seemed ashamed, and paid for the child. After the conductor left, she gave the traditional joy cry and pulled two more children out from under her.

I finally got to go home to Assiut. My father was there to greet me but not my mother. I asked where she was. "Your mother isn't feeling well and is staying in the guest room." I could hear her inside crying and crying. She stayed in the guest room for the two weeks of my vacation. My father took her the food and medications she needed.

Back at school I made friends with a new boy, Hank. He was Roman Catholic which was unusual. Because I liked him, I became interested in what it meant to be Catholic. There were only three in the whole community. I was interested in how they worshiped. I told the headmaster I wanted to go to Mass with Hank. He said I would have to get written permission from my parents to do such a thing. I was sure my parents would be fine with it. One of my father's most admired friends was a Jesuit priest. It took six weeks for the answer to come back. The mail was slow and censored. I went with Hank to Mass a few times and was fascinated by the mystery and ritual.

Another time, the school choir sang at a Catholic Church. As we were leaving, a couple of priests were sitting outside smoking cigarettes. We were shocked. Smoking was sinful in our world. And then the second shoe dropped. It was whispered that they drank wine. This was too bad to be true; they seemed like good, friendly men.

At school, I got criticism from a housemother. I was walking by her one day and she stopped me.

"Walk down the hall as I watch you." Then she called me back,

"You don't swing your arms like normal people." I did not know what she meant.

"You walk like this," and she held her arms straight at her sides without swinging them at all.

"You are supposed to walk like this," she said, swinging her arms back and forth as she walked.

"Try swinging your arms." I did but my arms went with their matching leg, left arm with left leg, right with right.

"Wrong, you have to coordinate opposite arm with each leg." It took me a long time to get it right. Once again, my natural was unnatural. The school held a retreat at the desert estate of a Muslim friend of the headmaster and his wife. It was about thirty miles away from Alexandria. The desert started with a rough stone covered surface and then became sand of rolling waves. There were some general sessions and then the students were invited to go out away from others for private prayer time. I went off by myself and walked for twenty minutes.

I was alone. As I stood praying, I heard a voice say, "You are my Temple." I shivered; I looked around. There was no one there. And then it came again, "You are my Temple." I slowly realized then that it must be God speaking to me. I was amazed and overcome. A bell rang and I returned to the main building. I told no one of my experience, afraid to be mocked. I felt empowered to go on with my life, in spite of my deep unhappiness.

Egypt was a client state of the Soviet Union. The Soviet Union wanted to promote its culture and artistic abilities. The school had arranged for certain students to attend a performance by the Bolshoi Ballet. I was included because I studied ballet.

At last, the night I'd been waiting for. I knew swearing was bad, so, oh my goodness, the Bolshoi Ballet. For several days I planned my outfit from my meager wardrobe. I wanted to look formal for the event but only had my one Sunday outfit. The good news was that those dress pants fit me well. I was conscious that they were tight on my bottom.

What could I wear on top but a plain white shirt and open it at the collar. No, the only thing that would do was show my skinny chest. Better use one of my three ties. The mauve one had food stains, so that wouldn't work. My green one which matched my eyes was a little short, which left the red one. A bright color that would help me stand out. The fact that it was a clip on made the knot perfect.

The school van was ready by 5pm. I was too excited to eat so was one of the first aboard. I took a window seat so I could look out and not have to talk to any other boys. If a girl sat beside me that would be great. The trip into the Alexandria concert hall seemed long. I tried to slow my breathing. The chaperons handed out the tickets willy-nilly. I was thrilled to receive a center seat in the upper balcony.

Just like my mother, I had trouble controlling my bladder when I was excited. But this time, I was determined not to miss any of the performance. I did not drink any water for five hours before the van left. The performance seemed like it would never start. I had one of the boy bullies on my left, but a nice girl on my right. The enemy boy had his own friend on his left so ignored me.

The lights went down, the curtain rose. The dancers came out like angels flowing on clouds. The men were incredible in their vests and tights. After my own awkward lessons, I could see perfection. I longed to be like them and wept during Swan Lake. I never wanted to go back to that school where there was no peace or beauty.

Another cultural event the next year was a jazz concert featuring Louis Armstrong. His strong personality and voice stood out. During intermission, I went outside and stood near the corniche, the walkway along the Mediterranean. Mr. Armstrong came out, lit a cigarette, and said hello to me. I was enthralled, mute, and just nodded back.

 For the summer, my sister and I, with our parents, traveled to Cyprus to stay in a mission camp in the mountains. The flight to Nicosia from Cairo went smoothly. We passed through customs and got a taxi to take us to the camp. As we headed up the mountainous two-lane road, a truck approached us on the right side of the road. I got scared and shouted, "We're going to crash…" But the driver just passed the truck on the left. Another truck was barreling down but by this time my father had figured out that in Cyprus they drive as in England, on the left side. We continued racing up the steep winding mountain roads with deep ravines to the sides. Finally, we reached the camp. In the morning, we heard, "Graps, Graps, Tomatis, Tomatis" as a local Greek merchant with donkey came through bringing grapes and tomatoes.

We went hiking to a tiny town three miles away. About halfway along, my mother had to go to the bathroom. She decided to go off the road and down a little hill. She pulled her pants down and suddenly she was sliding, heading into thick brambles. My father dove after her and grabbed her just before she hit the thorns. I found the near miss both horrifying and a little funny.

Our next stop was Lebanon. Because of the ongoing fighting in the city, we could only be on the outskirts of Beirut. At night, from the city's lights, we could see why Beirut was known as "the Paris of the

Middle East." Then on to Jerusalem. We walked the Via Della Rosa; the route Jesus took to his crucifixion. We experienced the Church of the Holy Sepulcher, the site of Jesus' crucifixion and burial. I was deeply moved.

I had a nightmare experience in Jerusalem. We visited Hezekiah's tunnel which started outside the city and burrowed under the city walls. My father and I followed the guide. The tunnel started ten feet high and seven wide with water at our feet. As we progressed, the roof lowered, the sides drew in, and the water rose. It got worse and worse. I started panting, getting dizzy, feeling frantic to get out. I wanted dad's help but remembered that he had claustrophobia. When we finally exited, I cried in relief and safety. We returned home to Egypt.

Back at school, I tried to concentrate in classes and ignore my attraction to other boys. Suppressing my desire was difficult, especially with Jim. He had a bunk bed in the next room and some afternoons would go there, lie down, and read a comic book. I would wait nearby in my room pretending to be napping when I only wanted to hear some sound out of his room. Finally, I'd hear movement and my skin would tingle. Should I go in again? Would I be safe? Would other boys discover me? I felt I had no choice. I'd wait until Jim had time to get a comic book and settle himself. Nothing could happen without the comic book.

I slipped into the room. Jim was on his bed, stretched out, head in the comic book. Walking over slowly, I shivered, and my saliva built up. I sat on the bed looking for any movement from Superman. None, so I carefully put my right hand on Jim's right thigh. His muscles tightened but there was no rejection. My breath was shallow as I pulled Jim's zipper down with my left hand. White undies showed through the gap. Jim raised his hips so I could pull down his blue jeans and underpants. After a few minutes, the comic book pages began turning faster. Finally, it was done. Jim closed the comic book. Without looking at or touching me, he pulled up his jeans and left the room. Desire turned to emptiness. I sneaked out of Jim's room, went to my bed, and cried. We were thirteen.

Word came that my mother and father were leaving Egypt for New York City. They were leaving me at boarding school with my sister. This was incomprehensible. The housemother attempted to explain, saying that my mother was sick and needed treatment that only doctors in New York offered. Alice wanted to stay in school. She had good friends and would graduate from high school that year. This news added to my ongoing state of anxiety and fear. I became desperate to escape to New York. The persecution from the boys I had sex with was increasing. They would tease me again and again in front of other kids for being a sissy, a girl. My only release came when I joined a small group of girls in the old gym. We danced secretly to Chubby Checker singing about dancing with an older queen.

I decided to write a letter to my parents telling them the secret of my sexual nature and experience. I believed this shocking confession would force them to take me out of Schutz. I asked Alice to help me with it. In the letter I stated, "I fear I have homosexual tendencies and need to come to New York." In telling them the truth, I had also used what I thought was their greatest fear for me.

 The responding letter, four weeks later, was crushing. "If you have a problem, go and consult with Reverend Smith. You cannot come to New York." My hope was crushed. This rejection meant I had to remain in Egypt until the end of the school year. I cried bitterly. I knew Rev. Smith would never understand. He would surely threaten me with hell, little knowing I was already there. I made it through 9th grade but with terrible marks. I was too demoralized to have the energy or desire to apply myself.

NEW YORK

At last, I was leaving Egypt for New York. I had trouble believing there could be freedom from the bondage of boarding school. I packed my two suitcases and waited. The school van took my sister and me down to the Alexandria harbor and the Excalibur. The merchant ship took on a few passengers. Although I had arrived with only two suitcases, the wharf was piled with eighteen family crates and trunks indicating that our family would never return. Furniture, rugs, *mushrabiya* antique wooden screens, kitchen, dining room, living room items, all had been carefully packed and boxed. The customs inspectors were taken aback but the *bucsheesh* tips the mission staff prudently distributed smoothed the way.

I rushed up the gangplank almost tripping on the last step, finally able to look down on the city of my suffering. Internally I screamed, "Bye bye you fuckers." I hadn't known the word until sixth grade when I heard someone whisper it and I asked the teacher what it meant. The Mediterranean Sea which had kept me captive was now offering me freedom. The grime of the desert sand and dirt were left behind. Alice and I found our cabin and settled in before the ship's foghorn sounded. I raced up to the railing and waved madly at the dutiful contingent of one seeing us off.

In the special dining room for passengers, we sat with two other kids, a sister and brother from Texas. I thought their accent was a bit off but was gracious to them. I was a liberated fifteen-year-old and wished to start my new life. The meals were so much better than at school and the stewards were kind. There wasn't too much to do but I would lean on the railing, watch the waves, and feel the power of the ship moving me away to my new life.

In the port of Marseilles, I donned a tight pair of jeans and a jean jacket to go ashore. Wearing these I felt strong and tough as I headed down the gangplank and into the port. I had studied French, and my long dormant spirit of adventure rekindled as I sauntered down the quay. I wished that those cruel boys could see me now. I spat on the ground at the thought of them.

After walking for twenty minutes, I passed a man on the street selling knives. Did they look neat. The harsh speaking Algerian vendor let me pick each up and feel their weight. We bargained in Arabic and French. The one that I liked the best (a small switchblade with mother of pearl sides) fit in the palm of my hand. I had an allowance for the trip, and this seemed like a great investment. I knew that I would never let it go. I squeezed it into my pocket and felt safe for the first time I could remember.

The ship docked in the Italian port of Genoa early one evening to unload merchandise before departing in the morning. Alice and I decided to go for a look around the town. We walked until tired and, coming across a fountain in a quiet plaza, sat down. It was around 10 pm. We were the only ones there until a woman appeared, walked slowly around a cove of small trees, and sat on a bench. She had a casual elegance matching her strapless gown. We admired her and wondered who she was. Several men walked by looking her up and down. She met their gaze boldly. Finally, one of them took his hand out of his pocket and we could see a flash of liras. She smiled at him, took his arm, and they strolled away.

Alice and I got to know the other two kids from Texas as we spent time together. At one point we ran out of things to say so the brother, Laurence, said h e could tell some jokes. I knew only one joke that my father told but said OK. Laurence went ahead to tell several elephant jokes. We were floored. These jokes made no sense, and we suddenly worried about going to America. If these jokes represented the American sense of humor, we wondered what the rest of the culture must be like.

After a stop in Boston, we arrived in the port of New York City. In a daze, we disembarked and headed for customs. Things seemed fine until we came to the customs official.

"Empty your pockets," he ordered.

"I really don't have anything in them," I responded as I unloaded them but kept my knife secure in my hand.

"Open your hand," he commanded. I was going to tell him that my hand was injured and couldn't open but the look on his face dissuaded me.

"I only have a little knife in it," my voice quivering."

"Let me see that," he barked. It felt like a death knell,

"It's really small and I won't do anything bad with it, it's very special to me," I pleaded.

"This is a switchblade, I give you a choice, you can either walk over to the water and throw it in, or you can turn around, get back on the boat, and keep going. What's it gonna be?"

It was the slowest walk of my life. I reached the edge of the pier, kissed my beautiful knife goodbye and let go. I have never forgotten the sound of that little splash. I couldn't breathe. I hated New York.

Figure 12 New York City, St. Hilda's

The mission housing on Claremont Avenue up near Columbia University was small and crowded compared to our home in Assiut. My father was now working at 475 Riverside Drive, nicknamed, "The God Box", for all the denominational offices there. He was in the Presbyterian international mission office. I was finally living with my parents again. It was soothing to wake up in the morning, hear their voices, and sit down to breakfast with them. Dad managed to get me a scholarship to 'St. Hilda's and St. Hughes,' an excellent private high school run by an order of Episcopal nuns.

First, I had to take an aptitude test. I excelled at the test however my 9th grade scores coming out of Egypt were so poor that St. Hilda's said they would take me if I were willing to repeat 9th grade. Mom, Dad, and I discussed the offer, and it seemed worth it to get into such a fine school. I was already young for my grade level and now I would just be one of the older students in the class.

The boys wore matching ties, white shirts, grey pants and a blue blazer with the patch of the school on the breast pocket. Proud wearing the school uniform, I felt I belonged. My home room teacher was Sister Mary Elizabeth who had a Ph.D. in history from Columbia University. She was strict but fair. All the nuns wore full habits. There were only fourteen kids in my home room. We'd get together at lunch and talk. I learned that many of them had parents who were professors at Columbia University or Union Theological Seminary, and I gravitated toward them. There were a couple Jewish girls and one, Lexi, with long auburn hair, became my friend.

They all lived in housing around my new home turf. On the weekends, we'd go for a coke at one of the local cafés like Chock Full of Nuts near Columbia. If we had enough money, we might get a milkshake. Up until then I'd only had one milk shake in my life, and that at the Nile Hilton in Cairo. Also, in Egypt, hamburgers were a real treat and along with hotdogs only available on July 4th at the American Consulate in Alexandria. The new thing for kids in New York was cherry cokes. I loved them. I was on a tight allowance compared to my classmates but made the best of it.

Latin was a tough course taught by Ms. Niver who appropriately looked ancient. It started out not too bad…. amo, amas, amat… then got harder. I discovered that Dad had taken Latin and enjoyed it. I could get him to help me, and we'd spend time together. Another way to get his attention was to talk about civil rights. My father felt very strongly about justice and racism. In the spring of 1964, he took two weeks off and went to Selma, Alabama, to learn and protest.

By 1963 the war in Vietnam was heating up. My oldest brother Neal had just graduated from college and came to live with us in New York. The apartment now turned into three bedrooms and I got the smallest. Neal went out a lot and began dating the oldest daughter of a professor. Her sister Abigail was in my class at St. Hilda's. Their parents had a fine two-level apartment at Union Theological which had an interior staircase of dark wood. Their home was enormous and elegant in comparison to ours.

The school year of 1963-1964 was a perfect year. I thrived at school and socially. The abysmal conditions of my existence at Schutz seemed a distant memory. I now experienced myself as smart, likable, and even popular with male friends as well as female. Lexi lay on top of me several times with her well-developed bust, but it didn't do anything for me. The Beatles came to New York for the first time. The girls went crazy over them. Along with the other guys, I wasn't impressed. I was taught how to do push-ups by Johnny, a cute Puerto Rican neighbor, who had clearly been exercising.

Close to my birthday in November, something unimaginable took place. My class was in a free session overseen by Sister Mary Elizabeth when another nun rushed in and gave her a note. Her face blanched and she started to cry. Quickly she collected herself and requested silence. She said, "Something terrible has happened. The President has been shot. Let us all bow our heads and pray for him." It took days to get back on a regular footing with the shocking news constantly on our minds.

Our school would gather some mornings and go to Mass at the Episcopal Cathedral of St. John the Divine. I was introduced to a new form of worship which fascinated me. Only the Episcopal students could receive communion. It could get very hot and sometimes girls fainted and fell off their kneelers. The cathedral was an extraordinary accomplishment and ongoing project, so peaceful and awe inspiring.

My father attended one of my special school programs in the cathedral. The rector asked him to help with the service. He was obliging and then suddenly realized that they thought he was an Episcopal priest. It was too late to tell them, and he continued in the procession robed and performing as he was told. I did think I saw a priest that looked just like my father. Later he got a great kick describing his experience to fellow Presbyterian ministers.

Having had such an extraordinary year, it never crossed my mind that my world could change again. But one morning, my father told me that we would be moving to the small town of Monmouth, Illinois. His work was ending in New York. He had accepted a position at Monmouth College as chaplain and associate professor. It was an old Presbyterian school that our family had been associated with since its founding in the 1850s. My world disintegrated. I had just had the best year of my life. I would have to leave my great group of friends. I was in shock and denial.

My mother was also hesitant to leave New York. I learned much about her and what drove her and Dad out of Egypt. She started as an athletic, beautiful, creative young woman. By the time I came into her world, the years had worn her down through the demands of motherhood and mission community expectations. Her once vibrant spirit had gradually been squeezed out of her. My brother Neal had seen bottles of wine secreted under her bed. Later came the medications. In her mind, the whispering regrets returned of how she could have once married a millionaire.

Her final crisis came when my father's work was moved to Cairo and they left their fine home in Assiut. Taken to an apartment, my mother was in a new Egyptian neighborhood knowing no one. Becoming suicidal, she would find herself on the new roof obsessed with ending her suffering. Rushed to New York for treatment, she met Dr. Fine, a psychiatrist. She attributed her recovery to his skill. She would later say that when she first met him, she was incapable of picking a pin up off the floor.

Looking back, I was struck by the realization that what I had experienced in boarding school, isolation, fear, judgement, loneliness, was like what my mother had faced in her life in Assiut. For both of us, our life in Egypt was like being on the rack but instead of being stretched, we were being shrunk.

I loved New York, the activity, the excitement, and most of all my friends. I was increasingly depressed knowing that I had to move to nowheresville Illinois. It felt so unfair after I finally found what felt like a real home. My parents were concerned and wondered what might help me with the transition.

My brother Paul, who had all kinds of friends, told us about a possible summer job for me upstate. It was at a place called Lake Mohonk Mountain House founded by a Quaker family over a hundred years earlier. The job would be waiting tables, something I'd never done. Paul said the place had a relaxed environment. It seemed they were shorthanded, and chances were that they'd take me if I just showed up and looked decent.

With my parents' encouragement, I made the plunge. Paul said he'd drive me to Lake Mohonk. His driving skills seemed more of a risk than the just showing up part. He was a great diviner of super deals and arrived in his new car. This one was a winner. Purchased for $29, it chugged along. The primary problem was the clutch petal just lay on the floor. Paul had a solution for that challenge. Since he was a boy, he had been able to do amazing things with his toes. They could act like fingers. He was able to grasp the clutch petal between his big toe and the next two, hold on, and pump.

Other than the slow speed, the ride was exciting. I hadn't been out of the city since Christmas, and never to Upstate New York. The trees grabbed at the car as we hit the narrowing roads. The difference between this countryside and the Egyptian countryside was stark. From striving for life in desert sands to verdant green pressing in on every side. I closed my eyes and felt the cool coming through my window that couldn't be closed. After numerous roads and routes that diminished progressively, we saw a little wooden sign declaring "Lake

Mohonk Mountain House."

Employee-related offices and dorms were off to the right. Among all the trees it wasn't possible to see the real Mountain House. I was nervous about the interview but just presented myself. They said I could start the next day. Because of my lack of experience, I wouldn't wait tables, rather I'd be a roll boy. I'd never heard of such a thing. It was explained that I'd have a leather strap around my neck which connected to a heated silver box. The lid of the box was curved so that it could roll forward and back. Within the box various sweet breads and crullers were arranged.

Most of the patrons were elderly women so the salutation I learned was, "Good morning madame, would you care for a cruller?" I had never heard of a cruller. I would flip open the lid and hold my tongs at the ready. Mrs. Wriggle and her sister were in my section. I was told that one of them owned one side of Fifth Avenue, and the other owned the other side.

After this brief training, the next morning I put on my uniform and followed my fellow servers up to the actual Mountain House. It was enormous and rustic like a Swiss chalet. Several floors and a grand deck which encompassed part of Lake Mohonk. The large lake seemed several miles around and was surrounded by tall evergreens reflected in the water. In the kitchen area I learned to prep my roll box.

Most of the wait employees seemed to be late high school or college age. I was initially nervous and shy but gradually eased my way into the daily pattern. I felt quite elegant in my short white jacket, black pants, and silver box resting on my mid-section. I was glad not to be a waiter with more issues to handle and items to remember. The employees were friendly and there wasn't a sense of cliques.

I gravitated to other roll boys and a few of the waitresses. Several trails radiated out from the main building. Of various distances, they accommodated all age groups. I grew fond of coffee and would take a mug out to the lake on a break. More fun was strolling along, mug in hand, with a few new friends on one of the easier trails.

In our wooden dorm was a boy named Hans. As a freshman in college, he was older than me. He was wiry with curly brown hair and an easy laugh. He was friendly and so we hung out together. We'd walk together up to the Mountain House and usually manage to get off simultaneously. A waitress friend of his, he, and I would occasionally hike together.

One day as we were changing to go down to the lake to swim, I saw Hans standing in the doorway of his room pulling on his swim trunks. He was naked. He smiled. A thin guy with an enormous member. Speechless, I went back into my room not knowing what to do with this information.

Several nights later, someone suggested we go down to the lake and skinny dip. I was horrified and thrilled. I loped back to my room to make sure I looked ok, my hair combed, shirt tucked in. I realized it didn't make sense considering the pending activity but still was a bit fanatical about my appearance. I also wanted to have others go in before me since I'd never skinny dipped and was ashamed to admit it.

When I got to the lake, the elevated voices told me I'd missed some drinking. Hans was already in the lake with one of the waitresses. My friends were hanging around acting nervous and challenging each other. I thought this could be a good way for me to show Hans that I was a real guy. I went to take my shirt off but was so nervous that I ripped a couple of buttons off in the process.

Undressing from the waist up was the easy part, but taking my pants and undies off was the challenge. Hans encouraged me, "Come on David, you can do it…. the water is freezing." I was shrinking in the cool evening, so I left my undies on until the last second. Turning sideways, I slipped them off and jumped into the lake. I screamed under water at the cold. I became aware of new body sensations. I had never felt what it was like to be naked and encompassed, the water holding all of me at one time, including my penis and ass. I realized for the first time that my nipples could be hard. I felt whole and free and forgot about the others briefly.

I floated in Hans' direction. I pretended I didn't see him and backed into him. Having his silken ass touch mine was electrifying. He chose to ignore me and just pay attention to nearby girls. I splashed some of the guys, swam over to the tiny beach area and walked out. I felt proud. I had exposed myself, skinny dipped, and rubbed assess with Hans.

I sorely wanted to relive the experience but the next time the group went skinny dipping, Hans didn't join us. It felt great in the water, but my anticipation of a repeat connection turned into disappointment. Realizing that our physical contact might have been different for him, I worked to let go of focusing on him so much. It helped but I did have a sense of emptiness that summer.

MIDWEST

From world renown New York City to a midwestern town of 10,400, proved another cultural cataclysm. I did find some other 10th graders whose parents were involved in teaching or administration at Monmouth College. This included a group of boys who lived in my neighborhood. We became friends quickly. They told me they'd been experimenting sexually with each other for years but then the other shoe dropped. Just before my arrival they decided that they were too old for it and stopped. So much for exploration. I found one of them painfully cute. None the less, they provided an easy introduction to small town high school life. I also made good friends with some of the girls. The pressure to date was strong. I did my best but couldn't push myself beyond some light kissing.

My favorite class was Spanish. It was my first introduction to the appealing language and the teacher, Mrs. Cameron, was excellent. Mexican American, her English was better than several of the other teachers. I felt I had to do something sporty and became the swim team manager. The title sounded impressive at first since I wasn't much of a swimmer. I mostly handed out towels after practice but did get an athletic letter for being a member of the team.

One small Italian American team member was a little effeminate and got teased. I felt bad for him but was afraid to be connected to him. They drafted me for football and I lasted half a game. Volleyball was a little better. When the yearly athletic testing came around, I excelled in push-ups and chin ups. Thanks to Johnny, my New York neighbor, I had been doing them on my own. I pushed myself to the limit and walked around for days with my arms bent. The teacher in English Literature liked me and had me sit right up front across from her desk. She arranged the non-academic types along the back wall. Some of them were cute in a rough sort of way. I envied those sitting near them.

Eventually I made good friends with a boy named Roy who lived with his family on the outskirts of town. I felt so good being out there with Roy on the weekends. We would wrestle in his bedroom. I found it sensual and wanted more. Weekend after weekend I would hope, "Maybe this this time, maybe I'll be able to kiss him this time. Maybe he won't fight me off so hard." But Roy would just laugh my attempts off. His casual rejection really hurt. I'd escape to the corn field nearby to cry. My mother and Roy's mom became good friends. At some point, Roy's mom just dropped my mother. My mother said it was because Roy's mom had periods of depression. I was very fond of his mom. I felt she was a great mom and secretly wished she'd been mine.

I went to the Friday night football games with the other guys and cheered but didn't care. Quietly, I would support whichever team was the underdog. The team found one girl fascinating. The guys talked about her as being easy. They said she was Catholic so could do it and then go to confession and be forgiven.

I expressed myself best through a strong singing voice in church every Sunday and in the school glee club. I didn't read music but could pick up the songs by standing next to someone who knew what they were doing. I was also good at memorizing, and this helped me with the drama club. "The Importance of Being Earnest" by Oscar Wilde was one of the plays chosen. I played Earnest. At the time I had no idea that Wilde was homosexual and wrote with a subtext in mind.

JAPAN

Figure 13 Full Kimono

The summer after 10th grade, a cultural program invited me to work with a group of Japanese students from a high school outside Tokyo. They were in the U.S. studying English at Monmouth College. My mother assisted the director of the program. It was great fun doing chores in their dorm, talking with them, learning of their culture. For two weeks there was a homestay and Hirosuke, one of the students, stayed in our home. He happened to be the grandson of the founder of Tamagawa Gakuen University and Schools where they were enrolled.

As a result of the homestay, his family invited me to come to Japan, stay with them, and study Japanese. My mother was thrilled with the opportunity and strongly urged me to take advantage of it. A trip to the Far East seemed like a real adventure and I agreed.

Meantime, a visa had to be obtained, and the process seemed endless. I was forced to begin 11th grade until the visa came through. Classes included second level math, science, and biology, never strengths of mine. I half applied myself knowing that I would be leaving any day. But the time dragged on and I became increasing anxious. I had no grasp of the subjects. I kept slipping further behind. I became terrified that I might be the first member of my family in four generations not to make it to college. For us, a college degree was the minimum.

Dreams of frantically wandering high school halls trying to find the right classroom haunted me. Some mornings I'd cry at home before having to face my difficult classes. At last, the visa arrived. Plans were made immediately for my departure. I flew Ozark Airlines to Chicago to catch the flight to Japan. One ominous feature of Ozark was a Safety Rope curled above my head.

I was met at Haneda Airport by the Bentley of Dr. Kuniyoshi Obara, grandfather of Hirosuke and the Founder and President of Tamagawa University and Schools. The school had a fine reputation and was based in part on Christian principles. I was whisked away to my new home, a sprawling traditional Japanese home. The Obara residence was a large, long wooden house with several inside gardens connected by wooden walkways. Shoes were never worn inside, always slippers.

My room was at one end of the house, had no doors, and opened by sliding a paper covered frame back and forth. The floor was of *tatami* woven straw and there was no window. However, by sliding the door frame back I had an immediate view of an inner garden. I would roll out my thick cotton sleeping *futon* mattress every night and roll it back each morning. At night if I needed to use the bathroom, I would have to rise in the cold and hurry along the walkways to get to the outhouse.

The kitchen was in the center of the house and the domain of Michiko, a rustic young woman with red cheeks. In the family dining room, we sat on a cushion on the *tatami* mat floor at a raised table that had a heater under it. Our legs and feet rested in a space three feet below the level of the tatami. I never got to see the other end of the home which held the sleeping quarters of Dr. and Mrs. Obara. Dr. Obara was a large gentleman with a stock of white hair. Mrs. Obara was a petite dignified woman who always wore a kimono. How gracious they were as hosts.

I was invited to visit Yamagata, a remote prefecture on the main island of *Honshu*. It was the ancestral home of Sato, one of the university students who worked in the Obara home.

Zen, the nephew of Junco *sensei* teacher, daughter of the O'Bara's, went with me on the journey to help with the language. The first thing I noticed upon entering the home were the paper Japanese and American flags made by the youngest daughter of the family. The father said that he was proud of his son Sato because it was very unusual for the oldest son of a family from their farming area to be able go to university.

Sato's father said he was Christian but had not given up smoking and drinking. I said there were differing thoughts about that. My visit turned out to be making history because I was the first *gaijin* foreigner ever to appear in the village as well as the first *gaijin* that anyone had ever seen. Mrs. Okada in Tokyo told me that when she was young, she met some people from Yamagata and when she heard them speak, she thought they were speaking English.

Sato's mother brought in some different silk clothed dolls to show me. One of them was of a nun. Slippers were put out for me, and the outhouse toilet paper was changed from newspaper to soft tissue. Beethoven was playing on the stereo.

The next day, after a meal of ramen, a Shinto priest arrived. He was inhaling deeply on a cigarette. Samurai used the yellow and white style of his robes when hunting. The sleeves could be put behind the back and tied. His white footwear had holes in it. His yellow silk robe was dirty. The *shozaku* white robe he had on was what a samurai would wear when committing *harakiri* suicide. He had studied fifteen years in Tokyo schools to get his license to become a Shinto priest.

The disheveled priest sat straight and shared a cigarette with Sato's father. Then they prepared for the ceremony to make the land fertile. A small table arrived with a rice bowl and candle on it. The father brought in about ten thin bamboo rods, three and a half feet in length. The priest broke them into the right size. Attached to the bamboo were thin pieces of paper. The priest put the bamboo sticks in the rice and lit the candle. On his head he placed a black head-cover then placed a paper god in the rice. He rang a bell beside the table many times while chanting to the god. As he chanted, he held a wooden board.

He bowed twice, clapped twice, and bowed again. He read prayers to the god. Refolding the paper, he bowed twice with the board. After a final bow he took a strict sitting position.

For his services, Sato's father gave the priest a meal with sake. By tradition a host was to always make sure enough cups of sake were drunk by the guest. The father and the priest offered the sake to each other. Zen, serving as my interpreter, was very diplomatic. I sensed he was telling me one thing and when I spoke, something different to the family. I went outside into a beautiful Japanese garden. A light was trained on the garden, a deep blue sky was in the background.

Next morning, wearing *kimono* and *geta* wooden sandals on my feet, we went to see Mt. Omari. Wearing my *kimono*, I rode a Honda motorbike most of the way. Area mountains were tall but between them was flat farmland. After lunch, I had my picture taken both on a horse and in a field working.

That evening we visited a Shinto shrine. A bell rang. Twenty of us in kimonos clapped our hands twice to alert the gods to our presence. Then we went in front of the altar and joined a group of men around a fire. Sato's father and the mayor of the village were in attendance. With the sound of drumming, a small wooden temple arrived carried on the shoulders of male villagers. The priest wore white and a black head-cover with a long black ribbon.

The priest opened the door to the small temple and waved a stick with paper attached. Then he waved the stick over us as we bowed together. He took out a paper with writing on it and chanted to the gods. Several costumed men entered wearing *onni* devil masks with long red noses and small brushes for hair and eyebrows.

 A wolf figure animated by two men danced in rhythm to the music. After the dance, the priest went behind the high altar and opened it with a key. He lifted the curtain and let the gods out. He then shut it and walked with the key over to the small portable temple. He opened it and the gods went inside. Some *sake* was served, and we filed out. The drums and flutes went first and then the temple with the transferred gods. I was a porter for the temple most of the way around the village. At midnight, I was told that the people of the village were raptured that I had visited them, their main temple, and helped carry the portable temple. We returned to Sato's house.

Two months later, another trip was to *Karuizawa* close to a mountain range. I was in a simple Japanese home with a garden. They were excited to serve me what I might find unusual. Treats of fried grasshoppers and chocolate ants appeared. I did well eating both and all were happy. The third night at two in the morning, I woke up with something terribly wrong. I came out of sleep and realized that my bed and the room were shaking. It took a moment, then the word earthquake entered my consciousness. A feeling of complete helplessness came over me. Despite the cold, my sweat flowed in fear. The tremors lasted several minutes. No one approached my room, so I gradually recovered and went back to sleep.

Okada *sensei*, my host father, planned for me to travel around southern Japan during a winter break. The parents of a fellow student, Teruaki or Tam, were asked if Tam could accompany me. They agreed and off we went. Part of the way we took the *Shintokaido* bullet train. What fun it was to be speeding faster than any ground transportation in the U.S. We went from Tokyo to Osaka and then on to Kyoto. We stayed in traditional Japanese inns, sleeping on *tatami* floors in rooms heated by braziers. Sometimes we would drink *amasake*, a weak hot sake used in the winter.

It was on this trip that I first heard of Lafcadio Hern, a world class writer who had come to Japan in 1890 and was so enamored that he stayed, married, and became a Japanese citizen and scholar. He wrote many books about Japanese culture and folklore. I felt a strong respect and a desire to emulate him. I too wanted to be immersed and transformed. I desired to cast off my American coat and take on the mantle of a kimono. As I had experienced in Egypt, the States, and France, I yearned to become acculturated and fit in to where I was, yet I could not escape the sense of being a stranger.

During our adventure, I developed strong feelings for Tam. I found him cute, open, intelligent, humorous. We spent all our time together, traveling, eating, sightseeing, sleeping in the same room. After a week of this, I felt more drawn to him. One night after dinner, we retired to our bedroom for sleep. Tam was lying on his back, and I jumped on top of him and tried to kiss him. He laughed and escaped my grasp gently but firmly. The budding romance ended before it began. I did not try intimacy again. We continued our friendship journey.

Having started on *Honshu*, the main island of Japan, Tam and I traveled to *Kyushu,* the island nearest to the Asian continent, and then *Shikoku,* the second smallest after *Okinawa*, and back to *Tokyo*. Visiting *Kyoto*, the ancient capital of Japan was extraordinary. So many beautiful temples with incense, gardens, and paths. Such a sense of peacefulness. Then came *Hiroshima*. We went to the museum of the atomic holocaust. I was very aware of being an American and experienced guilt and shame viewing the horrifying photographs and relics. A fellow beside me looking at the same exhibit gave a strong curse which I knew was for my benefit. It was the only time I experienced anti-American sentiment.

The week before Christmas I moved from the Obara's extensive home, into the home of his daughter Junko *sensei* teacher and her husband Okada *sensei*. They were the parents of Hirosuke. Their home was modern, reminiscent of a Swiss chalet. I had a bedroom on the second floor at the back of the house. It was small with a window facing the front courtyard. The evening before Christmas we were all in the kitchen with the TV on in the den when I froze in disbelief. Wafting in from the den were the voices of the Supremes. I dashed into the room to hear, "Baby, baby, baby, where did our love go? Please don't leave me, all by myself." I was suddenly so lonely and under such reverse culture shock, I started crying and moving to the music. I realized how much I was missing home. It was not clear to the family what had happened when I tried to explain.

On New Year's Day we visited the home of Okada *sensei*'s mother. She was very gracious, and we had an enjoyable time. At the end of the day, she gave each of us, Hirosuke, Mayako, and me an envelope. When we got home and opened them it was a gift of money. She had given me the same amount she gave to her grandchildren. This impressed me deeply. Even more, her husband, Okada sensei's father, had been a high ranking general during WWII in charge of the protection of the Japanese homeland. After the war, the American occupation forces took him prisoner. He was tried and hanged. And this was his wife who had been so gracious and generous to me.

It took several months but finally one evening at supper in the kitchen I understood a complete sentence. I was so excited. They were just talking normally and not for my benefit. I also learned several curse words directed at me by Hirosuke. He did not appreciate the special attention I received.

Occasionally, I went from our home in Machidashi into Tokyo with friends to attend movies. This was a great activity to practice my Japanese and have fun at the same time. We would go by train and subway. In American movies with Japanese subtitles, during amusing parts, I would laugh loudly at the dialogue. Then, several seconds later, hundreds in the audience would laugh at the subtitles. I did not think of myself as being different because of my intimate involvement in Japanese life and culture. I would however become aware of my difference when at times on public transportation it was clear that I was being stared at and talked about.

The head of the English department for the junior high where I was taking a few classes, was Dr. Kotsuji. He was a kind gentleman, chain smoker, who made sure that I was getting my lessons. At one point he invited me to his home, and we had a charming time. About halfway through the year, I noticed that he wasn't at school. I inquired about him and politely wasn't given an answer. I ultimately discovered the reason. He had been demoted as head of the English department and feeling dishonored, had taken his own life. This tragic loss left me with great sadness.

The Japanese loved to visit the public baths. I had some apprehension around the practice but went forward. It was like being in a public swimming pool but naked and only with men. The water wasn't unbearably hot as opposed to the time I took a bath at Dr. Obara's and came out of the water colored red and white.

Before Christmas I got quite sick. I was diagnosed with asthmatic bronchitis, making it painful and difficult to breathe. I stayed in my room for some days. During that time, I had a record of Spanish songs and decided to memorize several. I especially like the song 'Malagueña' and taught it to myself. I was feeling more drawn to Spanish than Japanese at that point.

The school went on a four-day ski excursion for a break after Christmas. I had never skied before. Different members of the family gave me various ski clothes as well as skis to use. I managed to do minimally well. The real challenge was the food served in the resort. I thought I might starve. All we had were *bentobaco* lunch boxes which held dry rice, dry fish, and *umeboshi* salted plums.

In school, one of the activities that impressed me was the morning assembly. Students and staff would gather in the courtyard and line up. Then the Japanese flag of the sun raised slowly. We would bow to it as the national anthem was played and we sang, *Kimigaa yoowa*. I felt a little self-conscious being the only westerner and an American bowing to the Japanese flag with WWII only having ended twenty years earlier. My desire to fit in and respect for Japanese culture overcame any reluctance I had. I bowed as deeply as any other student.

Figure 14 Kendo Class

All the boys in the secondary school trained in the martial art of *Kendo* swordsmanship. The armor included thick cloth undergirded with metal, a bamboo rib cage protector and a helmet for the face and head. I was the least of this *samurai* band but loved running in the armor. We practiced the strokes descending from above our heads to the head of our opponent, then a side stroke landing on their side. It started out fun, not too painful, and challenging.

But then came the hard strokes which bypassed the armor on my side. I would cry out in pain and the master *sensei* would give me a cold stare. He was of the *samurai* class, powerfully built and short-worded. His shouted instructions of *DO MENG DO MENG* guided the strokes. My height invited attack from the other more compact students. One time I escorted the *sensei* down to the train station, each of us in *kimono* and using *geta* wooden sandals. I felt proud walking beside him and did my best to communicate. The master's brevity was helpful.

The junior high was a series of one-story wooden buildings with wood floors connected by passageways. I had been attending for several months when one morning I was running late and ran directly into a passageway. I immediately felt uncomfortable, and it took me a moment to realize the problem. I had forgotten to remove my outside shoes and change into slippers. I was horrified and looked around with embarrassment. My second reaction was one of pride, for I had acclimated to this Japanese way.

Another class was *shuuji*, the art of Japanese calligraphy. Not only was I not artistic in terms of the visual arts, but I was also left-handed, and the *sensei* insisted that I write with my right hand. The ink had to be a perfect consistency made by rubbing a solid ink bar against a stone base which was holding a small amount of water. I at least got the ink right, but the challenge of forming the *Kanji* Chinese characters was great. I assumed I was the poorest calligrapher in all Japan.

Even going for a haircut was an adventure. I was taken to the local barbershop on the main street of our small town of Machidashi. The barber had never worked on western hair. Used to thick Japanese hair, my head was shorn quickly leaving little. The coup de gras was the shaving of my forehead.

One afternoon I visited a school friend's family home. I found this friend warm and attractive. The mother and grandmother were extremely polite, lowering themselves gracefully to the floor and bowing repeatedly with their heads to the side. My friend's little brother was there just chatting away with me. The boy was cute and precocious. I enjoyed him but also found myself jealous of this three-year old's grasp of Japanese. I found out later that the family had originally come from Korea to live in Japan. I soon picked up the sense that some Japanese look down on Koreans due to their earlier colonization.

Just as I was initially unfamiliar with Japan and things Japanese, I was impressed by the lack of knowledge by some Japanese concerning America. In the Obara home, there was the cook named Michiko. She was interested in me and enjoyed asking me questions. One day she asked me where I lived in America. I said in Illinois. She asked me if it was in Chicago. I tried to explain. Then she looked at me quizzically and asked if Americans had telephones. I assured her that they did. She got a smirk on her face and said, "But I bet you don't have television."

In the rainy season, the wooden *geta* sandals were an on-going challenge. They had a wood base with two two-inch wooden pieces attached to them, and a cloth strap to keep them on. They allowed the wearer, both men and women, to rise above the streams during heavy rains. Keeping balance and moving along with others took great perseverance. Dressing in a kimono was an art and, depending on the occasion or season, required various layers. I preferred the *uugata* the summer kimono when appropriate. It was one layer over underwear. Those for men had somber colors, but for women extraordinary bright silk patterns.

Spring held a special holiday. Okada *sensei* decided that to honor the holiday there would be a program in the chapel. Part of the celebration would include my giving a speech to the students and their parents, in Japanese, of course. I had no choice in the matter. I was panicked but he said he would help me. First, he wrote it out in Japanese, then he said the Japanese as I wrote it down phonetically.

I then went on to memorize it. There wasn't enough time for me to really understand what I was saying. Repeatedly, I practiced it. I had to memorize it because Okada *sensei* wouldn't allow me a copy on the stage. The program began, I was the third presenter. I walked onto the stage feeling naked. I started the speech and made it halfway through and then blanked. There was no way to recover.... I did not know what I had been saying.

At this point, Okada *sensei*, who was sitting in the front row, called out my next phrase. I immediately said in Japanese, *soo desu ne,* meaning "oh that's right." It was enough to get me through the end of the speech. Parents and students came up after the program, applauding me and giving gracious compliments on the excellence of my Japanese. Their praise felt great but most undeserved.

As I prepared to return to the United States, my hosts gave me some lovely gifts to bring home to Monmouth. For my mother, a beautiful porcelain geisha doll wearing a delicate silk kimono. I received pearl cuff links and a pearl necktie clip. I also brought back an eighteenth-century wooden Buddha with some of the gold paint still on it.

When the time came for my departure, I asked my parents if I could return to the States by ship. There had been several plane crashes at Haneda, the Tokyo airport and they agreed. At my farewell party at the Junior High, Okada *sensei* requested that I sing an English song to the large group. What came to my mind was, "He's got the whole world in his hands." They really enjoyed it.

Departure day came and I was taken to the port of Yokohama. I was sad to leave what I had come to love and respect about Japan and the good friends I had made. When I got to my cabin, I discovered that I had a Philippine roommate. He was a year younger, and we became friends. He taught me how to curse in Tagalog, the Philippine language. This made me proud. Our journey took us to Manila first and then across the Pacific to Hawaii. From there we headed for San Francisco. When the national anthem played as we entered San Francisco harbor, I wept for joy.

Figure 15 High School Prom

Back in Monmouth, my family was deeply worried for my future. I had missed 11th grade and did not know what to do about it. Through the great kindness of Mr. Pape, the high school principal, I received credit for my life experience in Japan and only had to go to summer school. I continued to 12th grade and graduated on schedule in June of 1967.

GEORGETOWN UNIVERSITY

I applied to Princeton University because my grandfather was an alumnus, to Columbia University because I had taken an intensive Japanese program there, and to Georgetown University because it had the School of Foreign Service. I was accepted at Georgetown. The fact that it was a Jesuit university meant nothing to me at the time. I really didn't know anyone in Washington, D.C. but there was an "Aunt" Muriel, my father's first cousin. She had been a professor of English Literature at George Washington University for over twenty years.

I packed up my bags in Monmouth and landed on Muriel's doorstep for the few days before moving into my dorm, the International Student House (ISH). Muriel was petite, intellectual, and very energetic. Shortly after arrival she had us visiting sights and doing errands. One errand was loading the trunk of her car with several cartons of select wines. This shocked as well as impressed me. When she dropped me off at the dorm, a couple of the residents gave assistance. One of them declared, "Boy, this sure is the way to come to college!" as he started up the stairs with a box of wine. Muriel stopped him dead in his tracks, "Young man, you bring that right back," and he did.

Drinking in D.C. was legal at the age of eighteen. From my dorm the local liquor store, Dixies, was just down a steep set of stairs and to the left. Later I became well acquainted with those stairs as I made my weekly shopping. Considering my behavior, it seemed no coincidence that they were featured in "The Exorcist".

A booze and dance party happened the first school weekend. All undergraduate schools were invited to the gym. Included was the nursing school, overwhelmingly made of young women. All kinds of free drinks flowed. Cocktail parties were completely new to me, and I hadn't ever imbibed in alcohol. Uncomfortable and nervous about the expectation to interact with the nurses, I took my first hard liquor drink. I didn't know the names of mixed drinks, so rather than trying to order one, I downed the partially empty glasses left at the exit table. The drinks tasted horrible, but I started to relax and socialize. One nurse seemed shy, so I talked with her.

After a time, students continued leaving and the exit table filled up with more leftover drinks. I felt better and better. I lost track of the shy nurse and just inserted myself into whatever group was in front of me. Struggling to wake next morning, I discovered myself under a bush, on campus, and disoriented. I snuck back to the dorm to ease my first terrible hangover. Somehow, I managed to remember the nurse's name. I looked her up and asked her out. One time turned out enough for me.

I had no experience with social drug use. When my roommate Ted and his best friend Mike smoked marijuana, I was horrified and in a quandary. I believed marijuana was wrong and bad for their health but did not want to confront them directly. My solution was to inform the dorm floor resident, Larry. He welcomed me and listened to my concern. He seemed to agree. A few days later at the floor meeting, Larry addressed the issue of drugs and how serious an infraction they were. Later, when alone with Ted and Mike, they cursed and said if they ever caught who had ratted on them, they'd kill him. I managed not to react.

My two years at Georgetown included incidents of increased public distress at the growing war in Vietnam. At the same time there was the Civil Rights protest movement. The student body at Georgetown was mostly conservative so it was a small number of us involved in protests. I demonstrated in several large protests against the war including the March on the Pentagon. I witnessed police brutality but escaped injury or arrest myself.

Dr. Martin Luther King, Jr. led two of the civil rights marches I was on. What a deep sense of belonging I felt as part of this work for justice. My father was encouraging as he shared his insight about justice and racism. My third experience with Dr. King happened when I squeezed into the first-row balcony of the New York Avenue Presbyterian church. His voice, charisma, and appeal to justice were so powerful that I had the sensation of floating down to the podium to touch him. His compelling preaching remained one of the most profound experiences of my life. Dr. King was assassinated the following year, and Washington burned. From the roof of Copley Hall at Georgetown University, I could count smoke columns from 14 separate fires ignited in a raging reaction to this great national loss.

As my political activities expanded, my inner turmoil grew as well. I had a strong sense of being "homosexual" but did not know anyone else who was. So, I searched for information. I heard several of my classmates joking about a couple of queers who lived in a nearby Georgetown home. One night I got up my courage and went to visit them. When the door was answered, I just blurted out that I thought I might be homosexual and would it be all right to speak with them. The two gentlemen were older, kind, and invited me in. They offered me a drink and we sat in the living room while I was asking questions. All I could remember later was that the one I was sitting next to had on eye liner. I was shocked and hastened to leave. For a time, I had no desire to pursue my quest.

Near the end of the semester, Georgetown invited the great poet Allen Ginsberg to speak. He was to address the student body in the elegant Gaston Hall. Everyone wanted to hear him. I had heard that he was homosexual. I joined the press of the crowd. Just as I got to the seating, it was closed off. I had to see him, so I went onto the stage and sat with a few others. He came out with his notebook. Short, balding, and real. I was at times only ten feet from him as he walked the stage delivering his poems. I was transfixed.

At the end of my first year, I did hear about a gay bar on Wisconsin Avenue near the campus. The information came from a couple of dorm-mates talking about a queer bar and how their buddies hung around outside to beat up some faggots in an alley. I did not have the nerve to go there but kept thinking about it. At the beginning of my sophomore year, the bar was still on my mind. One night, with a couple of drinks under my belt, I walked over to Wisconsin Ave and looked for "The Grill." It was impossible to tell from the outside what might be inside. I paced up and down the sidewalk observing.

Getting up my courage, I pushed the door open. A screech pierced the air as the old hinges moved. Highlighted in a triangle of light, I crossed the threshold. I could barely see but heard chairs shuffle and dimly lit heads swiveling to view me, the new entrant. Holding my breath, I took the next step into a small gathering. I didn't know what to make of them. They were older men, some in semi-drag, all white, but what a mix. Trying to look, yet not stare, I experienced a strong feeling of being different and standing out. How could I be a part of this strange murky world. I gulped down a couple drinks and fled.

As the year went on, I developed a casual friendship with Wilber, a precocious African American boy of sixteen. His family in D.C. was middle class with a mother who was an engineer and father who was a chef. Still in high school, Wilber was taking courses in linguistics and foreign languages at Georgetown. He was brilliant, had a loud braying laugh, big smile, sparkling eyes, deep black skin, and apparently a muscular body. He liked to hang around the International Student House and study with us.

Internal turmoil over my sexuality was increasing. I found myself pacing the dorm's hallways in distress. One evening Wilber was sitting in my room and observed my behavior.

"David, what's wrong with you?"

"You wouldn't understand,"

"I think I do understand," he retorted.

"No! No one can understand," and I kept pacing the halls. Back in my room, Wilber said,

"I think I understand what's going on!"

"No, no you can't possibly understand!" I continued pacing. For the third time I headed back to my room. Wilber closed the door and said,

"I do understand! You're gay and so am I!"

Our friendship deepened. Wilber invited me to his home for dinner to meet his family. I brought him home to Monmouth for spring break. One afternoon we went to see the movie version of the musical "Oliver" at the Moline theater. We loved it. After the film finished and we headed to my dad's car, we saw a group of guys standing around who started to yell, "Nigger, nigger, nigger lover" and more. I was afraid for us. We jumped in the car, and I drove off feeling disgusted. What contrast to the gentle feelings after seeing Oliver. Wilber handled it far better than I did.

Wilber became my first lover. The only place we could find to be alone was in the basement of my dorm in a storage room. We had found an old mattress on the floor. We began going down there occasionally. The feeling of danger was acute but did not hold me back. Wilber was more experienced, and I felt a sense of comfort with him. He told me he was a protege of Noam Chomsky and was learning a great deal. We remained friends for the next forty years. We checked in on each other periodically. After Wilber moved to New York City in early 1990, we would have dinner together whenever I was in the city.

SUMMER IN FRANCE

At the end of my sophomore year, I applied to Georgetown's French language summer school program at the University of Dijon. The program would be my last official connection with Georgetown. I had decided to transfer to Monmouth College starting my junior year. I shared with my parents that I was struggling with my sexual orientation. My parents felt concern and encouraged me to make the transfer. They felt I would straighten out in a healthier, more co-ed environment. Also, my tuition would be free because my father was the Chaplain. Part of our arrangement was that they would pay for me to live in a dorm on campus.

For the French summer program, students made their own flight arrangements and met initially at a small hotel in the center of Paris. Our hotel was right down the street from the Folies-Bergère, a cabaret music hall. What an exciting time going out, drinking wine, finding our way back. I already had a good start on the language. My confidence was reinforced when a young woman coming down the stairs in the early morning spoke to me in French. We exchanged pleasantries and I thought to myself, "Well done, Davíd. You've already fooled a young French woman." Later, at the hotel meeting of Georgetown students, I saw her in our group. I went over and she said that she too thought I was French and had been delighted that she fooled me.

One of the highlights of the stay was attending the Folies-Bergère. I had never been to a burlesque performance. The theater was packed and the only seat available was in front on the extreme right where I could see into the wings. The curtain went up and the perfectly built women did their kicking and fine dancing with special emphasis on their exposed breasts. I was so close, I felt I might be hit on the head. After each piece, I could see dancers as they exited. They grabbed their breasts and lifted them up as they ran into the wings.

After a few days in Paris, we students headed by bus towards Dijon. Georgetown arranged for my stay with a French family. Madame Richard, the lady of the house, gave me two large, old iron keys. One was for the front door and the other to my room. I had almost no interaction with the family. Every morning, I headed out to the university for classes in French language, culture, and history. At night I would stumble home after glasses of *vin rouge* red wine at the cheapest possible price. On several occasions, I found myself frantic at the house door, confusing the keys and in great need of the toilet. Madame was not pleased.

I made friends with both international students and French students. We had four days of holiday in honor of Bastille Day, July 14. One French friend had a cousin living in a small village. He invited four of us international students and four French students to the countryside. Most importantly, the last things packed were bottles of cheap red wine. The journey was like rolling into another world. Roads shrank, the hedges moved in, and dirt kicked up as we hit the country roads. The villagers welcomed us with rustic suspicion and ample food.

We were quartered in a large shed away from the farmhouse. It had slanted wooden walls, low ceilings, and a thatched roof of dubious waterproofing. Dark, dank, dismal, perfect for eight university students on holiday. We stacked the wine at the door for immediate access. The guys were warm, generous, fraternal. I longed for more. Bumping into one of my French friends, I looked for special meaning. He laughed and gave me a shove. It was too good-natured.

The village held a fair in celebration of the historic storming of the Bastille fortress which ushered in the French Revolution. A bowling contest with short pins and a small worn red leather ball was led by a group of shrunken old men in semi-circle, puffing, jeering, cheering, swigging. Rules opaque, assumptions made, guffaws rendered. I knew little of bowling but emboldened by my cups of wine, I joined in the bonhomie and won the most rounds. With tempered pleasure, they handed me the prize of a sommelier saucer with silver cigarette lighter in the middle. I lit up a Gallois and felt very French. I held onto the prize for decades only to have it finally rust away.

What an exciting time being in the country with friends, wine, and …. that was it. After the holiday, we went back to Dijon and school.

Wine in a box seemed iconoclastic for France, but for poor students willing to embrace the cheapest, it was a fine solution. Leaving a party one weekend, I fumbled my way down a path and finally to a street. Wine box in hand joyous tones escaped my lips. "*Allons enfants de la patrie, le jour de glorie est arrivé,* the French national anthem.

Among the international students studying French was a German boy whose spirit impressed me. He spoke no English, I spoke no German, so we created a linguistic cocktail in French. Also memorable were two American brothers. The slightly older one had progeria syndrome and at twenty looked much older. They both played the guitar well, so we put together a performing group hoping to make some loose change. They played the blues and I sang.

Another student in the group, a Dane named Frederick, stood over 6', thin, with sun-browned skin and a half arm that went down to his elbow and had some tiny digits. He was very coordinated and after a time his disability just seemed natural. I found him attractive and in a clumsy way tried to get close to him. One night we were in Frederick's room drinking, he was lying quietly on his bed, and I was in a chair. Something about his woundedness drew me towards him. Someone I could care for. I moved closer believing that I was being welcomed. I gently lay beside him and went to kiss him. A loud snore broke through Frederick's lips. The romance was over.

About two thirds of the way through the summer semester, I came down with mononucleosis, called the kissing disease. I certainly hadn't been kissing anyone. In the French manner, I was taken from my homestay and isolated on the 5th floor of a large empty dorm. Two meals a day were brought up and a painful penicillin shot applied to my rear every other day. As one cheek recovered, the other was injected. There I remained for two weeks before returning to the homestay. How unfair, to be in France and put in solitary confinement.

During my homestay, I noticed that my dirty laundry was disappearing and returning cleaned. I thought it was especially nice of Madame Richard to do this. On my last day with them, I went to say good-bye and she handed me a bill for $150 for laundry service. I was shocked and said I didn't know that was the arrangement. She gave a hard smile and kept her hand out. I gave her my money. This left me with barely enough for bread, cheese and wine for the two remaining weeks.

I decided I would fill the time by taking a train with a friend to Marseilles and then hitchhike from there. We hit Marseilles but not wanting to spend money on a hotel, we slept drunk under some trees beside the train station. After leaving the station, we hitched to Monaco, arriving in early evening. Some wine and cheese and off to the beach. There was no sand, only small pebbles. We ran into some other students, and all bedded down to dream our spirit dreams. One boy, a Czech named Jacob, was cute and friendly. We spoke into the night. Around three am we were awakened by men in uniform ordering us off the beach. Grabbing our things we headed back into the city. We found an abandoned house and sneaked into the basement. I lay as close as I dared to Jakob. In the morning, we exchanged addresses before parting, and I hitched for Geneva.

In the evening, a ride dropped me in the countryside outside of Florence. It was dark, but I found some straw on the ground, gathered it, and laid my sleeping bag down. The dawn light and a rumbling sound awakened me. I turned on my side and saw I was at the bottom of a hill with a beautiful mansion at the top. I turned to my other side to locate the increased rumbling. A farmer aboard a large tractor was working the field creating a peaceful morning setting. Suddenly, he saw me and aimed his tractor right at me. I raced to throw my stuff together and yelled as he chased me back towards the highway. I would have to forgo Florence.

I had been hitching for over an hour and was becoming discouraged when a car pulled over. A mother with a young daughter picked me up. Most drivers had been men. We spoke French and I learned they were Swiss from Geneva, my next stop. They warned me that I was supposed to have at least $200 to be allowed across the border into Switzerland. I had about $25 to my name at this point. The mother instructed me to hide in the corner of the back seat. I was terrified of being denied entry. The border guard, charmed by the attractive woman, did not see me and allowed us to cross.

Rolling through the mountain tunnel into Switzerland, how very fine I felt, chatting in French, lolling in the backseat of a high-class car, being driven to my destination. The mother knew of a youth hostel in a wooded area on the outskirts of Geneva. She dropped me nearby.

The hostel had shared rooms, bunk beds, and a cafeteria with apples, cheese and of course cheap red wine. The next morning, I hiked into town and headed for Lake Geneva. With the lake in the middle, the city of Geneva was like two arms stretched around a great fountain reaching for the sky. The romantic setting was so beautiful, I longed to have someone to share with.

I walked around town viewing the historic buildings and banks then slowly back to the hostel. As I entered the wooded path an attractive guy around my age was walking with a friend towards me. I heard German being spoken. I felt shy, but at the last moment we looked at each other. My throat constricted and I couldn't get a word out. He nodded and kept going. I thought about him all afternoon, hoping to see him on his return. I built my courage up but to no avail. There was no second chance.

 I got going early in the morning to hitch out of Switzerland and into France. I was not lucky. For the first ride, a middle-aged man stopped. He seemed friendly and we chatted in French. After a while I started to feel uncomfortable and eased my way toward the passenger door. When the driver put his right hand on my leg, I knew I had to get out. I said that I had forgotten something important back in Geneva and had to return. The driver unhappily stopped the car. I waited until he was out of sight and began hitching again.

I just made it to Paris, arriving the day before my flight to New York. I was exhausted, but worse, I only had one dime left to my name. Transportation to the airport was part of the pre-paid program. I had no idea what I'd do when I reached New York. During the flight, one of the American brothers from our music gig came down the aisle. We started talking and I mentioned my financial dilemma. He reacted immediately, saying he was sure his parents in New York would help me out.

After we arrived at Kennedy Airport, I called Mom and Dad to wire money and went home with the family to Long Island. I was taken down to the basement where I crashed from exhaustion. In the middle of the night, I woke in pitch black with no sense of where I was. I started feeling around and found only empty space on three sides. I heard the constant sound of running water. I was terrified thinking I was on a ledge with a river running far below and no way to escape. I fell back to sleep. In the morning, I realized I was in their basement. My parents wired the money to get a bus back to Illinois and start my junior year.

MONMOUTH COLLEGE

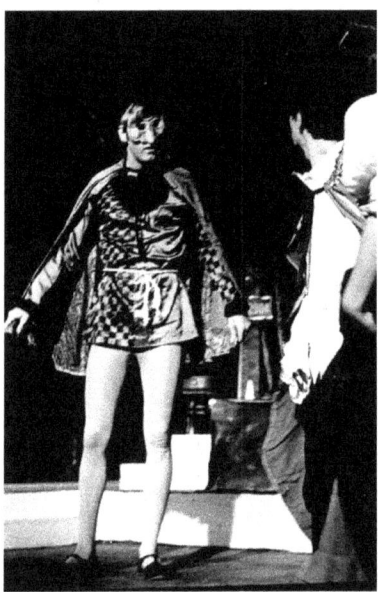

Figure 16 Harlequin

My major at Georgetown was International Affairs. At Monmouth I began anew with sociology hoping for something both engaging and practical. I started making friends through classes and hanging out at the student union. I kept running into a group of students who were majoring in theater. They seemed to be the loudest and most interesting of those who could call the union their second home. At first, I sat close to their usual booth catching some phrases. They would play the jukebox, hangout, and smoke. Theirs seemed the life. I got tickets for a couple of the school theatre productions. I loved the mystery, suspense, and energy that the actors projected. I was hooked. To the chagrin of my parents, I changed my major to theater and communications.

Now I could officially hangout with the cool theater majors at the union. Smoking was required so I continued to work at it. I observed how they did it and followed all the cool moves except for one, I managed not to inhale. My mother was an early smoker who quit using massive amounts of chewing gum. No one in my family smoked. Other than psychedelics, smoking was the one thing I knew not to do.

In the dorm, guys talked about girls all the time. I wanted to fit in and participate. I did my best at showing interest. Thank God it was a drinking campus, and we could bring beer and wine into the dormitory. I felt more comfortable once the bottle went around. The theatre gang was significantly alcohol inspired.

I took general courses required for completion of my B.A. and stayed busy with Theater Arts. Theater was like being paid for doing something I loved. School work was all consuming, having classes in the day and then rehearsals in the evenings. Before one show ended, we were already in rehearsal for the next. I had never felt so alive. I wasn't just surviving; I was caught up in the great dance of creativity.

Some of us theater majors formed an independent theater troupe and put together a Shakespearean piece drawing from various of his plays. We scouted around town to find an appropriate setting to produce it. An abandoned church was located. It was perfect and we moved there. Haley was the creative mind behind our project. As a troupe we became close, sometimes sleeping in the church. We ate, worked on the set, practiced instruments, sang, and drank of course. Haley was lovely and one night I invited her to my dorm room. We had a bottle of Southern Comfort to help us along. In a stupor, we did our best. In the morning, I could not remember what had happened.

Like my 9th grade in New York, I developed solid friendships with my fellow actors, and they really liked me. There was a young short Italian guy who showed interest in me. We had a drunken one-night stand in my dorm room. I was afraid to do more and crushed his feelings.

One day, I looked in the mirror as I exited the dorm shower and thought, "I am pretty attractive and have some good muscles." Self-confidence was a new experience, and I liked the feeling. Two of the girls in the department seemed interested in me and maybe more than just as an actor. Suzi was very fun and with a good singing voice. She and I ended up often being cast as the lead man and woman in the department productions. We spent a great deal of time together both related to the theatre and socially. When we worked late on a script, she would stay overnight in my room, lying close to me but we never made physical contact. Later on, a mutual theater friend told me she had loved me and how hard this was on her.

One time there was a party in a wooded area outside of town. The booze was abundant, and it helped me socialize. With Suzi, I left and stumbled to the car. I started it up and hit the gas. There was a crash. The car was in reverse. The rear bumper and the exhaust pipe had smashed into a tree. What the hell. Suzi didn't want me to drive home to Monmouth, but I was adamant. We compromised by going to her home in Galesburg. I woke up with her mother handing me a cup of tea. When I went to look at the car, there was a plug of wood up the exhaust pipe. I made up a story for my father. I was afraid if I told the truth, he wouldn't allow me to drive again.

For Christmas vacation my father put together a weeklong program in New York City at Union Theological Seminary. Monmouth students, including me, would be studying the impact of poverty in the homeless population. Different activities were lined up, plus presentations. One night, Joe, another theater major, and I decided to have a night on the town. We left the group, went to a gay bar, and started drinking. When the bar closed at 2am, we decided to just keep going, it was New York after all. We learned of an after-hours gay joint in Soho.

The bar was dark, small, with a cross section of hard-core drinkers. We kept drinking. Thirty minutes later two older men joined us at our table. They asked a lot of questions about who we were and what we were doing in New York. We felt uncomfortable and said we needed to return to the seminary. They offered to drive us there. They wouldn't take no for an answer.

When we were close to the seminary, one of them said,

"This is what's going to happen. One of you is staying in the car with Pat, show 'em your gun Pat. I'm going up with Joe to the rooms. Joe, you go in and collect money. If you try anything Joe, we'll kill David. Everything goes right, we'll let you go."

I was frozen, I couldn't think of anything to do. When Joe came back after the students were robbed, I said,

"OK, let us go."

"Hold on there fellas, we've changed our minds, get back in the car Joe or we'll kill you."

Joe got back in the front passenger seat, and I remained in the back seat; the car took off.

"Where are you taking us, what are you going to do with us?"

"Ohhh, you'll see."

The impact of the booze I had drunk evaporated. I was struck cold sober. They went a few blocks and then turned a corner to get onto the Westside Highway. As they were slowing down to make the turn, I shouted at Joe,

"Get out, Get out!!"

Simultaneously we each grabbed a door handle, pushed, and rolled out of the car onto the street. We had no time to recover, we stumbled for the safety of the seminary. One of the students had taken down their license plate number and called the police.

The kidnappers were caught, arrested, and thrown in jail. Joe and I had to go down to the precinct, identify them, and make statements. I shook with hatred at what we had experienced. Both had records and would be put away for some years.

About four months before graduation, I was in a quandary of what to do once I was out of college. I had no sense of how to proceed. I talked with my parents several times about this. They suggested that I would make a good teacher. One of the things my father had done was teach English, and I'd done some basic teaching and tutoring with Japanese students. I didn't think I wanted to deal with high school students, so I decided on the elementary level. I chose a Master's at Teaching (MAT) given by George Washington University in D.C. What a relief to have someplace to go.

Shortly before graduation, my theater friend Patty and I decided that we would hitchhike to Maine right after graduating and hang out in my brother Paul's cabin in Eastport, Maine. Patty was lovely with a perfect hourglass figure. We had kissed a little bit, but she already had a boyfriend, Ron, who was also a good friend of mine.

We headed out. I discovered it was easier to hitch with a girl than alone. We made good time and arrived in Eastport within two days. Paul's cabin was rustic, and we inhabited the loft on one side. It was cool at night and there was just a big iron stove to heat the entire place. I did find Patty attractive. We ended up for several nights, after much wine, attempting to 'do it.' Things worked well up to a point, but I could never actually complete the deed. I thought I wasn't straight enough to manage it. My brother Paul came up from New York for a few days while we were there. I was proud of Patty and happy to show her off to Paul.

I returned to Monmouth for the rest of the summer before going to D.C. for the teaching program. I got a job as a dishwasher at Mellings, a motel restaurant. I did find some pleasure in getting plates and pots scraped and into the large dishwasher. Things went well until some forks got trapped in the disposal. I was called to the manager's office and let go. It was my first experience of being fired.

My father then got me a job with the maintenance crew of the college. It seemed great until I was asked to climb a forty-foot ladder to scrape and paint the gymnasium windows. The fundamental truth returned that I was terrified of heights. I had to carry a can of paint plus a brush and scraper up a ladder for forty feet and to balance there without holding on. I was spotted with one hand gripping the ladder and fired again. This second dismissal put an end to my summer jobs program.

WASHINGTON, D.C.

I needed my own housing in Washington, D.C. so left Monmouth in the middle of August to find a place before beginning the program in September. I was fortunate, the only other guy in the master's cohort, Jim, knew of an apartment building. It was on New Hampshire Avenue above DuPont Circle. It had a one bedroom but could be turned into three living spaces.

 I took the apartment and put word out for two other tenants. I found one springy straight guy, Billy, and a young woman, Michelle, who was of French origin born in Algeria. She was what was called a *pied noir* black foot, meaning French who were born in North Africa.

Michelle kept pans of wax on the back of the stove. I asked her one day what they were for. She said that she would heat the wax and apply it to her body to remove all her body hair. She offered to help me do it, but I graciously declined. I learned a practical life skill from her though. Take a small brown paper bag, grease it with oil; take a fresh chicken; grease the chicken; put the chicken in the bag, place the bag in the oven and set it to 400 for 40 minutes. It was a miracle. The chicken would come out perfectly delicious and ready for the table. At last, I could cook.

So began the master's program. I was impressed with the intelligence and quality of the other students. I managed the academic aspect well for the first semester and made friends with several of the women. I remember one, Susan, who had an outgoing personality and a small gap between her two front teeth. She was from New Jersey and in the summers worked the toll booths on the Jersey turnpike. She had all sorts of experiences with truck drivers who came through. They would make chauvinistic cracks at her expense, but she developed a great defense. Just as they were pulling away, she would smile and call out, "Fuck you very much." A group of us celebrated Thanksgiving together as well as a Seder, the Jewish Passover meal.

At the beginning of the second semester, practicum assignments for student teaching were given out. I requested a gentle teacher I liked who taught sixth grade. The director of the program, Nan, assigned me to a third grade with a strict disciplinarian, Ms. Layman. When I asked Nan why, her reply was women's intuition. I tried but was not able to manage younger children. As Ms. Layman sat there observing, the children became more and more out of control under my tutelage. After several days of their dancing on the desks, I decided I couldn't live in dread any longer. I told Nan I would leave the program unless I was assigned to another teacher and grade level. She did not change her mind, so I left.

I was paying $70 a month for my share of the apartment rent so I was able to stay in Washington. I decided to return to my theatre roots and took some classes at a small theatre school on P Street N.W. The director of the class was a guy named Timmy, a most interesting looking fellow with long hair, pointed countenance, and very thin body, especially in tights. He formed us into a little company practicing long hours of physical and dance movements, short imaginative pieces, and moments of meditation. He had studied at Juilliard in New York and Method Acting. Timmy was our theatre guru, and we were his devotees. We threw ourselves into whatever he asked of us.

We were introduced to many theater pieces. One couple with us lived a hippyesque lifestyle. They were soft and gentle and had a daughter named Flora. Diet was a key part of their lifestyle. They found direction from one that was called the mucusless diet. As they remained faithful to it, the rest of the group was much distressed. Their chosen foods produced constant gas which was omnipresent at all our theatre efforts.

A guy named John had the most theatre training and served as Timmy's second. He was of Irish descent blessed with high energy, flights of fancy, and well familiar with the bottle. I became infatuated with him. I spent time at his group house on Capitol Hill where parties were often held on weekends with a considerable variety of guests. Living in the house were a juvenile patrol officer, an aspiring writer, John, and several others.

For John, I was an attractive guy to date. I however, wanted him to be with me all the time. I got drunk at one of their parties and went to a nearby park, wrapped my arms around a tree and wept bitterly. John found me, laughed, comforted, and returned to the party without me. I went back to my apartment where Billy, straight and jumpy, was in his room. I was frantically drunk, desperate, and considering throwing myself out the 6th floor window. In the midst of this emotional storm, I experienced my consciousness being on the ceiling in the corner, looking down at me, observing my frantic state. A little later, Billy came in, and though most uncomfortable, gave me calming support. He moved out soon after.

John continued with Timmy and the troupe. For my own stability, I left John and the theater effort. The last time I saw John, a year later, I was going to a doctor's visit on M Street. I saw a man moving very slowly, head bowed, with intense effort, one foot, then the next, then the first, shuffling towards me. I stood frozen. How could this be? It was John. His hair, still long and free, was the only familiar sign of the man I had known and loved. He was heading towards a doctor's office that specialized in AIDS treatment. There was no AIDS treatment.

ALIVE

Shortly after leaving the master's program at George Washington University, I decided it was time to strike out and get an apartment of my own. A studio was almost affordable. Striking gold, I came across one on I Street and 21st, bordering the university campus. It had the basic one room of peeling yellow paint connected to a diminutive kitchen, bathroom, walk-in closet. Located on the second floor facing I Street, I would be able to sit on the radiator and watch students go by.

The second time I went to see the apartment, I met Pat, the tenant, who had three days left on his lease. He was about my age but short, compact, with dark curly hair seemingly everywhere. A collection of mechanics magazines was stacked in the corner. He filled me in about the place, the manager, and the neighborhood. Pat suggested that I should come back that evening to see what the area was like after dark. This seemed a little different, but I had no other plans. I showed up and knocked on the door. I was greeted by disco music and Pat in a tight t-shirt and shorts.

He was cute in a stocky sort of way as he led me ten steps to the kitchen and got out a bottle of wine. At first we sat on the long window sill watching the street life. Pat suggested that we might be more comfortable on his worn green sofa bed. Several drinks and poppers later, I couldn't believe my good fortune in finding this apartment.

The student center of George Washington was right around the corner. I could easily grab a cheap bite anytime. Having just been a student there, I felt very comfortable using the facility. One noon, heading for some lunch, I glanced across the ramp and there was a cat, a beautiful long- haired one. She was arching her back and viewing the stream of students oblivious to her presence. I could not help myself and went to pet her. I was stunned. Despite her thick coat, her spine was sharp to the touch. Her external display belied her reality.

Desperately thin, I had to act. She allowed me to picked her up and carry her, a long cat as light as a feather. I hurried around the corner and upstairs before she could change her mind. Back in my studio, reality struck. As she began to cry it was clear I had to run get food to quiet and nourish her. This done, I sat on my sofa bed and contemplated her. Fur matted in spots, nails cracked, tail swishing as she examined the room and me. I still wasn't sure… but she came over, rubbed my leg, and jumped into my lap. I had no choice, I had to keep her. As I held her body, I felt a pang of sadness then fright. I could have missed seeing her, not touched her, and just gone by like all the others.

I named her Kibbes. I had never been responsible for another living being. Questions attacked my mind, was I allowed to have her, would management find out, would she cry a lot, would I act responsibly. I had no answers but she was beautiful and needed me. I changed a little that day; I began to think beyond myself.

I was unemployed, money was scarce, and I didn't have a lot of practical skills. But I could do basic typing which I learned in 7th grade. Responding to newspaper ads went nowhere. Someone mentioned the possibility of temporary employment. My savings account had gone from $900 to about $300. Rent was due at the end of the month. I visited a temp agency, and they determined my typing would do.

For a couple of weeks I went on various day assignments, was loaned around, "Hey, does anyone need a temp, he's got a couple hours left?" I came to hate the word 'temp'. A job for several months in a travel agency came in. I interviewed and got it. Wow, something steady. I worked for Helga, a naturalized US citizen originally from Austria. Dark husky voice, dark sun-browned skin, and an equally dark outlook. Her brown hair was pulled back severely from her strained face. I did my best to accommodate. I strove to be pleasant no matter what I faced. I figured if I presented well, I might be acceptable on the work level. Polished shoes, white shirts, pants with the new permanent press, and ties that didn't express too much character.

I hated getting up in the morning but managed to arrive on time. It was so important that I have Helga's just right coffee waiting for her entrance. As the door burst open, she would launch her sweater into a chair as she strode to her office. "Where's my…..ok, never mind".

My desk was just around the wall, I could hear everything. She liked that I was only a cough away. When my response lagged, she would shout, "Quick like a bunny you"! "You" being short for David. At lunchtime I'd rush out to get whatever delicacy she was inclined to. Considering the pay, I brought my peanut butter and jelly from home.

I wasn't great with machines so when the Xerox machine jammed, it was Helga's show. She would approach the copier as an enemy whose weaknesses she knew well. With a smirk she'd release the levers, relieve the machine of the crumbled sheets, slam the doors shut, give me one hard look, and retire with honor into her office. I could never forget that her husband had been in the military.

The walk to the office from home was about twenty minutes. This exercise and time to think was good because I was being drawn into the night life of gay D.C. It was lovely having Kibbes to greet me, love me, and sleep with me, but a different yearning was rising. After the experience with Pat, I felt a need to meet other guys. Staying home with Kibies, watching my little black and white TV was nice, but as the evenings moved on, my desire to be close to someone grew.

I couldn't afford a car and taxis were expensive. I heard about a meetup area called 'The Block' that was walking distance from my place. I decided to check it out for possible weekdays. One evening around 10pm, I strolled over to Georgetown and started to wander the streets in the vicinity. For a while there was nothing but fine homes and healthy trees. Then I noticed a guy lounging against the fence of a home. I pretended I was just strolling along but allowed my eyes to dart for a moment towards him. I was caught,

"Hi, how ya doin there" he drawled. I was too embarrassed to respond so just nodded my head and moved briskly onward. I didn't even have the chance to see if he was cute or not. I turned the corner and passed several other guys striving to be subtle in an obvious way. I just couldn't interact but went home knowing enough about this resource.

That weekend I decided I needed to work on my Block style. I put on tight jeans and a T-shirt and paced around my apartment. I pretending I was passing a guy. I went over different ways to initiate, respond, and disengage. I was amazed by how many guys hung out there. It was a fine neighborhood and one home was pointed out to me as belonging to Henry Kissinger, Secretary of State. I grew accustomed to speaking to the guys, discussing the weather and where we each lived. The Block was most crowded once the bars and discos closed. Late hours made for a hard workweek when occasionally I would invite a guy home.

After twisting to Chubby Checker songs at boarding school, I never

thought I'd like dancing as much until Disco came along. Boy, did I throw myself into it. Not only the dancing but the entire ethos, the demimonde which the music created. It was a magical culture. Aretha Franklin turned me on with her lyrics,
"R. E. S. P. E. C. T., Don't know what it means to me." This line of hers was related not just to women and black freedom but was inculcated into the nascent gay movement. Dancing disco was a freeing from the constraints that held us.

At first, I would visit discos with my friends, drink, and let myself go. The music made all strangers friends, and all friends closer as we sang and boogied down. Then I wanted even more. I wanted to stand out, so I got some clothing from the Salvation Army and started to put myself together.

It took time to get it right. I bought tight bell-bottom brown pants, a silk shirt, and a fur jacket to match. What I was lacking were the right shoes. Regular shoes just couldn't be worn with this fine fare. I needed a pair that my slim wallet and body could manage. At last, at a budget discount, there they were…Platforms with rounded black toes, brown body and thick 3.5" black heel. Best of all, they fit. I practiced walking in my studio so I wouldn't make a fool of myself.

Then came the night I was free to strut my stuff. Oh, what a night…flashing colored lights, globes spinning, drinks flying, bodies gyrating, and new shoes stomping. I only fell twice. Feeling fabulous, I was in with the in crowd.

Meeting in discos, I could see how well a guy could dance. Also, that way I'd be with friends and have company in case nothing worked out. With my passion for dancing, my disco moves would brake out, and I wouldn't be so focused on connecting.

I remember one guy of Greek origin with the name Nicholas. He was small with smooth brown skin and thick black hair. His complexion was marred by acne, but I was able to overlook it. He loved to put on my fur jacket and walk around naked. I wanted to see more of him but he disappeared. He wasn't the first, it happened often.

One night at the disco I met Donnie from Buffalo. I instantly fell for him. He needed a place to spend the night. He had alabaster smooth skin and curly blond hair. It was summer so quite a bit of him was exposed. I told him he could just spend the night at my place without any expectations. He agreed and we ended up in my sofa bed. It would squeak every time one of us rolled over. We ended up in the middle, face to face laughing. A kiss and we sailed away. Donnie was around for a couple of days and I was in love. The next weekend he said he needed to return to Buffalo. I was shocked. I thought he might want to move to Washington for me.

We exchanged information and said we'd be in touch. I thought about him a lot. I believed that if I visited him, it could cement our relationship and he'd want to move to D.C. A month later, I flew to Buffalo. He was nice, friendly, introduced me to friends. We all went out a couple of times to eat. I had my own guest room and each night waited for Donnie to come downstairs.

Never happened, he made sure we were always with others. I went water skiing for the first time on the Niagara River above the falls. We were a group of gay guys in the boat. I managed the skiing well until I didn't, crashing headfirst into the river as the current pull me along. With help I made it out safely. I went home physically and emotionally bruised, never to hear from Donnie again.

My desire to continue acting did not recede. George Washington University theater department was one possibility. I auditioned and over the next year performed in several shows. I was the lead in a production of "The Egg", had a role in "A Midsummer's Night Dream" and in "Boys in the Band". Stonewall, the first gay uprising against police harassment, had happened just two years earlier in New York City. The gay rights movement was growing but it was still challenging to appear gay in such a public setting. I had seen "Boys in the Band" in London during college and it had a powerful impact on me. I wanted to promote the human face of gay life to the world.

Also in the cast was a cute Italian American. We became friends and ate together several times after rehearsal. I was nowhere near affording a car and he had access to one. One evening I went with him to his car, and as we were talking, he leaned into my lap and we became better friends. He was not out to his parents, taking a role in the play was a way of broaching the topic.

I was cast in several productions at the Folger Shakespeare Theatre on Capitol Hill. It was a wonderful, small stage, small wings, small dressing area, and small house, but very classy. I had a bit part in "The Winter's Tale". One day during a rehearsal break on the steps of the theater I shared my peanut butter and jelly sandwich with one of the lead actors. Her name was Kathy Bates. She was a fine actress and friendly. Also in the productions that year was Stewart Pankin.

I auditioned for a theater company named Library Theater. Its mission was to encourage reading in public schools throughout the Washington metropolitan area. It looked interesting and I was hired. We put on productions of children's books like *Curious George* and *Little Red Riding Hood*. In a '56 Chevy pickup, we toured public schools with our props and costumes and were paid $7 per show. Usually, we had one or two shows daily during the week. My income was low enough to qualify for food stamps.

During this time, I decided to move into a group house made up of three men and four women. I was not allowed to bring Kibbes with me. I found her a home with a friend who loved her. Chores, including meal preparation, were assigned on a rotating basis. It was a large family home on Riggs Place, N.W. above DuPont Circle. What an interesting mix, a couple of lawyers, a social worker, a house cleaner, and including me, two actors. The other actor was my good friend Samantha. We had become friends through intense months of theatre training.

The concern of the group house was there already was one gay man living there and would it be too much to have two. Samantha was a small woman but highly energetic and persuasive. For her, the result was worth any extension of the truth. She lobbied hard to get me accepted. Her day job was as a legal secretary where she could type 125 words a minute while talking and chewing gum.

Figure 17 Halloween with David

The five of us who composed the Library Theater crew drew close. Fred and I became friends. He introduced me to David Goldstein, one of his housemates, a childhood friend from New Jersey. I was immediately attracted. David had curly brown hair, was just over 5'6", had a slight acne problem, and lots of energy. I also discovered that his skin was smooth as alabaster, and as we dated it drove me nuts. Their group house was in Northwest, down Wisconsin Avenue from the Washington Cathedral.

David moved to Washington from San Francisco. While there, he worked in a macrobiotic restaurant. Taken from ancient Chinese principles, all food was divided into groups based on yin and yang. The perfectly balanced food was brown rice. David was a real devotee, and I was moved to emulate him. This meant fixing extra meals just for myself. I gradually worked my way into no sugar (too yin), no meat (too yang), fish once a week, much tofu, green vegetables, little fruit, and lots of brown rice. Being no cook by practice, what I produced was nothing compared to when David prepared a meal.

My bedroom was in the basement which gave me much needed privacy for a rent of $57 per month. The group house system worked well and I felt mostly accepted by the others. Samantha and I were best friends at this point.

Gay bars and discos continued blossoming. The pounding of the music drove me to heights I hadn't known. The big discos were located in S.E. Washington and required a taxi ride to get there.

The most popular gay disco was the Lost and Found. It was the largest gay disco on the east coast.. It had a restaurant, a central dance floor, two bars in the general area, then a back bar run by an older bartender nicknamed MayLing. He wore leather chaps and black vest and looked more like an elderly pirate than bartender. But did he ever run his show.

I attended church sometimes at the Metropolitan Community Church, a basically gay denomination with churches in a number of urban areas. I felt comfortable there and able to be myself without hiding. I especially enjoyed singing the hymns. David was Jewish but came with me a couple of times. Over a period of a year I was happy in my acting and relationship and didn't anticipate any significant changes.

It was around this time I decided to apply for a job at the Lost and Found. I already spent so much time there drinking and dancing, why not see if I could be employed there. I was hired initially as a bar boy, meaning I was responsible for seeing that the bars were well stocked. For the beer, I had to roll large kegs from the storeroom, through the crowds, to the bars. The call liquor was much simpler to manage. The place would get packed as the night went on with a long line of patrons striving to get in. It was frenetic and time would fly.

After three months of this employ, I was offered a job as bartender. What an honor, to be bartender in the largest gay disco outside of New York. I loved the prestige and the tight T-shirts we'd model. I got a fast tutorial and became familiar with names of drinks. After a few weeks I was slinging the drinks and developing my own clientele. As part of the bartender culture, we would occasionally give complimentary drinks to good, high tipping customers. My favorite mixed drink was the "slow comfortable screw", a combination of Southern Comfort and orange juice. Being asked for one, I enjoyed responding, "I'd love to".

Like many aspiring actors, besides waiting tables, I thought I'd give modeling a try. I got a recommendation and put together my book of various poses and settings. I signed up with Central Casting and Adair Agency to be available for both acting and modeling. I got called for several industrial training films. For a short time, I was used both as a regular model and as a character model such as farmer or priest. I had a couple photo spreads in the Washington Post and the Washingtonian Magazine.

Figure 18 Little Red Riding Hood, Wolftrap

On another front, there was an article in the Washington Post about our Library Theatre company on location at Wolf Trap. A photo appeared of us preforming *Little Red Riding Hood*. I was in the photo but completely covered from head to toe in a heavy cotton wolf's costume. It was summer and the costume had been used by several of us repeatedly. At one point I was choreographed to land close to some elementary school kids. One girl began to yell, "You stink, You stink". An ignominious end to a challenging role.

The next summer I was hired to be part of a summer stock troupe to perform on a paddle boat on the Mississippi River. The boat, docked at Davenport, Iowa, had been overhauled and turned into a small theater. David and I discussed our impending separation. He reassured me of his love. I felt sure of him, so I headed for the Mississippi.

DAVID McCLANAHAN

Figure 19 Character Model

Figure 20 Real Estate Ad

Figure 21 Head Shot.

Figure 22 For Fun

Our floating troupe put on five productions. As we did one, we were in rehearsal for the next. It was a hectic schedule. Among the shows we put on were "Harvey", "Wait Until Dark" and "The Fantasticks".

David came out from Washington to visit for a weekend. It was wonderful to see him and I proudly introduced him to the other actors. The theater company had rented out dorm rooms from a local college and we each had a private room. That summer featured John Denver's, "Almost Heaven, West Virginia", which I loved and played frequently during private time with David. He seemed a little remote but I decided it was the pressure of only having the weekend together. I had bought a white flowing robe with blue vertical strips which I enjoyed wearing when we were together.

After the summer run ended, I hurried back to Washington and David. We were together and all was well. One evening, David and I shared a cup of green tea and made love. After, he lay beside me, his alabaster shoulders above the sheets. Dark basement lightened by his laugh. Shadows passed through the sidewalk level window. Full, whole, complete, I was at peace.

"I need to share something with you," he said.

"Yeah," I lazily replied.

"I've been thinking, and I think I want to see other guys too.... It doesn't mean I don't love you or don't want to be with you...."

"You want to be with other guys?"

Yeah, I think so."

"You mean.... I'm not enough?"

This possibility had never crossed my mind. I was so in love and happy with him. The more we talked, the more I knew that such an arrangement would not work. I could not imagine his being with another guy. So, we broke up. My basement room turned very lonely.

I did continue the macrobiotic diet. Compliance wasn't as easy now that I had no one to share with. It was hard to maintain a balance and I tended towards the salty, yang end. Yang contracts and I started losing weight. I was committed and ignored it. Samantha began referring to how skinny I was. Feeling the indent of my hip bones didn't bother me. I would look in the mirror and not really see how thin my face was. I was 5'11" and weighted 129 lbs. Later, I realized that I was borderline anorexic.

I continued with the diet a few more months until one day our troupe stopped at a McDonald's for lunch. I had my prepared lunch but suddenly had a craving for a juicy burger and so ordered one. My stomach rapidly rebelled. I decided the only immediate treatment was to coat my stomach with a thick chocolate shake. I slowly felt better and then to make sure, ordered another shake. My fast-food binge was the demise of my macrobiotic life.

Turning over a new leaf, I began working at the John F. Kennedy Center for the Performing Arts. I started out in a new customer service called Instant Charge. It was a great opportunity to save patrons from coming to the Center for tickets, instead they could just pick up their phone and call us. There were three banks of telephones. We agents would gather in the morning before showtime for coffee and the latest Center gossip. Once the lines lit up it was nonstop. We took orders for the Opera House, Concert Hall, and Eisenhower Theater. One of the great perks was the opportunity to sneak in to see the performances. Some house managers were stricter than others so a delicate dance needed to be done.

Barbara Streisand was to perform one evening. Having heard how exacting she was, I wondered if she might do some pre-concert rehearsing. So, on my afternoon break, I walked to the third tier and gently opened the door. Oh my god, there she was on stage in blue jeans and jersey. She was giving directions to one of the crew, and then she sang. I was mesmerized, alone in this great hall listening to Barbara. It was hard to sneak out and return to Instant Charge.

When the New York City Opera came to town they always needed extras for non-singing parts to compliment the scenery. I made friends with a couple of corps dancers from New York. They told me I was just the right size for several of the costumes, the only requirement to land on stage. How exciting it was to escape and share the dressing rooms with the singers and dancers. I was delighted later to refer to the time I'd been in an opera with Beverly Sills. The difference being I was a silent extra upstage near the wings, and she was the diva downstage center performing.

I had the great privilege of being invited to play a silent role in the opera *Madama Butterfly*. My part had a bit of acting involved. I was the photographer at the wedding. It took rehearsing and choreography and wearing a period suit. After my scene in the first act, I was able to change clothes and rush into the house for the second act. One time there were no empty seats so I sat in the aisle and wept at an aria.

 Usually, I would go to the opera with Aunt Muriel. I told her I wasn't able this time but didn't mention why. Opening night all went well. The great Mexican Diva Gilda Cruz Romo was the diva. I loved this opera. On the weekend, I went to Muriel's for dinner. As we were talking, she mentioned that she had been to see *Madama Butterfly*. I told her I was the photographer. She was stunned, she said she thought he looked like me but completely dismissed the thought.

The great Diva, Leontyne Price, was performing at the Kennedy Center. This time I wasn't able to get into the house, but my friends from the ballet said they would sneak me in backstage. What an honor. I was taken into the wings and met Ms. Price. I would never forget how gracious she was.

 Leonard Bernstein came to the Center. Such power and fluidity in his movements. Audiences loved him and acclaimed him as the nights progressed. I had been invited by a friend of a friend to a party at the Watergate penthouse. Filled mostly with young gay men, I felt at home. Going down a hall to the bathroom I passed Mr. Bernstein and recognized him. I was thrilled and slowed my pace. I looked interested and he invited me to join the small group. After a few minutes, the great conductor turned to me and asked,

"And what do you do?" I had taken a short break from the Center and was somewhat embarrassed to say,

"I am unemployed". He smiled and then started to laugh. He said,

"I do so envy you, I know exactly what I am doing every day for the next 8 years!"

I was offered a new job at the Kennedy Center. There was an opening as Eisenhower Theater stage door manager. It sounded interesting, different, and I took it. It involved sitting on a stool in a narrow office space across from the stage door. I would have those entering sign a registry. The process generally went well until one night I did not recognize the great English actor Sir Ralph Richardson and required him to sign in.

The Eisenhower was considered one of the East Coast's pre-Broadway staging theaters. It also ran a number of both modern and classical pieces. I was able to meet a number of great classical actors including Julie Harris, John Gielgud, and Sir Laurence Olivier. The job was fun or boring depending on who appeared through the door.

Towards the end of 1976, I met Joan, a woman working on the administrative end of a production. We talked a little about show business and my interest in theater. Joan said that there was a production she was involved with coming to the National Theatre. After D.C. it was headed to Boston for a three week trial and then on to Broadway. She gave me tickets. It was the vaudevillian show, "Hellzapoppin". The two stars were Jerry Lewis and Lynn Redgrave.

The next time I saw Joan, she asked me,

"How did you like the show?" I said,

" It was entertaining and the style was new to me". Without warning Joan asked,

"How would you like to work on it and come to New York with us?". Amazed, I said,

"Wow, well….yeah, Really?" What an opportunity, to have a job in New York, and in theater, unbelievable.

I had been sharing an apartment off of Foggy Bottom with a massage therapist friend, Jenny. I was worried about giving her the news but she was surprisingly cool about it. The apartment was basically hers and I rented the extra room. Both of us were interested in various spiritual practices. We shared in various vegetarian diets, had done EST, and were subjects for a master class in Rolfing, a rarefied form of physical therapy led by Ida Rolf herself.

It did not take long for me to prepare for departure. I hardly owned anything. Jenny was fine with my leaving my bed, chair, and my beloved spathiphyllum plant, the only green thing I'd ever been able to keep alive. I did have my fine disco outfits and platform shoes which could fit into a couple of suitcases. I left knowing I would be able to return if it didn't work out.

I hit the discos for several nights to let people know I was moving to New York and had a job in theater. Boy, did I feel proud being able to say that. My friends and mostly acquaintances duly congratulated me and seemed impressed. Clearly my value in their eyes had gone up. I had dinner with various friends and promised to keep in touch.

Catching the train up to Boston, feeling I had it all, it didn't matter that there was no one to see me off. I felt like giving the finger to D.C. which had never really appreciated me. Now someone was seeing my gifts and giving me an opportunity to shine. The Boston Biltmore Hotel was in rough shape but for the first time I could claim staying in a suite. The show had come to town. I accepted the fact that the actual work I was doing was mundane. I had been chosen and that's what mattered.

During one rehearsal I met Lewis, a guy whose mother was an investor in the show. We hit it off. The family members were practicing Christian Scientists and involved with the *Christian Science Monitor*. My parents had subscribed to the newspaper for years. Lewis and I liked each other but there wasn't any chemistry activated. In the second week of the run, Lewis said he had a friend, Samuel, he wanted to introduce to me.

The three of us got together after the Saturday evening show and headed for a restaurant. Samuel had long blond hair and an angelic face. After eating, Lewis said he wanted to head home but for the two of us to keep going. We had some more conversation but after a brief gaze into one another's eyes, I popped the question, "Would you like to come to my hotel suite?" I'd never been able to say that before. The answer was, "Sure".

I kept red wine in my accommodations and offered this to Samuel.

"Another ?" "Sure." Some more talk while holding hands and it was getting late so I offered for Samuel to stay the night. If he wanted, we could just sleep. He said, "ok". We got in the queen sized bed on different sides and just lay there. I didn't want to make the first move. After a couple minutes Samuel reached over and touched my hand. He had smooth white skin, warm to the touch. His blue eyes and long blond hair drew me in. We enjoyed each other. In the quiet time after, I asked Samuel what he did for a living. "I'm a prostitute." I was very surprised but felt I had given him a comfortable break from that life.

LIFE IN NEW YORK

I didn't have any idea of where I could live in New York. I'd felt so excited about going I hadn't focused on this essential aspect of the adventure. Beginning to worry, I asked for ideas from some of the production crew. I got nowhere until one of the younger guys, Tim, said that he might have a possibility. He had an apartment on the Upper East Side on 76th Street, but really wasn't using it. He was staying at his partner's place, and I could use his apartment if I wanted. Wow, first the hotel suite and then an apartment on the Upper East Side.

As scheduled, the show closed its three-week Boston run, and I prepared myself for New York. I already had everything with me in two suitcases. I left Boston and headed for the Big Apple. Meeting Tim at the address, we climbed the five floors. Used to living in D.C. apartments, I was shocked by how small the place was. It was a railroad apartment, a narrow hallway with three tiny rooms. Tim said I could do what I wanted in terms of freshening it up, painting the walls, whatever. When Tim left, I went outside to regain a sense of space. Little did I know how fortunate I was.

"Hellzapoppin" had its big Broadway opening on a Monday… and folded on Thursday… I was in shock. In my mind I had built a new world around this entré into New York and the theater scene. How could this happen? Joan, feeling a bit responsible, said she might be able to find me something else but wasn't sure. I decided to deal with my anxiety by painting the apartment. I wasn't enthusiastic considering past painting experience, but I decided to try. I bought some blue paint and brushes at a hardware store and hauled them home. I started with the first room in the late afternoon. I chose a color that would help relax me, a gentle blue.

I went to bed happy having done something positive. I awoke in the morning with a smile on my face. Proud of my effort, I went into the next room. Oh no, the gentle blue had turned into a garish turquoise that hurt my eyes. I wanted to change it, but it was too late. I couldn't take it back and I couldn't afford more. I had to continue the job with clenched teeth. I signed up with an employment agency that sent me out on sporadic day jobs. Short assignments weren't easy but helped me get more oriented. Meantime, Tim said he needed his place back. I needed a new place to stay.

At first, I panicked and called Jinny to see if I could move back to D.C. She said her boyfriend had moved in and they were very happy. I then called an old Kennedy Center contact who had moved to New York. Mark said that his partner Henry had use of an apartment on Riverside Drive on the Upper West Side and it was available. Henry was staying with Mark. The apartment was owned by one of the great opera divas, Minion Dunn, who was on tour in Europe. I went from the railroad apartment into a luxurious environment which included a doorman. My bedroom had a large walk-in closet with some extraordinary gowns. I put my few items on wire hangers next to them.

I got a temp job working at Pfizer Pharmaceutical not far from Grand Central Station. My manager was named Sandy. She was smart with a strong personality. Her husband worked in a design firm. I worked for Sandy for two months and we enjoyed being together. One lunchtime she said, "Come with me," and off she raced. I ran after her and we ended up on Fifth Avenue. She escorted me into an elegant shoe store. Sandy said it was time I had a decent pair of shoes. She had me try on several and thought the Gucci loafers were the best. She paid and we returned to the office. The shoes cost more than I made in three weeks.

On another occasion, Sandy and her husband were going away for a long weekend. They lived in Princeton in a lovely home surrounded by woods. Sandy asked if I'd be willing to house-sit for them and care for their two Russian wolf hounds. My stay would include the use of one of their cars. I felt I was being invited into a magical land. I packed my best outfits and hit the train. I went into town to a diner wearing my Cartier scarf from Goodwill. There was only one small burn mark on the silk which I could hide as I wrapped it around my neck.
I felt chic and well-to-do. Coming home I made myself a snack and sat

at the grand dining room table. I had just taken a bite when Sasha approached me. She fixed her eyes on me and growled, fulfilling the meaning of her name, "Defender." I was terrified and tried to ignore her. It did not work, she kept threatening. Deciding I really wasn't that hungry, I dropped some toast on the floor. She continued staring at me but then gave in. I was saved, though I did go through about a loaf of bread in two days.

Initially, I had only one good friend living in the city. Lou worked for AmTrak and somehow had scored a small rent-controlled apartment on the Lower East Side. Then my old housemate, Samantha, contacted me and she wanted to come to New York. She was welcome but I couldn't offer any real help. I felt guilty sitting at an elegant desk in a doorman apartment building saying I wasn't able to host.

My luxurious stay was short lived. Ms. Dunn's European tour was coming to a close. I reached out to the theater crowd. An acquaintance, Amy, was on the production staff of a show going on regional tour. Her apartment was on the Upper West Side on 103rd Street in Spanish Harlem. It was on the 6th floor and the elevator often didn't work. Amy had two long-haired dogs and a Himalayan cat. It was a very hot summer in the city and the animals insisted on sleeping with me. I could manage until the electricity went out during a weekend heatwave. It was like sleeping in a fur lined oven, but we all survived.

In my free time, I got involved with several consciousness raising groups. One of them was named Sirave founded by a UCLA trained psychologist and his actress wife. It was hard core in terms of digging down into the psyche and gaining new insight. There was also acting out one's birth for hours to experience rebirth. At one of the sessions I met a woman named Suzi and we instantly connected. Suzi was a divorced mother with three teenage kids living in Yonkers. She brought her son John and he acted out a powerful rage that burned within him.

Suzi invited me to spend a weekend with the family and I did. I had saved a little money, so I was able to treat them to pizza. The kids, Freddy, Deena, and John really liked me. After that, I would sometimes go up for a weekend. I felt part of the family. I was like a father figure to Freddy who was fourteen at the time. We went canoeing and did other activities together including giving him back rubs like my father used to give me. At one point Suzi and I attempted intimacy, but it didn't work for either of us.

My next job was in the box office of Joseph Papp's Shakespeare Festival on the Lower East Side. The Festival had both Shakespearean productions and avant-garde shows. It managed the "Shakespeare in the Park" program of Central Park. I met a young ballet dancer who was connected to one of the productions. Danny and I were drawn to each other. Danny had a cute round face, warm lips, and a dancer's body. He lived on 14th Street, Lower West Side, with an older female roommate who worked in theater management. Danny and I spent our free time together going to cheap dance and theater productions. He worked but his dance classes were the center of his life. Although he had little money, he was generous with me. He would bring me treats when we were going to a show and take me to dinner sometimes.

I relocated down to the East Village. The friend that had gotten me into Minion Dunn's apartment knew of another older female actress on tour. I was not familiar with the East Village and Bedford Street was very different from the West Village. Winter was coming. With a shortage of temp jobs, I had almost no money. My only sweater was no real protection from the wind. One cold afternoon, there was a knock on my door. A postman handed me a box from a close friend, Vanessa, in D.C. The contents made me laughed with joy. It was a beautiful full-length Harris Tweed coat she found at Goodwill. It was perfect with just a small tear in the lining of the right pocket. I was warm at last.

Danny and I continued going together for six months. One day I woke up in my apartment and just didn't have feelings for him anymore. Danny was as attentive and generous as ever, but I decided I would cut it off. Not knowing my state of mind, he came to my apartment. I apologetically told him that we needed to stop, that my heart felt like a stone within me, my feelings for him were gone. He was shocked and left. A few days later I was doing some freelance work for the TV show, "The Doctors," and received a call. It was Danny. He said through his tears, "Don't go near any dark alleys, if I catch you, I'll cut your face."
A few years later, I realized how cruel I had been. I went back to New York twice to find him and apologize but never saw him again.

Yet another necessary move found me in a friend's apartment in Chelsea. Then good fortune smiled on me. There was a sublet of a sublet available on 45th between 8th and 9th Avenues. The apartment was on the first floor. It was one room with kitchen and rusty shower stall. What a great location, Broadway shows were in every direction. Of course, I couldn't afford them. Across the street a restaurant called Ted Hook's Backstage was featured. I decided to be a waiter again. I got the job and did the brief training. A major requirement was we had to look great in the uniform, a tight brown polyester jumpsuit with zipper from crotch to neck. The tighter the better. I passed the test.

I wasn't that great as a waiter, but pleasant and clients tolerated my service. When it got busy, passing a row of tables each making requests felt like running a gauntlet. The restaurant was popular with the theater crowd, both audiences and actors. Ted Hook was friend to many.

One night I had Eartha Kitt in my section. She ordered leg of lamb but served in a special manner. I had no idea what she meant. I went frantically to the kitchen. I spoke to an experienced waiter. He graciously offered to take over her service and I was relieved. Liza Minnelli was another favorite who came in later in the evenings. My favorite customer was Judith Jameson of the Alvin Ailey American Dance Theater. She would order a simple hamburger with no frills.

Wilber, my friend from Georgetown, called to say he wanted to move to New York from Washington, and could he just stay for a few days while he followed up leads. Considering my tiny apartment, I hesitated but decided to go ahead. He arrived with two suitcases and his raucous laugh. It was now me, my two six-month-old hyperactive kittens, Pigeon and Tebbs, and high energy Wilber, all in one room. We slept back-to-back as friends. Wilber frequently went out at night and did not return until early in the morning filled with wild tales. After a couple of weeks, I couldn't take it any more and told him he had one more week and then needed to go. He still hadn't found a place but did leave. Later Wilber told me that when he left, he slept in an empty condo building under construction.

While still working at Ted Hook's, Dad came to visit. I'd communicated some dissatisfaction with my life and my parents were concerned. In the afternoon we spent some time walking around and talking. I shared with him something of my life. I offered to treat him to dinner at Ted Hook's. He was delighted. I had a little concern about how he might take the milieu of the place but he seemed fine. After the meal, I really needed a drink and ordered my red wine. I knew Dad never drank alcohol but had a sweet tooth, so I suggested a Creme de Menthe. He hesitated and then said yes. I was surprised, and then he went on to have a second. We shared my ancient couch bed and both slept well.

Suzi, my friend from White Plains, was a devotee of Ken Keyes, author of *"Handbook to Higher Consciousness"*, a new way of experiencing life and relationships. A central mantra was "Always Us Living Love." I was moved by the message and became more involved. I discovered a commune in Kentucky dedicated to this philosophy. Taking three weeks off, I headed to St. Mary's, Kentucky. The campus, once a Catholic college, was beautiful. Everyone was assigned a chore, and I got baby care. I shared the responsibility of watching over three baby boys around nine months old. After they ate, I found my favorite activity was to take them one by one to a hammock slung between two trees. I would rest the baby on my chest, sing, swing, and rock him to sleep.

The commune held meditations and gentle discussions. One morning I noticed a young guy having breakfast by himself. I got cereal and joined him. He turned out to be cute and smart. As the time progressed, I found myself distracted by him. I tried to dismiss my thoughts, but we ended up in a bunk bed when no one else was around. Turned out he had a partner who was a flight attendant. I was angry with myself for breaking an unspoken understanding of the commune against fraternizing. New York, after the peacefulness of the Kentucky countryside, was jarring.

Samantha ended up being platonic roommates with a wealthy guy whose family was connected to the beginnings of Hollywood. He traveled and liked having someone in his enormous apartment. It was located on Riverside Drive in the West Seventies with great windows overlooking the Hudson River. Every so often, her roommate would divest his closet and buy a whole new wardrobe. Samantha would grab some items for me before they went to the trash. One thing I held onto was a small metal suitcase covered in travel logos from the countries he'd visited.

Studio 54 was the most popular club in New York. I knew someone who could get me in. I dressed impeccably for the night. I was proud of my outfit and the tight grey slacks that showed me off to advantage. The night went into full swing. Disco fever ruled. At midnight in mid-dance, I crouched low and pop, the back seam of my pants split. Thunder struck, I ran from the floor. To feel really sexy, I had chosen not to wear any underwear.

I was aware that my landmark 30th birthday was a month away. Although I tried, I had never fully been with a woman and decided I should know what it was like before turning thirty. I had stayed in contact with a young woman, Hope, from the Kentucky commune. She was leaving the commune and coming through New York on the way to her parents in Connecticut. I invited her to stay overnight at my place. She was young, bouncy, with long brown hair. I took her out to dinner. Not to Ted Hook's, I didn't want my friends and co-workers to get the wrong idea.

We had a cheap dinner with wine and on the way back to the apartment picked up a couple more bottles. It was fun to reminisce about different commune personalities and what we had learned. We started kissing and then went for it. I was amazed by the experience. Hope left saying she'd be in touch but wasn't. This was fine with me. At least I had completed my goal of fully knowing what being with a woman was like, and my birthday was still a week away.

One night a group of French guys came into Ted Hook's. I waited on them and after the meal, one of the guys slipped me his phone number. I called later that week and went out to dinner with Fredrick. What a nice guy, a sous-chef at Tavern on the Green in Central Park. He wasn't exactly my type being bony with sharp nose and cheeks, but he was fun. Fredrick had an efficiency apartment on Central Park West and we usually went there. I loved that on the mornings we were together, Fredrick would get up a little early to make café au lait, followed by an omelets and a baguette. His was the best coffee outside of Paris. We saw each other for almost six months. We talked about visiting his home in France. One night, it happened again, I just felt the relationship was over. I had fallen out of love with him, if I'd ever really been able to love him. He was crushed, and I moved on.

BACK TO WASHINGTON

After three years in New York, I moved back to Washington. I thought I could have more sense of community with my old D.C. friends. My dating began again, at first for one night, then for three, then two weeks, and finally for six months. I lived in an apartment in Adams Morgan off the intersection of 18th and Columbia Road. A gay restaurant bar opened right onto my building's front door and my efficiency was right off the lobby.

I had found Rick, a kind, thoughtful, skilled handyman. He had freckles, red hair, a pleasingly smooth body with boyish build, and an affectionate nature. He helped me with some basics for the apartment including a box spring to sleep on. Several pieces of my furniture came from the street. I met another resident who lived on the second floor. Raised in the South and from a genteel family, he worked for an association in government relations. His special claim to fame was being friends with Tennessee Williams. I did get to see his elegant 2nd floor apartment where his friend Tennessee would visit upon occasion. Once I saw them together in the lobby. Both appeared inebriated as my neighbor helped Mr. Williams through the repeated closing of the elevator door.

Figure 23 Church Dance

I needed a larger apartment and discovered one on 16th and T Streets, N.W. It was a large one bedroom on the 6th floor with a fine view of the neighborhood. I found a waiting job at a gay restaurant/disco, the Frat House, on P Street near DuPont Circle. It was popular and in a hub of gay establishments. Once again, I got to exhibit my mediocre waiting skills but was liked by the management. The Frat House became the center of my social life when I wasn't out with friends.

One evening I saw a young guy dancing who really struck me. A move I'd discovered, as an adjunct to just dancing, was to subtly back up into a cute guy and start rubbing my rear end on his. After a few bumps, if my partner responded in kind, there might be a connection. As the disco music blared, this small guy in a tight yellow and green sweater responded to me enthusiastically. I was turned on. Off the dance floor he was intelligent, and we hit it off. By the end of the night, I had invited him home to my new apartment on 16th Street.

Paul was hot. After our night together I drove him to the Maryland suburbs. We continued to date on weekends. He worked as a shoe sales associate when not going to university. After a few weeks all the travel was a hassle, and I invited him to move in. Paul had no furniture of his own and I had little, so this gave us an excellent activity to pursue.... setting up house. Paul drank a lot for a small guy, and I was right there with him. He was from New Jersey and came from a hard drinking family with a waitress mother.

I could not keep my hands off him. I wanted to be with him every possible minute. Fortunately, we each had separate friends for a little balance. Paul loved setting up house, getting the china. I got the silverware off the back of a truck hawking it on 16th Street. The spoons began to rust within the month. Things were tastefully matched. We located a decent queen-sized bed, couch and chairs for the living room, a TV and entertainment center. Thank God for credit. The cost didn't matter, it was forever. Life centered on sex, alcohol and discoing.

 My friends accepted the arrangement but communicated some concern over the impulsiveness of it all. I learned more about Paul and the rough life he had being gay in his family and neighborhood. He was hungry to embrace various symbols of the new life. For show, he loved wearing large colored handkerchiefs in his left or right back pockets to communicate various sexual interests. Red handkerchiefs were for hard core sex, blue was for screwing, left pocket was active, right pocket was passive. I hated it but went along to be part of his life. Cowboy hats and off we'd go.

As my need for Paul increased, his desire to go out increased as well. I felt anxiety and panic as each evening came and Paul wanted to party. The tension became too much after a year, and we decided to break up. I did not realize how attached I was to him until an apartment opened up one floor down and I grabbed it. I was living in hell knowing that he was one flight up and with other guys. When it got to be too much, I'd go upstairs and hang around his door, listening, hoping he'd come out.

I was unemployed again so didn't have work to distract me. I found myself pacing my efficiency apartment constantly trying to combat feelings of jealousy, anger, fear, resentment. Nothing worked. I realized I had to do something, or I was going to explode. A great solution came to mind. I'd go to grad school and start a new career as a psychologist. I started looking into programs in the DC area. I called the local mental health center to make further enquiries. After about ten minutes with the secretary of the center, she suggested that I might want to come in and get some counseling myself with a clinical psychologist. A week later I had my first session with Dr. Johnson, a clinical psychologist.

The mental health center was funded by the DC government and with only my unemployment income, I was able to afford counseling on a sliding scale. With Dr. Johnson's help, I soon gave up the idea of becoming a psychologist and instead turned to understanding my addictive behavior related to Paul. He also strongly encouraged me to focus on getting a job.

I found work three weeks before my unemployment ran out. I ran into a friend on the Metro who was working at the American Psychiatric Association on R Street, N.W. near DuPont Circle. He said I should go and check out the association. I did and was hired as a secretary. I became good friends with the woman who had interviewed me during the process. Years later she said that she thought I would be good for the APA and had recommended me to management.

Having a commitment to go to work and seeing the same people every day felt like a new experience. The APA Office of Meetings Management was made up of a demanding, hard drinking team. I began as secretary to the Assistant Director and shortly was promoted to secretary to the Director. The office had to plan for annual meetings as far as ten years in advance in order to get adequate space committed in cities we booked. There were other meetings to work on as well but the APA Annual Meeting was central.

Starting work in January, I was thrown right into preparing for New Orleans in May. The registrar had been with the office for almost three years. I was in awe of someone having held a job for that long. I hadn't worked anywhere for more than five months. Whenever there was a social event for the staff, lots of booze was present. Sam, a fine woman came on board to be secretary to the Assistant Director. She and I really hit it off, both having some involvement in a faith life.

We went down to New Orleans a week before the official opening of the annual meeting. I was placed in one of the lesser hotels but was able to walk to the convention center. My basic role was as a courier for the office and to assist at the Information Desk in the convention center. As many as 9,000 psychiatrists and thousands of additional allied professionals attended. Each evening numerous cocktail parties were given by pharmaceutical companies and other service providers. The parties overflowed with great hors d'oeuvres and selections of liquor.

The best part was getting familiar with New Orleans and its popular haunts such as the numerous gay bars. I woke up one morning with a stranger in my bed. I didn't remember having met him. We were polite to each other, and he left. I had no time to think about it, I had to get to work at the convention center. That morning, when I was answering phones, one call asked if the Assistant Director was there. In confusion I answered, "No I'm not", and hung up. The staff enjoyed a good laugh.

An assistant position opened in the APA Public Affairs Department and I was accepted. I liked the director and assistant director and it continued to afford me opportunities to travel related to work. Another gay guy, Henry, worked there but he kept a low profile.

Figure 24 AIDS Quilt

One afternoon in the spring of 1982, Henry came over to me carrying a copy of the Washington Post. He lay it down on a worktable and told me to read it. It was a small piece that included a term that I hadn't seen before, "GRID". It stood for Gay Related Immunodeficiency Disease. It talked about several cases that showed up in New York. Not much was known about the disease. There was no sense of where it came from, what caused it, or how it spread. I asked Henry if he was aware of any cases in Washington and he wasn't. The AIDS epidemic had begun.

Figure 25 With David

I heard about a new music group formed in Washington the previous year, The Gay Men's Chorus. I wasn't dating anyone and thought this could be a fun activity and means of meeting some interesting guys. Having done musicals and church music I hoped to be accepted. I auditioned and got in. I loved the positive angle of working on a project to create something with other men. I also met a tall, handsome, dark-haired guy named David. We were both tenors and stood beside each other in rehearsals. I had a good strong voice, but David was blessed with a high, angelic tone which people loved. I grew to really like David and his voice. After several rehearsals we decided to start dating and I appreciated even more of him.

I was living in a small efficiency off Logan Circle close to my work. David worked as a high-end waiter in one of the swank hotels, the Willard on Pennsylvania Avenue. The way he carried himself, his flashing smile, lean torso, and slightly superior aire, all contributed to a persona deserving of the highest renumeration at the end of a meal. In other words, he got great tips.

As we drew closer, we promised that this would be a committed relationship. We both had strong religious backgrounds and decided, when possible, to attend church together at Metropolitan Community Church. Over time, I had shared about my life, my relationship with my parents. I was proud of David and wanted them to meet him. On a trip north, they came through Washington and were impressed with David. Also his elegant mother visited several times and was delightful. David eventually was spending much of his time at my efficiency off Logan Circle. It was close to his hotel and he enjoyed just walking to work.

My apartment building had affordable rent for a reason. It was located in one of the red light districts of D.C. This was not immediately apparent until night fell and the working women came out. Observing them, I came to see how difficult their lives were. I had an altercation with one who tried to get in the building but didn't live there. I was pushing out the door, and she was pushing in. A police car came by and we both raced to tell our side of the story. She was yelling in the driver's side window, I was yelling through the passenger side window. After a few minutes of this, the police car just drove off.

As with many, my apartment was overrun with cockroaches. I got the great idea of buying one of the large insecticide bombs and using it to be rid of them. I set it off in the morning as I headed out to work. I planned to spend the night at David's. I had been careful to put my two cats, Pigeon and Tebbs, safely in the glassed-in porch and using wet rags along the bottom of the doors. The call came at 10am. It was the building superintendent. The building fire alarm had tripped and the super had discovered the smoking bomb. This incident was not good for relations and my pets had to go to the vet immediately due to their coughing. Fortunately, they recovered from the poisoning.

To get away from it all, we decided to take a holiday to Acapulco. David hadn't been out of the U.S. so all was new to him. We had a cheap fare and cheap hotel to match. It was August which could explain the low prices. We visited bars and had late nights. The vivid memory that I retain was of getting up late, walking along the beach at noon with no one there. We came across a beachside bar. Going in, the only other occupant was a tan dog sprawled across the cement floor, panting.

Back home, someone left a large chandelier on the sidewalk outside my building. It was in rough condition, but attractive. I hauled it to my apartment to add a touch of class to the barren environment. The ceiling was only ten feet high. Once hung, the chandelier leveled off around seven feet. David at 6'2 ducked whenever he was under it. One evening when we were eating at our small dining table, the chandelier unleashed and crashed, shattering glass globes everywhere.

David had little experience in the gay world when he arrived in Washington. He loved me and our life together but after two and half years he had the desire to date other men as well. My nightmare had returned taking me back to my first David and his asking the same of me. I was deeply hurt and couldn't understand. I believed I was all that David needed. Again, I had no choice. I suspected David was already seeing another guy in the Chorus. He went back to living in his apartment.

I enjoyed meeting friends in bars but after a while wanted another venue. There was a gay sports organization called Adventuring. I went on some hikes but didn't meet anyone interesting. I thought maybe I'd try gay volleyball. They had a pro league and one for amateurs. I started going to amateur night at a local high school gym near DuPont Circle. Everyone seemed more skilled than I was. When about to give the idea up, one attractive guy started to give me pointers. I was certainly more interested in the guy than the pointers, but fortunately at the moment, the two meshed.

ERNEST

His name was Ernest. He had a chiseled Slavic face and a lean athlete's body. He knew his volleyball and was studying ballet. It turned out he and his siblings were almost a volleyball team in themselves. I went a few more times and then popped the question. "Do you want to grab a drink sometime?" We hit it off. Ernest was twenty-four and I was thirty-six.

After just a few months, we decided it didn't make sense to keep paying rent and decided to look for a cheap house. Finn, a colleague, was venturing out for the first time as a real estate agent. He had gotten the elderly woman across the street from him to let him try to sell her house. It didn't even go on the market. Ernest and I leapt at the chance and made a bid. At this stage of my life, I was a good saver and was able to manage the down payment. It worked out, the 1913 Victorian row house on 17th Street, NW in Mt. Pleasant was ours for $89,000.

Once the rose-colored glasses came off, the reason for the price was more evident. The former owner, who had lived there for decades, was a hoarder. She left huge piles all over the house. The worst was the basement which was waist high in uncollectibles. She had thirteen cats living with her and the fine wooden floors were caked with ingrained feces.

Ernest and I had not discussed our approaches to a major multi-year project. The possibilities enthralled Ernest. There were French sliding doors, alcoves, a fine banister, an attic to organize, and an overall facelift of surfaces, including the removal of ancient wallpaper before painting. The renovations were a daunting project but Ernest embraced the work. I, on the other hand, hadn't considered the reality at all, never having been one to do manual labor. It reminded me of when I'd been fired from the college painting job.

I did strive initially to apply myself to the easier tasks at hand. Clearly, I wasn't gifted at painting, but it was work I could do acceptably as long as I didn't run over the masking tape used to separate the walls from the paneling. Ernest selected the color schema, curtains, the putty, all the basics and directed the two of us. I was want to whine after a short time, needed copious iced tea breaks and moving towards a dinner glass of wine early in the afternoon. I was always anxious to run any kind of errand. Ernest just slugged away. Members of his family would occasionally come by and pitch in with the daily project. How delighted I was to see their strong healthy bodies enter the front door.

Bottom line, Ernest did the work and I complained. I had gone into home remodeling with no concept of what was required. Nor did I have a sense of what toll on Ernest my attitude and resistance were taking. We agreed that if we could complete the dining room, living room, and foyer by summer, we would travel to Paris and London as a prize. Ernest had never been to Europe; Paris was my favorite city and London came in second. Often as Ernest did the renovating, I would be dreaming, looking at maps, tours, and just wishing for the time to hurry up. We met two of the three objectives by spring.

TRAVEL

Flying out was none too soon for me. I couldn't wait to be free of the constant burden of needing to do something for the house. The house had begun to feel like a lover Ernest had on the side.

At last, cocktails in hand, we were winging our way across the Atlantic with nary a care. Landing first at Heathrow, the luggage carrousel produced all our luggage. I had packed with the view that anything that might be needed should be included. Ernest packed simply and efficiently.

It was springtime in London, cool and rainy. Having disposable income, I was anxious to procure some appropriate attire. We found a shop after a few days of sightseeing that was stylish and not too expensive. I bought a billowy cotton pullover with a high collar. Ernest took a picture of me on the steps of St. Paul's Cathedral. After all the fine dining, I looked as big as Henry VIII. After our return, we settled back into our usual pattern of doing our day jobs and Earnest working on the house.

The next summer I staffed a conference of the World Psychiatric Association in Nairobi. I thought it might offer a perfect chance to visit Egypt on the way home. I hoped there could be some healing from my childhood trauma. Landing in Cairo, I took a cab to the Cairo Marriott. The next day, I visited the great Cairo Museum and made a day trip to the Pyramids and the Sphinx. The story came to mind that when Napoleon had invaded Egypt, his troops used the Sphinx for cannon practice with the resulting nose damage to it.

While at the pyramids, I met an attractive guy, named Cal, a US soldier on leave from the Sinai. We at once liked each other and decided to get together to attend the sound and light show that night at the Pyramids. It was an impressive display, but I was distracted sitting close to Cal. We shared drinks afterwards and decided to have lunch together the following day. The meal was excellent. I needed to get something at my hotel, and he said he'd tag along. Once in the room, I went to the bathroom. Cal said he needed to go too, and he came up beside me. I was in agony. Ernest and I had been together for two years and I had remained monogamous. This guy Cal was a beautiful, blond guy with clearly a great body. I turned away and walked out of the bathroom, ending that romance.

We did go for dinner and get drunk on a rather cheap tasting costly red wine. Enjoying each other's company, we promised to keep in touch. I returned to the Marriott and prepared to travel in the morning. My father had contacted a long-time Egyptian friend in Assiut and arranged for me to visit. I was suffering quite a hangover when I went down at 5am to get a cab to the train station. I explained what I needed, and to my horror, was informed no trains were running due to the Muslim holiday.

I had to go. The friends in Assiut were expecting me and my return flight out of Cairo was fixed. I communicated my urgency, and the bellhop suggested using a taxi. A taxi, all the way to Assiut!? I asked how long it would take… about 9 hours and cost $100. Realizing there was no option, I agreed. Wearing dark glasses and nursing my hangover, I crawled into the back of the cab. Silence at first, then the driver motioned to me, asking if he could play some music. I said *Itffuddal,* please, go ahead. He turned his tape machine on and threw me into culture shock. Out from the front seat blared, "It's raining Men, Alleluia, It's raining Men A-Amen." I could not stop laughing at myself, at the situation, and at the fact I had nine hours to travel by taxi into Upper Egypt over 400 kilometers from Cairo.

We arrived late in the evening at my father's friend's home after coming through the mountains around Assiut. For millennia the mountains were used as burial grounds. When we were kids, we'd go up into them and collect mummy beads to make necklaces for my mother. Also in the hills was a Coptic monastery dedicated to the Holy Family. Near the monastery was a cave believed to be where Joseph hid Mary and Jesus when they first arrived to begin their life as refugees in Egypt. I was in awe when I had visited the cave as a boy.

I was received as an honored guest by my father's old friend and family. He had planned a few activities for me. My particular interest was visiting the mission sites where my early life had taken place. The first place we went was Assiut College. My family lived in its compound. The streets leading there seemed more crowded than when I left in 1963. We briefly visited the main college building and then on to the 2nd floor of the building that had been our family home for fifteen years.

The grand apartment was unrecognizable. There were clothes lines covered with *jelabeea* robes and pajamas hanging across what had been our elegant living room. I went into the bedrooms now turned into cramped dormitories with bunk beds. I was shocked. I fled to the veranda for fresh air and let my tears fall. I was completely unprepared for this new reality. As I thought about it later, I had not considered the passage of time and its consequences. I strove not to appear ungrateful to my host. We then went by the mission hospital where I was born. It mostly matched what was in my boyhood memory.

My host, Dr. Ramses, suggested going by the PMI, the Egyptian preschool I had been taken to when I was five. I did not think about it and agreed. We walked into the hall, and I almost fainted from the powerful scent memory. I was overwhelmed by the feeling of having been abandoned there.

I was asked if there was any other place I wished to see while in Assiut. I remembered a lovely mansion located on the Nile as it flowed through Assiut. It was the Alexan Pasha home. I asked to visit it even though it would be empty this time of year except for the groundskeeper. I was the only one there. This small palace was as I remembered, a gem with a magnificent staircase, columns, and murals on the walls and a walkway down to the Nile.

After visiting Assiut, I decided to visit the site of the trauma I experienced at the boarding school in Alexandria. I took a train, second class, missing the goats and chickens in third. There were not enough seats, so I sat on a rolled-up rug for some of the trip. Upon arrival, the taxi driver eventually found the school. Alexandria had grown and I had difficulty recognizing anything. The school was on holiday so there were no students. However, my old nemesis, the principal Henry McClain, and his wife were in residence. I approached him with care, after all, the man had beaten me for running out of a prayer meeting the moment it had ended.

He offered me a beer. I was shocked, alcohol in our mission school. This was the same place where some boys weren't allowed to take off their shirts for basketball. I felt in another universe having a beer with him and Mrs. McClain. The buildings and compound were much smaller than I remembered. There was no quiet time or privacy for me to process my dark memories. Thank God for the beer and a pressing appointment which came to mind so I could exit gracefully.

I stayed at a Marriott on the Alexandria beach for a few days. The first evening I decided to go for a walk along the *corniche*, the pathway along the Mediterranean. After about twenty minutes, I noticed two young men following me. Fortified with wine, I stopped, feeling brave. I questioned why they were there. Our communication had to be in Arabic. It was a real effort to call up words from my childhood, but some did come. They said during the day they sold tourist items from booths in town. Then it became clear that they were selling something else in the evenings. It was a temptation, a rare opportunity, but my relationship with Ernest, my rational self, and the specter of AIDS overcame my loneliness and convinced me to keep going. Back at the hotel, I, cheered up by toasting myself for doing the right thing.

When I woke up in the morning, I could not move. I had severe pain in my lower back and left leg. I was captive to my bed. A vicious bout of sciatica had returned. The pain was excruciating. I called the concierge asking for a doctor. They responded with sympathy and within half an hour a doctor came to my room. His English was flawless, and his manner was formal having gone to medical school in London. I told him the three medications usually prescribed. He at once put in an order for them and left. They arrived within the hour and brought me back to normal within two days. The day following, I left for Cairo and my return flight to Washington.

In the fall I heard a rumor that TWA was going bankrupt. For over ten years I had saved frequent flyer miles with them which included a work trip to Maui. I decided I wasn't willing to lose them. Ernest and I talked it over and he was fine with my being gone. So, in September, I took off first class for a two-week trip to France. It was my virgin first-class experience. It proved luxurious, with great leather seats, flowing wine, and personal service. I appreciated the irony of having humble clothes and a large backpack. I spent time in Paris visiting churches and museums, but after some days a desire grew in me to visit to the French Alps.

I booked by rail and headed for Chamonix. It was a lovely town with a funicular reaching the highest point one can go mechanically in the Alps. I found a cozy room for myself and walked around town for a couple days, frequenting various cafes and restaurants. I decided to take the funicular to the top and hike several trails before returning to Paris. Before getting on the funicular, I went to the bathroom. I found myself in some discomfort but didn't think much about it. After we reached the top, I needed to go again. This time I was in pain and there was some discharge. I could not believe what was happening. I had been with no one other than Ernest for the last three years.

The hiking trail had an extraordinary view of the verdant hillsides and snowy mountain peaks. On one hand I was seeing a great wonder of nature and thanking God for it, on the other hand my mind was racing through life threatening possibilities and begging God to spare me. I wondered if it were possible that I had contracted AIDS. So many guys I knew were being struck down. I trudged along with my soul torn between splendor and a death sentence. On the path, I ran into a gentleman walking his gorgeous German Shepherd. He spoke German to me and I responded in French. As I began the descent I wondered if I were moving towards knowledge of my suffering and death. At this time having AIDS was a death sentence.

When I arrived Paris, I placed a call to a French physician and made an appointment. I was not able to see him for two days. My physical distress and my imaginings were hard to handle especially away from home. During the appointment, the doctor took cultures and said it would take a day for the processing. With fear and trepidation I placed a call the following day. The results revealed neither HIV nor a venereal disease. It was simply a urinary infection and the treatment was simple. Such a frightful load lifted from me. I returned to Washington with relief knowing I would not have to have 'the conversation' with Ernest.

APA

Life in Washington carried on at a normal pace. Ernest went through several jobs as I continued in my position at the APA with Dr. Sabshin. Several times a year I would staff either the Annual Meeting or a smaller meeting. I always enjoyed the opportunity. I loved to travel and it was especially nice to have the costs covered. In San Francisco there were approximately 15,000 registrants. The demand of it increased alcohol consumption on the part of the staff, and certainly for me.

 One night after visiting several bars, I connected with a guy in a bar and he took me home with him. It had been dark in the bar, and he kept the lights low in his apartment. He seemed to be keeping part of his body covered. I was observing this through drunken eyes and ignored it. Upon returning to my hotel room early in the morning, a light bulb went off. I realized that he probably had the bruise-like markings of Kaposi's sarcoma and was covering them. A great wave of fear passed over me. But there was nothing I could do at that point. I carried on. Once home, I tested negative for HIV.

The meeting next year in Los Angeles allowed for visits to Hollywood and movie studios. The APA had a number of affiliate subgroups which met during the overall meeting. The gay and lesbian members had their own caucus and I, with some other staff, would attend and support them. A large party was arranged one night in the home of one of the lead actors in the original "Star Trek"TV series. His home was situated in Hollywood Hills with a terrific view.

As staff liaison to the Committee on Addictions, which included gambling, I helped with the logistics for its meeting in Las Vegas. The site seemed to me both ironic and logical. Members and staff were put up in casino hotels at a great discount. As I hurried through the casino section to get to the hotel lobby, slot machines were clanging, the croupiers were addressing their special audiences, and waiters were rushing by. The one-armed bandits never seemed to get a break. What I enjoyed watching most was the horse racing. Gambling seemed to be the one addiction I was not drawn to, so for me it was the ideal setting.

During Ernest's life up to college, he had been steeped in the Catholic Church. He even considered seminary. He came from a family of religious parents, his mother having become Catholic when she married his father. His father died young and his mother's strong faith helped to keep the family going. Ernest's adult siblings continued to be involved in the church. Once in a while we would join a family outing which included Mass.

We were again struggling in our relationship. Ernest was more socially and culturally active, and I spent more time at home. We no longer felt attached to our neighborhood and started to question remaining there. The truth is that we were questioning our attachment to each other, questioning if we should stay together and move or break up. Ernest loved Rachel, our red Doberman. She really was his dog and more responsive to him. He insisted on an adequate backyard for her. He was involved in theater in Northern Virginia and suggested that we check on Del Ray. It was a quiet less upscale Alexandria neighborhood within walking distance of the Metro.

I still had my two small black and white cats, Tebbs and Pigeon. I adopted them in New York and brought them down when I moved back to D.C. in 1979. In truth, Pigeon was my favorite, she only weighed six pounds and liked to hitch rides around my neck. I gave her ballast by holding onto one of her back legs. I tried to give Tebbs extra attention to make up for it but often failed.

We found a nice two-bedroom home with a front and backyard. The work Ernest had done on our house on 17th Street paid off. We were able to sell our Victorian for enough down payment for the Del Ray house. Fortunately, it did not need basic work, and we moved in smoothly. The living room had a sliding glass door onto the backyard. It was a pretty view of tall, encompassing bushes with a small flower garden.

But the new home wasn't enough of a challenge for Ernest. I think my lack of attention inspired him to pour energy into something new. A back deck abutting the glass sliding door was it. His family had been a ready team in the past and were enthusiastic to help. Once again, I was serving iced tea and being amazed by the progress.

During the first couple of months, I tried to be more helpful. But the truth was that I didn't care. I was feeling an emptiness inside. When socially involved I was fine, but alone I felt anxious and lost. Over the years, Ernest and his family had a gradual spiritual influence on me. Although Ernest was alienated from the church, his religious training and philosophical orientation gradually drew me in. He had a close friend who sang in the choir of a local Catholic church, Blessed Sacrament. I checked it out and liked the people and the young priest.

I decided to take a step forward and started to attend what was called the "Inquiry Class" where different aspects of the church and teachings were presented. I took another step and joined the catechism class. If completed, it would lead to formal membership. I had some serious questions about the Church concerning homosexuality but also could see that this congregation was open and welcoming. The music director, who also led the catechism class, seemed open-minded and was appreciated by the church.

As I evolved in my faith life, my relationship with Ernest devolved. He was taking more time with his theater activities and his separate group of friends. Often, I was either at work or home alone. I'd have my wine and wonder what made sense for the future. Being with Ernest, I felt lonelier than when I was by myself. Neither of us seemed able to give what the other needed. But neither did we want to take the inevitable step. As we moved further apart, I put more of myself into the church. By the time of Holy Week in 1994, I was ready. I joined the Catholic Church during the Easter Vigil. Ernest's family came to welcome me into the faith. I wept for joy first and then felt deep sadness that Ernest and I were separating.

Ernest was methodical in deciding how our material goods, accumulated over our ten years together, would be divided. Long lists were made with value assigned to various items. On a fair basis he designated what each of us had arrived with and what we were entitled to leave with. I agreed to it all. One challenge was finding places to live. With my income I was able to find a fine one-bedroom apartment to rent on 16th Street, N.W. in D.C. I was able to keep Pigeon and Tebbs, but the building did not allow Rachel our doberman. Ernest on the other hand was low on money and could not afford either his own place nor a place for Rachel.

Our last project together was finding a home for Rachel. We went to the Doberman rescue society for leads. For three weeks our primary effort and goal was Rachael. At last we got the name of a woman who lived further out in the countryside. We were both praying that this rehoming would work. It was a dog's paradise. The family already had a young male Doberman which Rachel immediately dominated. There was land, horses, and loving owners. We lied about her age. Out of fear, we said she was seven. She was nine but looked and acted much younger.

Driving her out that last time and dropping her off was the hardest part of our break up. We wept together as she was taken into her new home. The new owner sent occasional emails of how happy Rachael seemed. After nine months an email announced her death. It said the owner felt that Rachael had been a real blessing to her. We wept separately.

My new apartment was in a nice deco building well situated close to Meridian Hill-Malcom X Park. The relaxed door staff and other occupants seemed nice but distant. My focus turned to the development of my faith life. I started going to Holy Trinity church located in the Georgetown area of D.C. It was Jesuit and considered a welcoming parish. It had been President John F. Kennedy's church. I became active with the committee that designated charitable contributions and eventually became a member of the Parish Council. Holy Trinity had a sister parish in El Salvador named *Maria, Madre de Los Pobres*, Mary, Mother of the Poor. In a poor section of San Salvador, the priest was Padre Daniel. A yearly mission program involved visiting our sister parish and being in community with its parishioners.

I signed up to go to El Salvador. The five of us volunteers were an extraordinary mix of wealthy and near poverty, religious and secular, male and female, straight and gay, young and old, life-long Catholics and new Catholic. We did not know each other at the beginning but came to deeply appreciate and cherish each other by the end. Our time was spent being with the youth and older adults at *Maria Madre*, but also traveling to a retreat location for three days with five members of the parish. Great generosity was exhibited.

Figure 26 El Salvador, digging latrine

Sister Mary Jane had been a nurse in El Salvador during the civil war. When we went to the small village she had lived in, a woman brought her a live chicken as a gift. What extraordinary generosity from this poor villager. A meal was prepared for us and it had little pieces of chicken in it, a feast coming from their hearts.

Padre Daniel helped facilitate the mountain retreat three hours from the parish. The faith sharing was profound. I was particularly touched by one young woman. Veronica, poor, little education, in poor health, had a beautiful way of expressing her faith life. After the retreat, we went to a play with several of the youth. It was a comedy and fun, but I had no comprehension of the humor. Jim, the other male in our group, was an attractive young guy of 18. We shared a bed together, but my focus was on the mission we had all undertaken. We also shared being wakened every morning at 5am by a rooster right under our window.

I was advised to start Pepto Bismol two days before we left D.C. and then take it every day while we were there to prevent intestinal problems. We were all healthy until the return flight when a fresh salad appeared. In post mission communications, I was the only one who did not become violently ill. Two of us have remained close friends after the passage of twenty-five years.

St. Aloysius was another Jesuit parish in downtown D.C. The parish was in a lower economic area and dedicated to caring for those in need. I attended it as well as Holy Trinity. Over time, I became close to a number of St. Aloysius parishioners. After knowing each other for a year, a few of us formed a small community of prayer. We included a young German couple, Dotti a nurse who had worked in Central America, and Jude, a beautiful young guy who looked like a Greek god but had an evangelical bent. We met weekly for a meal and our prayer meeting. We became close over a period of a year and a half.

On Sunday evenings, a gay Catholic organization named Dignity held services at St. Maragret's, an Episcopal church on Connecticut Avenue. As a new Catholic, I had a great zeal for worship and often included Dignity as one of my three Sunday Masses. It was dicey for the priest because Dignity was not officially recognized by the Catholic Church. I went there to be in a religious environment where I could feel fully accepted. I also hoped I might meet a possible partner although I wasn't dating at the time.

I developed a crush on Sam, a young man, who had been with the Jesuits for eight years. He was not particularly handsome, but he emanated a wise, gentle spirit within an athletic body. One of my female church friends was under his spell as well. He was fluent in Spanish due to working in Mexico. The most tangible thing that came out of our friendship was poetry that poured out of me at one point. Other than Sam, inspiration for poetry came from the Taize ecclesial community chants which I would either cry through or write poetry to.

I was introduced to the Jesuit Center for Spiritual Growth in Wernersville, Pa. It served as a retreat center located on 400 acres of verdant farmland. I went on my first retreat there after the mission to El Salvador. My retreat director was Sister Barbara who was deeply spiritual with a strong character and great sense of humor. The style of the retreat was Ignatian, based on the teaching and experience of St.

Ignatius of Loyola, founder of the Jesuit order. I continued annual retreats there for the next twenty-five years. The retreats I took varied in length from a long weekend to eight days, to two Thirty Day Spiritual Exercises. All my retreats were in silence except for the daily forty-five minutes with a spiritual director.

My work life at the APA continued as I strove to meet the needs and demands of my boss, Dr. Sabshin, a large and imposing gentleman. He had served as Medical Director of the APA since the early 1970's and was well respected throughout the world. He was internationally oriented and attended numerous meetings outside the U.S. Dr. Sabshin was born Jewish but did not have any religious practice. Nonetheless, he was sensitive and accepted my faith involvement.

After one trip to Russia, he brought me a beautiful, framed icon of the Virgin Mary with the infant Jesus. I was very touched. At another time, he visited Israel and brought me a beautiful Jerusalem cross. He was a deep thinker and protective of his privacy. He would spend considerable time deep in thought concerning pending issues facing American and world psychiatry. I served as his gatekeeper and tried to accommodate any member of the staff needing to see him, no matter their status within the organization. There was fierce competition for Dr. Sabshin's attention among the directors of the various departments of the association. Dr. Sabshin engendered a strong loyalty from those who reported directly to him.

One of the major issues which had faced American psychiatry was the placement or non-placement of homosexuality into the DSM, The Diagnostic and Statistical Manual of Psychiatry published by the APA. This publication served as the medical guide relating to mental illness. It was also used by the American Psychological Association, Nursing, and Social Work. Every several years through research and committee work, the DSM would be revised and updated. Homosexuality was originally indexed as a mental disorder. In 1973 the APA declassified homosexuality as a mental disorder.

When I began working for Dr. Sabshin as his Executive Assistant in 1984, the declassification of homosexuality was somewhat old history, yet I felt that he did not have a high level of experience or comfort around it. I came to believe that in the following years, through our close association, Dr. Sabshin became more comfortable and cared more about gay related issues. He gave me a strong base from which to live and grow and supported my going through the process of getting a master's degree.

By 1997 I had worked at the American Psychiatric Association for over sixteen years. Dr. Sabshin retired after his long and distinguished career. The time came, and the board selected Dr. Steve Mirin to replace him.

One of the secretaries of Medical Director's Office, Cindy, and I had become good friends. Over time I shared my personal life and my faith life with her. About nine months into the Mirin administration, Cindy turned to me one day and said, "David, why don't you become a priest?" I was struck by this suggestion for two reasons. One, because I hadn't actually contemplated the possibility for myself, and two, because she was not involved in any faith tradition. I realized slowly over the next couple of weeks that she may have known me better than I knew myself. I accepted that my time at the APA was coming to an end, met with Dr. Mirin, and was offered a modest severance to leave. I had developed friends and relationships with other staff and knew I would miss them. A nice retirement party was held, and I moved on to whatever my future held.

I took the following nine months off. My intention was to use this time for travel and a non-stressful discernment process concerning my future. I was living in a condominium I bought at 1825 T St., N.W. I purchased this efficiency for $45,000. It was in an excellent location, only an eight-minute walk from DuPont Circle. After the stress of my work environment was gone, I crashed. I had some anxiety about where my life was going, but on the whole, I was able to relax and enjoy my freedom. I decided I would go on several Ignatian retreats, a Franciscan retreat, and travel to London and Paris. I was seeking God's will for me.

EUROPE

In early September of 1998, I attended my last therapy session with my psychologist. It had been seventeen years since we began. I was sad but also excited and solid in my decision to finish. He said some encouraging, positive things including that he would miss experiencing my increasing growth in spiritual life and that he had learned and grown from me in this area.

I gave him a cloisonné brass camel, the idea coming to me in the night. In the morning I had run out and found a camel in the Chinese shop right down Connecticut Ave. He was touched by it and the attached note. I wrote that he had helped to carry me through the desert and at times we had come to an oasis, then on again, with deep appreciation and love.

Preparing for London and Paris, I got my hair cut and highlighted. A good friend, Patricia, came over and raved about my new place. Dinner and wine were excellent, and she was great fun. It was the first time I used the dining room table. We sat at the two ends by candlelight, with the windows open. She shared that she was considering becoming a nun. Then slipped into thinking about being open to a relationship. As a housewarming gift she gave me a beautiful ceramic mug made by a famous artist monk. She said I'm the only friend she could, in fun, scream with. Occasionally we would scream with delight at the same thing.

Before the trip to Europe, I prepared for the wedding of my friends, Bill and Joan. I dressed up in a black linen suit with a white shirt and wore my New York Art Deco tie. I went to the choir rehearsal and poured myself into the music. I was probably too loud as usual since no one mentioned how nice it'd be for me to join the regular choir! However, a few people did say how nice it was to see me up there, singing my heart out. Joe Lacey, S.J., gave a powerful homily using the "Song of Solomon". He said that the sacrament of marriage was powerful and creative like the first Chapter of Genesis. I felt joy for my friends and sorrow for those of us who were denied the sacrament.

At the reception, I joined Patricia and the others for a glass of wine then went down to dinner. For the banquet, Patricia and I were thankfully seated beside each other. I ended up letting myself go and dancing for three hours. Unfortunately, I had dyed some of my chest hair a couple of days before to get the little bit of white out. Sitting down in the middle of a dance, I happened to glance down to discover to my horror that the dye had bled and stained the whole front of my white shirt. I grabbed my jacket off the back of the chair, threw it on, and continued with the disco beat.

On Sunday, the message of the sermon at St. Aloysius was about forgiveness and reconciliation, with President Clinton being mentioned. My close friend Dotti was there and afterwards we went to the Irish Times on Capitol Hill. She shared she'd been praying in the morning to feel loved, and she felt loved by me. In addition to her breakup, she said her grandfather might be dying in the next few days and it was too much loss for her to handle. I said I'd shortly be in Notre Dame Cathedral and would pray for her there. She was touched.

At the reception after the Dignity Mass, I went over to Juan Carlos, whom I had met a few weeks before. He acted embarrassed and apologized for not calling me. As he spoke, he kept rubbing his hand up and down my side. Then he realized it and apologized. It felt so natural that I wasn't conscious of it until he stopped. He said he'd call me after my return. I rubbed his arm and said, "Do". How intimate and sweet. I hoped he had felt the contour of my side and chest. What a boost to have hope of a positive connection. It was the strongest sense of mutuality that I'd had in a long time. I never heard from him again.

From Dulles Airport to Paris on Air France, I first sat beside a large friendly woman who required an extension to her seat belt. She expressed concern for my comfort. After explaining that I planned to stay up all night and the following day, she said she couldn't sleep on flights herself. A stewardess asked me in French if I wanted to move. She found me a seat beside an empty middle seat with a small quiet French woman at the window. After resettling, I offered the woman a Fig Newton bar. Her response was, "Oui, merci".

For dinner I had delicious *coq au vin* chicken in wine. Even the plastic cutlery was tasteful, white with dark blue highlights. Also served was Camembert with butter and bread. Speaking in French, I said to my neighbor, that I had forgotten if, like the French, one begins with the cheese and bread… She answered, no, no, after…but it wouldn't be a grave error! I laughed out loud, I think she got a kick out of it. Although it was chicken, I drank red wine with the meal, a demi bouteille of Cabernet Sauvignon. The Camembert proudly listed a 45% fat content. The French are, what can I say, so French.

Down the aisle, there was an attractive blond, heavy-lipped American lad in his early twenties. His partner was dark haired, short, stout, and transsexual. A little later, my neighbor was crying so I got up and walked around to allow her space. When I went back, I asked her if she were ill. She explained that her father had just died suddenly in an accident. I said I was sorry, that it was very hard. She thanked me. I waited a few minutes and said I still had my father and mother but they were quite old, my mother being 86 and my father 84 years old.

She asked about my stay in Paris. I told her I was on vacation, that there was much to do, monuments, spectacles, churches, that I wanted to go to Mass at Notre Dame. She said that for her this was an emotional time and her faith was very important to her. I was very pleased to be able to have this conversation in French and support her.

We arrived in Paris at 5pm. There was a two hour wait for the flight to London. I bought a *café et pain aux raisin* coffee and raisin roll. I tried to pay with the francs I had brought with me from the U.S. Rejected! *"C'est n'est pas bon"* They're no good. I had the old francs. On the flight to London there was a middle-aged Indian woman beside me. When I saw it was raining, I mentioned that I didn't have a raincoat. She advised, "One must always have a raincoat in London". She had been in Spain playing bridge, then shopping in Paris. She asked me the final results of the U.S. Open. They were unknown to me, so I asked the steward for her, and he didn't know either. One of the last things she expressed to me was a fear that London might disappoint me. I said I didn't think it would have time to.

Hauling my large green bag and knapsack onto the Tube subway, I headed directly for Earls Court tube stop. I sat beside kids apparently speaking English. They turned out to be from North Ireland, Belfast. Also in the car, French and Italian were being spoken. I stayed at the Halifax Hotel. I checked-in, unpacked, then left the hotel and got a one-day Tube pass and headed for Westminster Abbey. Coming out at the stop, I asked a woman where it was. She looked about and said she didn't know. It turned out to be a block and a half away. I decided to keep going all day to catch up with the normal sleep cycle.

In Westminster Abbey, Queens Mary of Scotland and Elizabeth I were entombed close together. A plaque stated that although they had been in conflict, each was trying to serve Christ as she understood. I was very taken by the Poet's Corner, especially Gerard Manley Hopkins, S.J. priest and poet, who died at forty-five years of age. Oscar Wilde was highlighted in a newer window section. The style reminded me of Marc Chagall. I felt awe at the grandeur of so many great men and women and a bit of shame at my ignorance of quite a number of them.

A sign for silent prayer led me to a heavy wooden door. Pulling it open, a plain small chapel was revealed. I prayed for guidance and strength to use my gifts as I am called to do. I wept. So much striving represented by the personages gathered in this sacred place.

St. Margaret's church featured a beautiful stained-glass scene of the crucifixion. It felt more real than Westminister Abby. Walking to the Banqueting House, I thought how earth-shattering the execution of Charles I must have been. The ceiling of the Banqueting House was brought to life by a Reubens fresco that Charles I had created to honor his father, James I. The fresco was opulent, with myriad angels drawing James into heaven. It also represented the vast spending Charles I went to in glorifying his father. It was symbolic of his other excesses as well, which led to his execution.

Forging onward, sleepless, to Covent Gardens down Kent Street. I realized I was going in the wrong direction and was reminded of Pogo's saying, "Having lost our way, we redoubled our efforts."

My new mission was to find the gay CRX79 Club. The bar was toasted as extraordinarily friendly. I found it and finally sat with a glass of red wine. I then headed to a health food store and again was scolded for using old money, this time, English. I was told to "Take it to a museum".

Pressing on, I took in a production of the musical "Rent". A white haired American behind me was loud and obnoxious. I found myself nodding out during the first act. At intermission, I bought some figs and juice, consumed them on the street, then back into the theater for coffee and chocolate. I changed my seat and was now wide awake. The performance was very moving. Power was coming from the personal experience and insights of the writers via the compelling performances. Love was the key, the center of all. Love is present in painful relationships and is what makes all relationships possible. Gay love, lesbian love, drag queen love, love of community. I wept greatly, thinking how I wanted an angel in my life. Juan Carlos kept coming to my mind.
I took the Oxford Tube bus for the Catholic Worker conference. Looking over the shoulder of a fellow traveler, I read in the *Standard*

newspaper it was looking bad for Clinton. It said video testimony might be broadcast, and the Democratic Party was deserting him. My thought was that Gore might make a better president.

I got to Oxford at 6pm, stepped out into the countryside of beautiful fields, cows, wooded areas, cottages. I joined other arrivals at the St. Francis Catholic Worker House. They were playing a game of imaginary introductions for new arrivals. Fantastical histories were made up as fun introductions. I joined in and on my turn, introduced a woman named Chris as working as a seamstress making wedding gowns for royalty. She introduced me as going to Egypt to have four wives.

Chris said she was knocked over by my mention of wedding dresses because she was struggling with the issue of marriage. She laughed when I told her I was gay and wouldn't be having any wives but had lived in Egypt. We went to a pub at 10 pm and had bitter lemon drinks. Art, from the Catholic Worker in D.C., asked me if I planned to go to Taize while in Paris. The famous monastery was three hours from Paris near Lyons. It was the second time the ecumenical monastery of Taize had been suggested to me. In my guest room was, "The Psychology of Romantic Love". I glanced through it. It suggested that since the Middle Ages romantic love had replaced religion, that sexual union was where the spiritual can be found in our modern culture. I found it thought provoking.

Visiting Oxford University, I went up the tower of St. Mary the Virgin church which predated the Reformation. It had a fine view of all the colleges and churches in Oxford. I then found out that John Cardinal Newman, beatified in 1958, had been a rector at Oxford. I stood in the pulpit where he preached. I remembered his cardinal coat of arms: "*Cor ad cor loquitor*" heart speaking to heart. One of his quotes that I much appreciated was about the importance of having intimate friendship beyond simple diffused notions of love.

Cardinal Woolsey founded the oldest college in Oxford, Christ Church, but having refused to acknowledge a divorce for Henry VIII, died of a heart attack on his way to the scaffold. A disk of the Christ College choir was playing. Heading for the Newman Center, I was almost hit by a car. I tried to recover with a glass of wine in a restaurant. In chatting with the maitre d', he as well mentioned having visited Taize. How extraordinary. It felt as if God's grace was guiding me there.

Paris was in my sights. I booked a ticket on the Chunnel train going under the English Channel. But first I made time to visit Tim Rogers, a retired theater producer whose condominium I bought in Washington. His extraordinary apartment building in London was next to the Royal Academy of Arts in Piccadilly. Lord Byron lived there in 1814-15. I shared some of my story with his cousin and she asked if I'd considered ordination. I said yes but believed my calling was to be in an intimate relationship with a man. She felt that a relationship was as sacred as being a priest.

I shared my dilemma about how to manage both Paris and Taize. Tim said he'd been to Taize twice and went to looked for his book about Taize. He got me the phone number to call for a reservation. I was touched by the degree of his encouragement, another example of the spirit moving and directing me.

I found my eyes were extremely tired and I was having trouble not only tracking the time but even the country. In the tube, an Indian fellow sitting next to me, I thought gay, gave me a great big smile, but my desire was only to focus on my journaling. When I got to the Halifax, I went to bed but what had looked so inviting turned out to be a thin mattress on wooden slats. Its hardness grew causing me to wake up every hour and a half. My hips were getting bruised. It reminded me of the bed on my first visit to Guatemala, a board-hard bed with a howling dog outside.

An insect, a mosquito hawk, landed on my head during the night but I ignored it. In the morning, trying to wash my hair in the sink, I found it in the bathroom. I hoped to escort it out so as not to injure it. It was coming in and out of the bathroom until I found it exhausted on the floor. I picked it up in my hand, took it downstairs, and out the door. I felt very good about giving it freedom.

Sitting in the Philbeach Hotel, in the Wild About Oscar Restaurant, I appreciated its reputation of being the best gay restaurant in London. Looking down on me was an oil portrait of Wilde. A recording of a French chanteuse played. An attractive maitre d', Mateus, said he could get me some mushroom soup. I went to the loo to freshen up passing an enormous wooden crucifix. How thankful I felt for such a remarkable and diverse day. A table of seven older drag queens sat across from me, having a drinky poo. If I wasn't looking I would have thought that at least one of them was a truck driver by his voice. All of them colorful and comfortable. They were talking about the time they went to a bar thinking it was TV night for transvestites, and it turned out to be lesbian television night!

The head queen announced she was writing a book. The loudest one responded, "Writing a book? She can't even read one"! Mateus made my bill only five pounds. It should have been fifteen. He seemed interested and available if I had wanted to pursue him.

Up in the morning, I went to Waterloo Station and took the Eurostar to Paris. I sat beside a charming African woman from Senegal. She started in English but when I responded in French she switched over and we continued in French. She was a biologist attending an international conference.

At Gare de Nord I lugged my knapsack and my monsterous green sac to the Metro Etienne Marcel to find my apartment. People smoking everywhere. Horrible, yet one must adapt while in Paris. Such a mixture of cultures and fashions yet mostly French. I finally made it to 5 Rue de Marie Stewart. I had just seen her grave at Westminster Abby. I was greeted by the boyfriend of Guilles, the owner. He had only a green towel around his waist. Ulala, *C'est Paris* it's Paris.. He took me upstairs to the apartment. The floor was tiled, shower in the corner, sink, two windows, small table, and a cabinet for clothes.

The next morning, sitting at a nearby café on Rue de Rivoli, I felt drugged, even though I slept from 1 am to 11 am. Hard to believe but the coffee served was weak, more like a dark broth. *Quelle horreur* How horrible, in Paris, *c'est possible*? Yet how can one complain of watery coffee when viewing the Hotel de Ville. I made the cultural faux pas of asking for butter to go with my baguette. The waiter looked shocked, swallowed, *de buerre?* Butter? Rolled his eyes. I thought I had slipped down from the ugly American to country bumpkin, except a peasant would know never to ask for butter with a baguette." *C'est la vie"*

I decided to go to the gay Catholic group called Jonathan and David. Guilles knew of it as did the waiter Mateus from the restaurant. I took the metro searching for 92 Rue de Picpus. Three of us there were new to the group. After some sharing and explaining of the group, there was an announcement of a dinner on Saturday night.

One of the new guys, Sederique, was in the metro station when I left. I asked him if he'd be going to the dinner. Very politely he said he thought so and we got on the metro together. He said his parents had no specific religion but that he believed in doing what felt right for him. He told me he liked to meditate in the woods. Coming from my recent background, I talked about my experience of church, the value of tradition, and the importance of community. He nodded and got off at the next stop.

I took a brief respite at the apartment and headed out again. A famous gay singing bar, Le Chantant, was to be in the Les Halles area, but the bar was gone. Instead, a bar called Barbar which was small and dank. A rude American spoke to me. His poor poodle was so cute, especially in comparison to him. I strolled through the intersection of Rue de Lombard and Rue de la Funniere, but the area didn't appeal to me. I ended up at the *Coeur de la Corrone*, the spot where Henry IV was assasinated. It seemed like a good place to end my evening. On my way home I stopped at a shop for some items. Once again, I had old Francs.

Next morning the door to Guilles' was open and I knocked. The night before I left him a note saying the toilet wasn't working and there was no hot water. He explained that the tenant had left for a week and turned off the water to the apartment. Guilles turned it back on. As we spoke he said that the French did not understand the American overreaction to the Clinton affair. He said their leaders had affairs, illegitimate children, mistresses all the time. I tried to explain that the transgression also had to do with the president lying and the cover-up.

Guilles said that he had many American guests over the years, but I was the only one who spoke French. He was friendly and said I should come by on Wednesday for *un verre de vin* glass of wine.

I went out looking for a restaurant named, *Des Mauvaix Garçons* some bad boys, for breakfast but it was closed until 8pm. So, I went to a nearby café and ordered an omelette with café au lait. Heard women at another table speaking Arabic. Their treated reddish hair made me think of the film, "Battle of Algiers". I found French men attractive in spite of their smoking. Many had thin faces, though they don't exercise as do Americans. I was reminded of Eric, my French boyfriend of six months in New York. I recalled our speaking in French, making love, his special café au lait. He was so generous but then came my disinterest. What a vicious and mysterious pattern.

A homeless gentleman at the Tour de St. Jacque refused money. So, I got him a sandwich. Near the Hotel de Ville I found the Place de Greve, the meeting place for those without work. The greve turned into a verb, *faire grève*, for the term to go on strike.

Wandering around I visited the establishment of my friend Miebeth's father, Quemper France China at 84 Rue St. Martin. Beautiful china was displayed in the windows. I noticed an old church right beside the shop, Eglise St. Merri, 76 Rue de la Verrerie, with gargoyles and statues. As I was admiring the forms, I heard a long musical note coming from inside the church. It was a musical program featuring a viola. Sitting to take it in, it seemed like dreadfully modern music, long in melancholy and short in tune. To me it did not represent the greatness of the Church, nor anything spiritual.

I experienced a feeling of desolation. It seemed no one there had any idea or interest in church and worship. I walked around and came across a beautiful marble crucifix and some great paintings of the saints. I hurt thinking how the Catholic church had fallen into such spiritual disrepair for the average person. That the remarkable historic and religious resources were unseen and unfelt. I had no idea how to find a Mass for Sunday *et voila*, a sign hidden off in a side chapel said there would be Mass at 10am. It turned out to be a Vincentian parish, the founder, St. Vincent de Paul. In the States they are known to be welcoming. What a blessing.

After an early afternoon café, I strolled to the famous Jesuit church of St. Paul and St. Louis in the Marais district of the 4th Arrondissement. It had a tall façade which hid the dome behind it. Constructed in the early part of the 17th Century, it was part of the counter-Reformation. Authorized by Louis XIII, the Jesuit designed interior focus centered on the altar. The mission was to bring the youth back into the church and enliven the worship of the people. Cardinal Richelieu celebrated the first Mass. Another glorious church treated mostly as a museum. So little sense of the vigor and zeal that built it. The Church seemed to be in need of another reformation.

I walked to the Hotel de Sully and rested in the wonderful Place des

Vosges. It held apartments commissioned by Louis XIII and the park in its center was used for entertainment and dancing. Louis XIII was said to have been in love with many men, as an adolescent and adult. A large statue of the king on his horse was in the center of the surrounding park. Victor Hugo kept an apartment at la Place des Vosges as well as Cardinal Richelieu.

Several men and a few women attended the David and Johnathan dinner. Sederique was there and it was good to see him. I was introduced around. I spoke to a priest for a long time. He was active with the organization and drove a bus for income. He lived in a poor section of the *bandlieu,* the massive apartment complex which encircles Paris. He said the division between the rich and poor in France, just like in America, was increasing. Most of those he worked with were immigrants and black.

Although the David and Johnathan group was founded as a Catholic group, the priest said that there was not much activity related to Mass and formal church. Many of the men had been hurt and rejected by the Church. However, the nature of the group's activities was Christian, with a hope of leading to faith. I enjoyed speaking with a number of the men. The conversations were not difficult. I was able to share about my life and faith journey while enjoying the great hors d'oeuvres and kir, a white wine drink with crème de cassis. I kissed a few guys on the cheek as I was leaving. They encouraged me to come back for Christmas and were surprised and pleased I was speaking in French.

Sunday morning at 10:30am, the bells of the parish of St. Merri rang out loud and demandingly. I got up to wash and had to light the water heater. Fortunately, I had matches with me. Figuring out how to manage the heater was certainly out of character for me. I washed my body and hair in the sink, used paper towels to dry, and raced to church.

La messe the Mass had just begun when I arrived. There were about fifty or so people. It was a mixed group with about half elderly. Included were nuns, African immigrants, and six children. The priest had a young African as Eucharistic minister. In the homily he spoke of justice and caring for the poor. I sang the French and Latin with great spirit and was moved by both the glorious environment and the Mass itself. At the end of Mass, the cantor gave me a big smile and asked if I lived in the neighborhood. She said I sang very well and did I sing in a choir. The priest also came by and asked if I lived nearby. When I said *Non*, he said, *C'est domage!* That's too bad. How uplifting it was to be spiritually inspired and appreciated.

I ate a lunch of beefsteak, green beans, and white beans, with bread and café au lait. It was the *plat de jour* daily special. A cute baby boy in a stroller entertained me. I kept thinking about getting to the Taize monastery. I called several times without success but remained open to the spirit leading me.

I decided to walk down to Sebastopol and across to the Île de la Cité. Such magnificent edifices everywhere. I went into Saint Capelle, built in the 13th century. It had such an array of stainedglass windows, strong and delicate at the same time. The history of the Bible filled 16 windows, a visual means to communicate the story to the many unable to read. Then walked to the Conciergerie, the prison for the Palais de Justice. It was here during the Revolution that Marie Antoinette, Danton, Ropspierre, and many more were held in 1793.

Seeing the information near the cell of Marie Antionette, I was reminded of her letter that my sister Alice translated from Old French to Modern French, and then into English for a wealthy family she knew who owned it. It was Marie Antoinette's last written communication before her execution in October 1793. The letter was filled with concern for her children and a desire to make a last confession to a priest, also her forgiveness of her captors.

On a little altar was a quote from another letter of hers. She wrote that she and her husband Louis XVI did not mean ill and that her children should not take revenge on their enemies. With such a small cell, it is hard to comprehend how shocking incarceration would have been for her.

I moved on to Place Saint-Michel and remembered how intoxicating it was in 1985 when Ernest and I first arrived in Paris. I then saw a phone booth which reminded me of another visit which included frantic phone calls to a Paris doctor about test results and fear of AIDS. But this time, Paris felt comfortable. I walked along the Rue de la Huchette near Saint-Michel trying to identify my former Algerian hotel on the noisy crowded street. I continued to Notre Dame which seemed to be having a facelift. Then on to the Île de Saint-Louis looking for the old church with the magnificent crucifix Ernest and I found.

I did some shopping at one of the two great department stores, Sameritaine. I went to the 6 pm Mass at Notre Dame. Then ate at the Auberge of the White Queen located in a building from the 16th century. No wonder going down to its toilet was like descending into the catacombs. Returning to the church of St. Paul and St. Louis in the Marais district, I found a very simple chapel dedicated to St. Teresa de Avila, a saint I greatly admired. On the wall was a notice that Edith Stein would be canonized the following October 11. She was an extraordinary Jewish convert and French philosopher who became a Carmelite nun and was exterminated by the Nazis.

I wanted to find the church with the crucifix that had so moved me. I went up and down the Quai along the Seine, one way then the other, then on to the far side of the Ile towards the Right Bank. Crossing another bridge, I saw a row of cafés leading up to a church and knew that this was it. I took my time entering, remembering the church from a dank rainy day.

The crucifix was of a dark wood. Every fiber of Jesus' body straining, his mouth open in a cry. It was moving. The décor of the church included many beautiful sculptures, a pieta, and a painting of Jesus being taken down from the cross. Young people were setting up for Mass and this gladdened me, that the church was still used for worship. How happy I was to have followed my instinct and desire.

I went to Notre Dame for its Mass and lit candles for my friend Dotti and her family. Music was only sung by the choir. Although it was beautiful and moving, it felt like a performance rather than as part of the community. It was all men at the altar including the Eucharistic ministers. After the Mass was over, the priest gave a long prayer in Latin dedicated to Mary, Queen of Heaven. The cathedral was magnificent; what a gift to worship there.

As I was leaving Notre Dame, I remembered St. Julian le Pauvre Church which was just across the bridge from Notre Dame. I recalled a concert Ernest and I attended there and decided to pass by. Low and behold, there was a concert being given of Lizt's Hungarian Rapsodies. Although it was about to start, I was so hungry I crossed the street and bought a banana and a Nutella crepe. Fellows behind me in the line were speaking Spanish. It was delightful to hear. They asked me in French how much the crepes were and I answered in Spanish, *vente dos* twenty-two. They smiled. I was enjoying myself so much I forgot to pay. Realizing my error, I rushed back and said to them, "*Es necesario de pagar*" It's necessary to pay! They laughed. I thought they were from Mexico, and it warmed my heart.

At. St. Julian's, the pianist, Pierpaulo Levi, was an extraordinary musician. He was a little guy, cute, big hands, and played with great energy. I have never seen hands move so fast, as if a breeze were coming off them. He was precise, creative, and passionate as well as humorous. He used his face to communicate. What a delight from a classical pianist. I did have a fantasy of inviting him to go for a drink but when it was over, I simply said, *"Merci pour votre passion et humour"* Thank you for you passion and humor. He answered, "*Merci*."

Tickets were being sold for the next night at St. Julian for a concert given by a Vietnamese counter-tenor performing music of the great castrati. I felt it would be meaningful to experience him in the 12th century St. Julian, founded on the site of an earlier 8th century church. The outside garden had the oldest tree in Paris, pre-1610. I continued praying for God to show me how I was to be of service.

The following day I slept for ten hours and even then, was tired. I took my time, and exercised listening to a Christian radio station, Radio Notre Dame. The station was both Catholic and Protestant. I was in a state of indecision whether to leave Paris and visit Taize. Heading out to Place de Victoire for the Banque de France, I found an enormous building surrounded by many *gendarmes* police. At last, I was liberated of my old French francs and given new.

Walking around I got lost and ended up at the church of St. Eustache. It was grand, like a cathedral. It seemed to have a practicing faith community connected to it. Picking up a piece of paper, I found the words, *"La fleur dit, 'Je suis', L'homme dit, 'J'ai'. Voila the difference entre la creation du Dieu et le monde des hommes"*. "The flower says I am, a man says I have, observe the difference between the creation of God, and the world of men."
As I left St. Eustache, I felt a gentle breeze and the fragrance of flowers wafted over me. All I lacked was a beloved. I had the thought that

Christ was my beloved as well and the creator of all the beauty I was experiencing.

My intention was to find information on travel to Taize, so I took the metro from Etienne Marcel to the Gare de Lyons. A 10am train and bus connection would arrive Taize at 1:30pm. In a call to the Taize community, I found I could go to an evening worship service, spend the night, have two meals, and catch the train back to Paris arriving at 7:30pm. I decided to do it. The operator asked me how old I was. When I told her she sounded shocked. She said I'd be in a small cabin with six others. The retreat house could provide bedding if I didn't have any.

I took a café au lait at the Café de Flore made famous by some of the great American writers of the 20th century, Hemingway, Gertrude Stein, and F. Scott Fitzgerald. I observed three French youths watching a group of six obnoxious Americans ask a French woman to make room for them. Cafés, were of course, set up to focus on the street with the pedestrians acting as the show and the café patrons as the audience.

Later in the afternoon, I was sitting in the St. Louis Salon de Té at the Sorbonne. Using my Café de Flore pen and imbibing in a delicious *Te au lait* tea with milk. The tea was very good and there was a fellow who looked like Tom Cruise to my left. I tried to get back into the Luxembourg gardens but a *gendarme* policeman said, *C'est firmé* it's closed. I went on to my concert which started at 9pm. I missed having someone to share such experiences with. My only sharing seemed to be with the memories of Ernest in various environs and of our passion. As I walked down the Rue de O'deon from the Place de O'deon, I remembered stopping at various shops. This time I shared only with God. I was on this journey with Him. I was trying to listen and follow the Spirit's movement.

Figure 27 Mom and Dad

In the evening after the Salon de Té, I walked down BulMich Boulevard Saint-Michel and then connected into familiar Left Bank streets. Back at St. Julien le Pauvre, the concert was just starting. I sat near the front. Duy Thong Nguyen was the counter tenor. The lights projected onto the walls of this 12th century church created mystery. There was an older French couple across the aisle from me who reminded me of Mom and Dad. She was complaining about their seating, he was going along quietly.

A large elderly woman pianist entered with a black gown bearing enormous epaulettes of white lace reminding me of my 12th grade literature teacher. She sat with frozen face and fixed eyes. The Steinway responded to her strong touch. The notes, stiff, predictable, but competent were completely at variance with the pianist of the evening before. As she commenced the second piece, a soprano voice emanated from behind the audience. We could not see the singer. He made his appearance in a violet velvet vest with white brocade and black silk pantaloons with white silk stockings. A Vietnamese countertenor singing Italian arias dedicated to past great castrati in the setting of a 12th century Parisian church. Where else in the world could one find such a scene.

After the first section intermission, the performer returned wearing a simple black linen suit with wide white collar. In parisian French, he introduced the next pieces. At the end he responded to the appreciation by giving three encores. The repertory included Hayden, Mozart, and Bellini. I wondered at the challenges he must have overcome to be there.

His piano accompanist, Wally Karveno, was 82 years old. Having lost a forty-four-year-old son, she dedicated her creativity to his memory. She was a French Metal of Honor recipient several times over and worked with challenged youth. At the break, I ate Turkish delight at a Tunisian patisserie beside the church. I saved some for my train trip in the morning. As the program continued, the elderly couple moved behind me and she talked incessantly, complaining that the audience had not been addressed formally as "messeurs et medames".

In the evening, I found a leak in the ceiling with a trash can below it, and water pooling under it. A pigeon was drinking from it. I thought how wonderful. Although in an alien captive environment, the bird was just doing what came naturally and taking advantage of its resources. As the Jesuits say, "Finding God in All Things."

Up early, a great number of parents, mostly mothers, walked their children to school. Most had only one child. I was sitting in the Gare de Lyons train station waiting for the train. There were all sorts of reasons I shouldn't make the trip… too much money, too tired, too many other things planned. Yet I had kept open to the spirit and the possibility. Everything had come together smoothly. I hoped for the strength to take in and appreciate whatever would be. I decided to use the travel time to write postcards to mail home with a Parisian postmark.

The countryside flashed by revealing both very flat fields and rolling wooded hills. My snack consisted of two hardboiled eggs, biscotti, apple juice, and dates. I've always loved dates. We would gather the dates off the palm trees in Assiut.

Off the train and onto the bus traveling through beautiful countryside with farm houses of stone walls and red slate tile roofs. Moving through the village of Prisse, I saw old Citroën cars on the road. They reminded me of the one we had in Monmouth. Dad bought it in New York City and getting anything fixed, was 150 miles to Chicago.

I arrived at Taize in the middle of lunchtime. I was surrounded by teenagers. No wonder the woman who took my reservation sounded shocked when I told her I was forty-nine. The music playing during lunch was "Let the Sun Shine In" from the musical "Hair". I joined the choir in the main worship building. The outside of the building was not impressive, but inside there were orange cloth strips like orange tongues rising to the heavens.

There were prayer benches for chairs. I joined the bass section having fallen from tenor due to the damage to my vocal cords by acid reflux. I knew some of the chants. Many languages were being spoken and the words to songs were in ten different languages. The kids were friendly and responsive with strong eye contact. One Polish fellow, Bartok, was very talkative. The map of the grounds was explained to me. I asked for a suggestion of a place where I could walk quietly. I was told "Source St. Etienne", which was the path that led to my cabin.

The countryside was so beautiful, high up in rolling hills. Walking I felt powerful feelings and a sense of being back on retreat in Wernersville. I remembered walking its grounds during the Spiritual Exercises. Arriving at a deserted cabin, the presence of Christ coming to me saying that his hands would hold me, his feet carry me, and his mind would comfort me. I now believed I must continue to trust the movement of God's spirit and flow with it as well as I could. Although I was not in fear, I was concerned about my return to the United States and what I would then do. I sat in a chair overlooking the vast ocean of rich green. I could not imagine having stayed in Paris.

Back to the *communaute* community for tea which was cool aid. I thought of Jonestown for an instant. I had requested quiet so was put in a cabin at the far back of the grounds. I was alone in a cabin of six beds, each with a very thin mattress on a board. I went to supper with the adults since adults were never to eat with the youth, only to be with them at prayer or at official mixing. To decide where to sit, I listened to conversations at a couple of tables.

Most were in German but then I found a table of an older French couple from Paris, an English woman, and a French gentleman with a stutter. All were very cordial and welcoming. We spoke in French with a few English words tossed in. The older gentleman worked in petroleum until computers came in and he retired. He said that the Clinton situation brought dishonor to politicians not to the American people. I said I didn't care much for politics, especially at this time.

During the meal we discussed the living set up in the *dormitoires* dormitories. I was chatting and realized that the woman at the end of the table told a woman that I had 16 beds in my cabin. I realized that I had thought *seis* six from the Spanish but in French it came out sounding "sez" sixteen. We all got a laugh when I corrected myself.

The woman from the older couple gave a French proverb, *"Un sac vide ne tient pas debout"*, The empty bag can't stand up, meaning one has got to eat. Then a French woman strove to properly pronounce the English word "full" with little success. The woman across from her said, *"C'est un nom de famille, n'est pas?"* It's a family name right? The table gave another great laugh.

Sitting in a large tent at the program for adults, a brother of the community explained a point concerning the need for the Holy Spirit. "If you want to be perfect, have compassion." He was speaking in French which was translated into German, then into English and then Italian. At Evening Prayer, there was no available chair so I sat unhappily on the ground.

Polish Bartok came into the tent, looked at me, and chose to sit beside me. I was touched. I told him how I had earlier tried to sit in a chair, not knowing that they were reserved for the Brothers, and that the policy was made very clear to me! We chatted closely. Then beautiful chanting began. I was moved by this experience of such complete beauty, such a blessed moment. Towards the end, Bartok shook my hand and left. I moved and sat near the elderly French woman from dinner.

I went to bed after 11 pm and up at 1:30 am to go to the bathroom. Outside, the stars were remarkable, there was no unnatural light. So I walked a little and thanked God for the magnificent firmament. I continued walking and thinking that God had touched me, reminding me that I loved to worship God and at the same time desired to love another with a romantic intimate love. Both desires are real and ever present to me. How I would live this, I had no idea.

I got up for 7:30 Mass in the crypt. The morning air was bracing. I was thankful that my hair did not crunch overnight so I didn't need to shampoo it. Just brushed my teeth and shaved with frigid water. The priest who presided was Italian speaking in French. There were four African sisters as acolytes and an African gentleman served as sacristan and cantor. Morning prayer was followed by a breakfast of bread, butter, jam, tea and cocoa.

At 10am a scripture lesson on the presence of the Holy Spirit in the New Testament and Old was given. Some of the points made I questioned, but the interpreters did a fine job of working with a difficult text putting it into German and English. I thanked them both later. The English woman and I spoke and she asked me about my home church. I shared about Holy Trinity and St. Al's and also Dignity, mentioning that I attended the meeting in Paris of Jonathan and David. She said there was a group in Britain.

I went to my cabin to lie down and pray, fell asleep for one hour, packed, and was late to 12:15pm prayer. My French compatriots joined me so we could take a picture of us with my camera. I hugged and kissed the older couple. The gentleman said, *"Partir c'est mourir un peu"*, parting is to die a little." I said, *"Comme un petit mort"* it's like a little death only to remember that this phrase is used to refer to sexual climax. Graciously ignoring this, I was told that I must return another time.

On the bus from Taize to Chalon, I found myself sitting with a young version of the actor Depardieu wearing shorts and having a backpack protecting a black and white cat. Passing miles of vineyards, I recalled my hitchhiking days outside of Florence when I slept in a field and the tractor almost got me.

The cows and bulls in the fields were grand in stature and girth compared to those of Central America. The difference was stark. The French countryside was full of fields, vineyards, villages, chateaux, flocks, and herds. The bus arrived in Chalon with just enough time to go to the bathroom and grab a café and croissant. I also bought some junk food out of a vending machine in preparation for the trip to Paris. As we moved on, I offered a chocolate to the woman beside me. She was surprised, carefully examined the contents, took one, and with a big smile said, "Merci".

On the train I shared a cabin with a young law student also named David. He was from Paris but a student at the Université de Dijon. Memories came back of my time studying there thirty years earlier. He sneezed and wiped his face with the cover of his magazine. I took out my journal and began to write. I told him that I had many memories but that I was not like Edith Piaf who sang, *"Non rein de rein, non je ne regrette rein"* No there is nothing, no nothing that I regret. I said, *"Mais pour moi, j'ai des regrets"* But as for me, I do have regrets. A man began singing loudly in the next cabin. I said to my French friend, *"il est bou"*

He is drunk. The fellow came into our cabin with a cigarette hanging out of his mouth, asking for matches. Both of us said we didn't have any, and besides it was a no smoking cabin. He continued up and down the corridor. No one could or would help him. He bothered everyone.

As I descended from the train in Paris, I saw a middle-aged woman weighed down with two large canvas bags. Suddenly, there appeared the staggering drunk fellow who introduced himself to her, picked up the two bags, and proceeded into the station behind her. I was sorry for the negative judgement I made of him. It was an excellent lesson. When another heavy middle-aged woman struggling with her great suitcase appeared, I was inspired and offered to help her. She gladly agreed. I went to pick her bag up and it seemed to weigh a hundred pounds. I struggled until she suggested that we share the weight. We did until I needed to head for the metro. She called me, *gentil* genteel.

The bag I was carrying was light so I headed to Sacre Coeur Bacilica in Montmartre to visit before heading home. I took the metro to Anvers, then took the funiculaire up to Sacre Coeur. I sat on the steps to eat some bread and cheese out of my backpack. Music sounded through the air and a nun sat behind me humming along. I entered the church and walked around. The interior architectural style reminded me of St. Matthew's Cathedral in Washington.

After, in Place Pigalle, I saw a few North African men and women strolling the street. I got a sandwich from an Arab shop. As I left I said, *"shukrin"* thank you, they were surprised. I went up and down narrow streets looking for the Abbesse metro stop. A heavy female prostitute spoke to me. I passed Arabic speaking drag queen prostitutes. One looked like Ella Fitzgerald but smaller. I never thought I would experience Arab drag queens. I stood on a corner and a healthy looking black and white cat meowed loudly at me. I petted her several times. It was late but there were many North African kids playing soccer in a park. Paris had a great number of immigrants who had come from her foreign colonies. The North African colonies including Morocco, Algeria, and Tunisia, became French speaking as well as their native Arabic.

Arriving home, I dropped by Gilles', my landlord. I think he was sleeping but said he was in the toilet and to come back in five minutes. I waited fifteen minutes and went back. I planned to stay for just five minutes. He was cordial and asked me about my time in Paris, about the David & Jonathan meeting, and other activities. He was surprised to learn that I had indeed gone to the Taize monastery. We chatted for at least thirty minutes. At the end, he offered to take me at 8:30am to catch the bus for Charles de Gaulle airport. I was very appreciative if not a little hesitant because of the early departure. I stayed up, packed, and went to bed which now seemed soft compared to the Taize cabin's.

Up, ready to go with a *"café a emporter"* a coffee to go. I said hello to people getting off the lift, but they did not respond. I remarked on this to Gilles. He said,

"There are many Jews in my section of town, and they never speak or say thank you if you hold the door." This comment gave me a shock and I didn't know immediately how to respond. I thought for a minute and said,

"I have had a number of Jewish friends and they act like everyone else." It was the best I could come up with in the time and the French. He said,

"I don't understand neighborhood behavior anyway." A little later he said,

We are now in a *mauvais* bad area in Arrondissement 18." What I noticed were North Africans on the sidewalk. I said,

"I usually don't use the term 'bad' for a neighborhood because it implies that all of the people there are bad. He said,

"I am talking about it not being an attractive, pretty neighborhood. What would you say instead, I said,

"A poor neighborhood". I had assumed there was some racism in his comments.

He drove me to the Place de la Chapelle to get a bus to the airport.

Gilles hugged and kissed me on both cheeks and wished me a good journey. He was well formed as I learned from the hug. He commented earlier that I seemed fit, *"Vous êtes en form."* I mailed the fifteen postcards I'd written so they'd have a Parisian postmark. The bus ride gave me the opportunity to write more with my Café de Flore pen.

I wanted to remember from Paris how the French coddled their pet dogs. Walking them frequently, having them in restaurants, and on public transportation. A French woman on the flight back had a small dog sitting beside her. For fun, I asked a young Ethiopian looking boy, *"C'est un chien, n'est pas?"* It's a dog, isn't it? He responded, *"Oui, Elle a un ou deux chiens"* Yes, she has one or two dogs.

As the plane descended, the woman of a French couple next to me was having trouble with her ears. So, the flight attendant gave her cups of wet napkins to put over her ears. I suggested that she swallow. We landed safely and I wished the couple, *"Bonne journée"* Have a good trip. On the bus into New York, I saw an advertisement for the Paris Suites Hotel, and to think that I had just been in Pigalle the night before.

I stayed at my old friend Lou's apartment for a few days before going home to Washington. Lou encouraged my pursuing a religious life. His apartment on the Lower East Side was only two small rooms and his nephew was visiting him. We went to a piano bar where his friend Luke played the piano. Lou wanted me to sing but I didn't, had two kirs instead. The three of us had to make do in the apartment. I was exhausted which helped me sleep initially, but the cousin snored, kept yelling "No", and the cat constantly meowed. I had a terrible headache in the morning.

Lou and I got to talk privately about his concerns over his nephew's life. Also, the pain of friends dying of AIDS. Two died in the summer, and now the death of his former lover's partner. Lou had been diagnosed with HIV years earlier and on the verge of dying when the retrovirus cocktail was discovered. It saved his life.

Though Lou was doing much better, he was afraid to go off of disability to start working again. If he became sick, his insurance would not cover him and he would be destitute. It was hard for him not to work. So much of his identity was tied up in his profession and work ethic. What he was doing instead was volunteering with troubled gay and lesbian teenagers. For years I did not want to tell people what I did for a living, feeling my work did not really represent who I was. My hope was now to find my true vocation.

Saturday morning I packed my knapsack for an overnight to Yonkers to see Joanna and her kids. I took Metro-North at Grand Central Station. After we got out of the city a youth got on the train with a bucket and some fishing poles. The guy in front of me asked,

"Going fishing?" He responded,

"Yeah, in Scarsborough". The conductor came by and the young guy was trying to ask for a schedule but couldn't come up with the word. I chipped in and offered,

"Schedule". The conductor retorted,

"Hey, no helping". I responded,

"Why not, that's why we're all here!" The young guy said,

"Right". It was a moment of human connection.

The young guy then talked profusely about sports, especially baseball. The night before I watched a Mexican soccer team play so I was able to mention something. Plus I saw the Cubs play years before in Chicago. I had forgotten how important sports were as a medium of communication, especially for straight men. I tended to poo poo sports events and be proud that I was ignorant of them. Now I was reminded how it was one way to be in relationship when there was no other real commonality.

When I arrived, Peter, Joanna's partner, said that they were all out reconciling with her former husband and father of the kids. I thought that it would make her rather late, but then again, she was always late. I once challenged her saying that tardiness was a control issue. I think she saw it but was late anyway. I was reading the *"Long Loneliness"* by Dorothy Day, so was fine. Having first met Johanna and the kids in 1977, I found it remarkable that we had been able to retain the closeness we built up.

I treated everyone to a simple lunch. We were like family and it was such a gift. Johanna, her daughter Dolly, and I planned a little party in my hotel room on the patio. We had some vodka and cranberry juice. Her son Sam never showed up due to bald tires. Fred, her other son, came with his girlfriend after 10 pm. I was pretty tired by then and he was apologetic. I overheard someone ask what our relationship was. He answered that I was like a father to him, a friend, and a teacher. His comment touched me deeply.

It should have been obvious, but Fred looked different after twenty years. I had difficulty connecting with that part of me that was so close and involved in his life when he was fourteen. My connection grew as we talked and had contact, hugging. He was physical with me and with strong deep eye contact as was always his way. I realized how significant I had been in his life. The musical "Grease" was put on, and Johanna's beautiful twelve-year-old granddaughter knew it by heart.

CONGREGATION OF THE MOST HOLY REDEEMER
The Redemptorists

Figure 28 In C.Ss.R. Habit

Back in Washington, I developed a strong prayer life by visiting the roof of my condo to greet the sun and find silence. I kept myself in good physical condition with a Nordic Track which I hid away in the walk-in closet when not in use.

In early fall, I went on a Jesuit retreat to Faulkner, Maryland in a house set above a river. It was a four-day silent retreat with spiritual direction.

Unusual for me, I asked my friend Patricia if she wanted to go and we went up together. The day before it was over, I choose a nun for spiritual direction. As I was sharing my discernment process, she asked if I had been in touch with the Redemptorists in Washington. She said she had helped lead some retreats with them and that she didn't think my being fifty would necessarily exclude me from their process. She knew the vocation director and gave me his name and also a book on religious vocations.

I had approached the Paulists and the Franciscans, and my age had been an issue. Also, the fact that I was officially Catholic for only five years. As I considered the Redemptorists, I noted that their formation house was in Washington and thought that with them I would still be able to have the support of my local faith communities and friends.

When I contacted their Vocation Director, he was glad to hear from me and invited me over to meet and have a meal with them. Though no longer a college, the formation house was called Holy Redeemer College. It was an imposing structure of grey stone, three levels, large refectory (dining room) and a beautiful chapel. Two of the Redemptorist priests were theologians on staff at Washington Theological Union, the seminary I would be attending if I were to join them. The order was divided into provinces and Washington fit into the Baltimore Province with headquarters in Brooklyn, New York.

I attended several of their discernment retreats and was by far the oldest of the postulants who were considering a religious calling. Postulancy was usually a two-year period. This was followed by a year in novitiate, a period of further discernment. It included going deeply into the history of the church, ethics, history of the order, and the nature of life in a religious community.

Over the months of visiting Holy Redeemer, I got to know the community and I was impressed by them and the staff who worked for them. I decided to take the leap and see how it went. I had felt that I wanted to be a brother rather than a priest but was dissuaded from this. They believed my talents, experience, and education were more suited to the priesthood. I joined them in May 1999, and began the Masters of Divinity degree program at Washington Theological Union (WTU) in September. In residence at Holy Redeemer were seven students and eight priests, some of whom were professors. I immediately enjoyed the courses and the intellectual requirement that went along with them. The student body consisted of lay students and students from the eight religious orders that together founded the seminary.

It was stimulating to be with students of varying backgrounds. A number of women were taking degrees as well. This gender diversity helped provide some balance to an otherwise all male environment. We had frequent chapel services.

I did my best to learn and fit in at Holy Redeemer. A particular challenge was morning and evening prayer where we used the breviary prayer book required for priests and religious. With my dyslexia and all the different sections and ribbons to keep place, I strove for months to master the mystery of its organization. Occasionally we took turns leading the prayer time. I would shudder when it was my turn.

Our bedrooms were large with very high ceilings and large wooden windows. The grounds were well kept and the food produced by the kitchen was excellent. For special events the community would have a banquet and invite guests. There were often interesting guests to share our meals. There were almost no brothers left in the order.

Redemptorist houses were located around the country including Florida, Illinois and New Jersey. If we wanted to go on a school break, we could stay in one of the other houses. Several were retreat houses on the beach and fine places to take some time off. Every need of ours was met.

My time with the Redemptorists was edifying. I learned a great deal in terms of theology, spirituality, living in community, and my feeling of being drawn to a higher calling. I also learned the importance of having at least one good friend in community. I spent a year in school and then went to the Novitiate in Glenview, Illinois for the second stage in the process.

The Novitiate was in a wooded area. Three novices of Vietnamese background, two others and I spent the year together learning the history and practices of the Redemptorists. We also met weekly with novices of other orders. I was able to make friends with Johnny, one of our two non-Vietnamese novices. Johnny was young, bright, conservative, and outspoken. In ways we were opposites but through a lot of dialogue became close friends. I remember one day we spent eight hours arguing about homosexuality. We only took breaks for lunch and dinner. He embraced the church's official teaching, and I questioned it due to the damage done to so many by the teaching.

Novice life was one of chapel, seminars, conferences, study, private prayer time and mutual activities. Our novice master/director was Father Joe, an older priest of humility, wisdom, and dedication. Having made it through the year, I returned and was able to take first vows. It was an inspiring ceremony in the chapel of Holy Redeemer College. A number of my outside friends and family were able to attend the ceremony. I continued with my theological education for the next year. During the year although consciously working against the feelings, I was attracted to several of the other Redemptorists. I felt committed to the order and process and in no way indicated my attraction.

I didn't know what was wrong, but something was missing. I was doing everything expected but felt empty. I was weighed down. I felt it in my room, as I went to meals, and in chapel. I realized that my fundamental dilemma was back. I had suppressed my sexuality, and the topic of homosexuality almost never came up in any context. Was I really called to be a priest and give up part of my natural identity as a gay man or was I to live in the secular world and be open. I didn't think my angst had to do with sexual expression, rather the ability to live honestly.

I had to share so I met with the Rector, Father John, and told him. Fr. John suggested that I have a phone conversation with a psychologist in Providence, R.I. who the Redemptorists often used. I followed the suggestion and had a series of weekly phone conversations with Kenny. What a great guy, honest, direct, supportive, and thought provoking. Kenny said, "You know David, Fr. John likes you, the permanent community at Holy Redeemer likes you. From our sessions, I believe you're fine material to be a Redemptorist."

For the beginning of summer, I was scheduled to go for two months to live with the Mexican Redemptorist community in Guadalajara and study Spanish. This assignment was something I requested. Fr. John asked me not to take any definitive action until after my time in Mexico. I agreed. In Guadalajara, I tried hard, interacting with the community members, and taking the four hours a day of one-on-one Spanish. After three weeks I started to crash. My legs felt they were made of iron as I dragged myself around. Spanish classes was excruciating, with no distractions. All I could do was make myself eat and attend class.

The mental and physical exhaustion went on for three more weeks. In the sixth week of my stay, I got a call from Johnny, the one real friend I made within the Redemptorists. Johnny called to tell me that he was leaving the order. His challenging, highly informed, and outspoken approach was not appreciated by the older priests. Johnny said he couldn't take it anymore.

I was crushed by my own doubt and loneliness. My depression deepened. How could I possibly continue when my only Redemptorist friend was leaving. After several days of considering my options, I decided I had to leave also. I called Fr. John and told him about Johnny and that I felt I couldn't go on. Fr. John asked if I could hold off from a final decision until the end of the summer. He said that he'd been in touch with Kenny. There was space for me after I got back to have a three week stay in Providence at a retreat center Kenny helped run. I agreed.

Over the next two weeks I felt a burden lifted off my shoulders. My energy level got higher and higher. I was doing much better in my Spanish class. One day I was able to translate between a U.S. student and the Mexican community. The next day I was friendly with a young Mexican woman and able to carry a normal conversation in Spanish. I was feeling stronger, more myself, and more fluent.

Arriving back in Washington, I made arrangements to go to Providence. The retreat house was in a downtown part of the city. It was a large home with different suites and a common area with a kitchen. The larder was fully stocked. I had money if I wished to go out to eat or walk to movie theaters along the canal. I was receiving massages from a skilled massage therapist. I met with Kenny every day or every other day.

One evening I went to see one of the Terminator movies. It deeply affected me. I stomped home with high energy, feeling powerful. I knew that I could take on anyone I passed if they challenged me. It felt great being this strong. When I got to my room I paced back and forth feeling the power flow through me. The following poem expressed my feelings:

JUNKYARD DOG

Sitting on the couch
Pretty much in a slouch
I got up the nerve to ask
Is now the time to remove the mask
And leave my junkyard dog to his task

Eloquent sallies exit my mouth

But always seem to go south
My humorous side, which I don't try to hide
Draws few laughs and most can't abide

My therapist stutters, my psychologist mutters
My friends ignore me, my enemies abhor me
Ceasing control, should I just let it roll?
Is it time to let my junkyard dog out?

'Tis certainly better than being enfettered
And ending up home in a pout
Nashing his teeth…he's just beneath…
Ah yes!!............ Ohhh what a relief.

A nearby department store had a sale so I went to check it out. I liked underwear and, feeling in great shape, tore through the men's department grabbing what appealed to me. In the evening when I sat down to count, I had bought twenty pairs of underwear.

I shared my experience of powerfulness with Kenny. He asked me a series of questions. I had a sense of what my behavior might represent but needed Kenny to put a name to it. A family member had bi-polar II disorder for many years, including hospitalizations. It had not entered my mind until this point that I also might suffer from it. Kenny said from what he was seeing, I most likely had the less severe bi-polar I varient, controllable with medication and counseling.

 Kenny still believed that I would make a good Redemptorist. But after further discussion and counseling I decided I needed to be free. Back in Washington, Fr. John hesitantly accepted my decision to leave. He said that if I wanted to continue in the master's program, the Redemptorists would pay for my tuition. I would need to cover room and board and could stay in the school housing. I had about a month before school started again.

I needed money to live on so decided to sell my only asset, my efficiency condo. The market was excellent so I made a considerable profit which allowed me to continue at Washington Theological without working. I was now seeing a well-known Washington psychiatrist was on one medication, then another augmented by a third when I felt anxious.

SEMINARY

I left Holy Redeemer College the beginning of September and moved to seminary housing. Washington Theological had an open environment with a co-ed housing facility. This made for a new and relaxed environment. Often groups of students would study at the several tables in the living room-kitchen area. My room was on the second level at the top of the staircase. Classrooms were two minutes away. Making such a dramatic change in lifestyle seemed not so difficult. I enjoyed my new freedom and focused on my studies.

Classes went well and I was keeping up. I especially felt the impact of the course on ethics taught by a Redemptorist priest. The approach to culpability and varying degrees of it, was an eye opener. Intent was extremely important in making a judgement on degrees of culpability.

For three months, life seemed to be moving along. I was making friends with my live-in colleagues. Towards the end of November, I started having trouble focusing in class and was anxious. Xanax was added to my regular medications. But the anxiety moved into depression. I would sit alone at the third floor window of my room, just staring out. I had trouble getting to class. Others were asking me how I was, which made me feel worse.

LOST

I seem to have lost my way
Nothing seems to pay
No energy for the day

One moment driven by internal force
Fully functioning and creative of course
Then nothing seems to matter,
Just the pitter patter of the rain

I've misplaced the manual
Does this have to be annual

Having stripped my gears
I reach out to my peers

But can they help,
None are seers

Can I make it plain
This empty space inside
I so want to hide

But my gear shift is shot
I feel so caught
Must this be my lot

How to explain
My past comes to haunt me
Can I let it be
Blindfold my instincts of panic and doubt
For I really don't know what it's all about

As Christmas approached, students were heading out to their families. I wasn't feeling that I had a family nor did I want to be with anyone. Two days after Christmas, sitting at my dorm window, the thought came to me that life would just be easier if I jumped. This scared me and I tried to stop the thoughts. I knew it was suicidal ideation and that these thoughts were dangerous. The self-destructive feelings continued for several more days. I had not realized how deeply I was affected by leaving the Redemptorist community and the vocation of priesthood.

 I was seeing a therapist so forced myself to go to the next appointment. It was a slushy winters' day. As I walked towards her office, a metro bus was about to pass me. I thought, "Wouldn't it just be easier to slip under the bus and get it over with." The next day I decided I had to take action if I were going to live. I called my brother Neal and admitted the state I was in and that I needed to be hospitalized. Neal strongly agreed. I called my psychiatrist and shared my desperate state. He asked me to stay put, that he'd call right back. He called back saying I should go immediately to Georgetown University Hospital and be admitted to the psychiatric unit. A local friend of mine, Joe, said he would accompany me.

I had to enter the hospital through the Emergency Room. It was a busy place but soon I was admitted. Joe carried my bag as we headed to the psychiatric unit. I entered, turn to the little window in the mechanized door, and waved goodbye to Joe, whose kindness I would never forget.

I was housed with the nicest guy named Mark. Our two beds were parallel in the room. After getting to know him a little, I couldn't imagine why Mark was there. It turned out he had tried to kill himself numerous times. This was the first time in years I'd slept in the same room with another person. In the morning, all the patients would gather in the dayroom for different activities. One of the activities was using magazines pictures to make collages. I found photos of wolves and incorporated them in my collage.

When I asked to see a chaplain, a young woman came and prayed with me. I stayed in the hospital three nights and four days. In my first conference with the medical staff, I mentioned a family member with bi-polar II disorder who was doing well on lithium. I knew family members often react well on the same medications. The team told me that they were recommending lithium to my psychiatrist.

On the third night I was told of my discharge the following day. I didn't feel stable enough to leave. The hospital was a safe haven and I begged them not to release me yet. The next morning I was told I could be in the day program for two weeks as I adjusted. I would spend four hours a morning at the hospital. I expressed my great gratitude to the head psychiatric nurse for her role in arranging it. I wondered how many patients did have to leave before they were ready.

Back at WTU, I was vulnerable and didn't want others to known I'd been hospitalized in a psych. unit. I pretended I'd just been away for a long weekend. One new friend in the residence, Annette, was studying at Catholic University for a Social Work degree. She had been with a Franciscan order of sisters for eight years including working with immigrants along the southern border of the US and Mexico. She expressed a gentle concern for me before I went to the hospital. By the end of the day program, I shared privately with her what had transpired with me. She was extremely supportive, and we became close friends.

I grew stronger as the weeks passed, convinced I had made the right decision in leaving the Redemptorists. I moved forward in finishing the Master in Theological Studies MTS. I tried to enjoy myself more.

Now that I had left my home with the Redemptorists, and was not becoming a priest, I had no sense of what I would do once I graduated. I was anxious having no sense of the future. I met with the vocation director of Washington Theological Union. Dr. Gerald was supportive and mentioned ministerial positions in parishes. I shared with him the process and issue of sexual orientation that had brought me to the point of leaving the Redemptorists. I suspected that in most parishes I would again feel that I could not be fully honest about myself. Dr. Gerald was understanding of the dilemma.

After our discussion, I returned to my room discouraged. Fifteen minutes later my phone rang. It was Dr. Gerald, he had just received a call from the supervisor of chaplain training at St. Elizabeth's Hospital, a large D.C. psychiatric facility for civil and forensic patients. She asked him if there were any Catholic seminary students who might be interested in her hospital's Clinical Pastoral Education (CPE) training program. Dr. Gerald called me right away. What timing, what a godsend. I immediately returned to Dr. Gerald's office to discuss the possibility. He contacted the hospital to express my interest. Within three weeks, I was admitted to the CPE program, contingent upon completing my master's program.

I now had to finish my master's comprehensive paper on time. The project required Biblical research, original thought, and concentration. I hadn't been able to focus on it before going to the hospital. The requirement was not just finishing the paper but I had to defend it before a faculty panel. I chose a topic I cared about, *"Lazarus at the Gates: Ministry to Marginalized Persons"*, and moved forward. Dr. Gerald was my faculty advisor and gave me guidance. I finished the paper, faced the panel, and was granted a Master of Theological Studies (MTS). I was subsequently admitted into the yearlong chaplain training program at St. Elizabeths Hospital. The head of the program, Reverend Anne, was a dynamic, strong, empathetic ordained minister and board-certified chaplain.

Right in the middle of the academic pressure, I had to find a new place to live. I focused on the DuPont Circle area of D.C. where I was most familiar and comfortable. Rents had gone up. At last I located a tiny five floor walk-up. It was a garret apartment with two small windows overlooking P Street. The one room had a kitchen along the wall and a tiny bathroom. Fortunately, I didn't have much in storage to bring over.

The period of finishing seminary and starting my chaplaincy training program proved to be extremely difficult. I was experiencing high anxiety, my psychiatric medications weren't effective, and I was drinking alcoholically. I was unsure of myself and my future.

After several months of imbalance, I was able to focus on my training at St. Elizabeth's. I drove there every morning and stayed for most of the day. The clinical pastoral educational program involved a number of different modules. Some of them were instructional, but much of the time was being with patients. Introspective exercises and group discussions were part of the training. My small cohort of five began by seeing civil patients in various sections of the large campus.

Many of the patients of St. Elizabeth's were poor and some were indigent. Beyond psychiatric illness, they struggled with severe life issues and yet many had a strong religious belief. The initial training focused on being present to the patient in whatever state they were in. To listen non-judgmentally was extremely important. Patients felt supported from knowing they were heard, accepted, and cared for. Frequent written verbatim reports on conversations with patients were required for group evaluation and suggestions of improvement on patient ministry.

The hospital's locked forensic unit held patients who had been sentenced by a court of law as "not guilty by reason of insanity". Some were violent offenders who committed murder. I was frightened when I first entered the two floor unit with Rev. Anne. But she was well known and liked by the patients. She possessed a strong presence, and I felt safe with her. We chaplain trainees had less contact with these incarcerated patients and they were fewer in number.

Having been in a psychiatric unit myself, I believed that I might have a special understanding which would help me in ministry to patients. In talking with Anne, she agreed such personal experiences were a gift in the context of a psychiatric hospital. She confided that several staff had themselves been psychiatric patients.

Another aspect of the training was putting together a prayer service that the civil patients were free to attend. It usually involved hymns, Bible reading, and prayer. Patients were encouraged to participate and share during prayer time. Spontaneous sharing might happen at any point during the service.

An early forensic patient of mine named Pedro was a member of the Jehovah's Witnesses. He was in his early 30's and physically powerful. I began by asking him to share some of his understanding of his faith with me. He was happy to have someone to talk to. He often asked to see me. I learned Pedro had thought that a stranger was trying to sleep with his wife and killed him. He had a history of erratic behavior and a diagnosis of paranoid schizophrenia.

Spirituality discussion groups with a theme were held. The discussions were open to whatever religious background or none that patients had. These group sessions provided an excellent way for patients to express what they were thinking and gave us chaplain trainees greater understanding. The dialogue and actions of patients were at times unpredictable. In one instance a particular patient was acting out in a threatening way. Concerned for the group, I asked her to leave. She left, but not before threatening to kill me. This happened to me three times during my training. Rev. Anne encouraged me to not just consider the behavior of the patient, but to look at what I may have done to contribute to the situation.

My CPE program was coming to an end and I needed to find employment. I heard through the program of a nursing home facility in the Maryland suburbs needing a part-time chaplain. The position was only fifteen hours a week but it was a start. I applied and was accepted. The nursing home was quite a drive from my downtown studio but I needed work in my new field. The private facility had patients from middle to high income backgrounds. I worked with a mostly elderly female population. I was particularly fond of one older Jewish patient, Mrs. Silverstein, who enjoyed having me read to her from the Bible. She would talk about her family who lived close by. She strongly encouraged me in my work.

Near the end of my time at the nursing home, Mrs. Silverstein's family held an 85th birthday party for her at one of the family homes. The younger members of the family were putting on a musical skit for her. The party was held at a beautiful home on a hill. One of Mrs. Silverstein's daughters was a well-known painter and her beautiful works of art covered the walls. There were also other works by well known artists and several large sculptures. Mrs. Silverstein was delighted to have me attend and meet her family and guests.

The Maryland job ended and I sought new work. A chaplain friend recommended me to the Pastoral Care director at Ave Maria Hospital located a little beyond the D.C. beltway. They needed night chaplains. Because of where I lived, it meant staying overnight to be there for emergencies. Although the work covered fewer patients, the medical situations were often grave and involved care of family members as well as patients, especially in the case of trauma or death.

The Ave Maria position was part-time and I needed additional employment. I was referred to a hospice service, ComfortCare. I interviewed and got to meet several of the other chaplains. I liked them and they, me, and I began. It was winter and I was still living in the garret apartment. Coming home from work, it would sometimes take longer to park in the DuPont Circle area than the commute itself.

Another significant challenge was finding the location of the patients I was assigned to visit. ComfortCare was in Montgomery County and most of the clients were there. Since the time I was young, I have had difficulty with cardinal directions, general directions, and the use of maps. Montgomery County was unknown to me. Planning my hospice visits sometimes took as long as the visits themselves. I sensed I was walking a fine line due to my geographic challenge.

But I was saved. The GPS guidance systems had just come out. The devices were shaped like medium sized rocks and saved my job. I got one for $400 and attached it to my front windshield. I immediately became completely dependent on it for work. I came out to clean off my car following a snowstorm. As I approached the passenger side, I noticed that the window was down, and snow had gotten into the car. More importantly, the GPS was gone. I blanched. I wasn't even sure I could find our central office without it. I called and explained the break-in and arrived late after purchasing another GPS.

I coordinated with hospice nurses, social workers, and aides. We chaplains made an extensive report on each patient we saw. The visits were in their homes or in nursing homes that used hospice. We strove to bring comfort to the patients but felt rushed due to patient load.

NEW BEGINNINGS

In my personal life, I decided to pursue Match.com to find a suitable partner, but was not having success. One day I got a response from an attractive Korean guy. It turned out both of us had been about to give up the attempt. Joo had given himself one more week and then was thinking of returning to Korea. For four years he had worked for a small firm in exporting. We decided to meet at the metro stop at DuPont Circle and go for coffee. He came up the long mechanized stairs and I found him attractive with short black hair, a smooth face, shy eyes, and gentle manner.

I invited him to my apartment. I made tea for us and we sat on the couch, sharing a little about ourselves. I was embarrassed at the size of my apartment, but he seemed comfortable. I asked him if I could kiss him and he demurely said yes. I did so gently and he responded in kind. We decided we'd get together the next Saturday. I told him how great that would be in that it was my birthday. I thought to myself, what a lovely gift Joo was, especially at this time in my life. He seemed to like me.

Joo was living in the Virginia suburbs in the basement of an older Korean man. I would sneak in through a small staircase and leave through a sliding door into a woods boarding the beltway. He was most thoughtful. When we connected the next week, he brought birthday presents for me. We celebrated early Christmas together before I went to be with my brother Neal and my nephew's family.

A chaplain manager at a health system in Richmond, VA called me. In November I had gone to a conference of the National Association of Catholic Chaplains and had causally met him there. He asked if I might be interested in joining their team of chaplains. The possibility was a miracle of timing and grace. We continued to correspond, and I was invited down to interview. The interview went well and I was offered the position of staff chaplain.

A full-time position as a chaplain…what a life saver and life changer. The major problem was the move would mean leaving Joo and I didn't want to do that. It was the first time I'd really been with someone in years. I presented my dilemma to him and he said I should take the position. He would commute on weekends to be with me. I was bowled over with his generosity and care for me. I accepted the position and started to make necessary arrangements to disengage from Washington.

My life had changed so much over the last years that I had only a few close friends. With Joo's support, the transition was not so difficult. All that I owned fit in a small moving van. With both regret and relief, I left my two jobs and headed for Richmond, VA.

I located a complex that looked interesting, Georgetown Apartments, and found a nice split level apartment. What a quiet environment in comparison to D.C. I could sit in silence in the small brick patio, or go out my front door, and be on a quiet street with nice homes. The apartment was only a couple hundred feet off Monument Avenue. As Joo and I became familiar with Richmond, I realized what a fine location I was in.

I moved on the weekend so Joo was able to help me set up my new home. Things seemed to fit in their appropriate places without a need for much more. I decided to buy a larger bed and use the folding futon bed as a couch for the living room. There was plenty of light and a large kitchen, wasted on me, but occasionally Joo cooked. I had several weeks to settle in before my orientation with the Richmond health system began.

The staff chaplains worked in various hospitals in the Richmond metropolitan area. The hospitals served different populations depending on their location. For most of my tenure, I was assigned to the largest hospital. Over time there were varying denominations of chaplains on staff. I grew close to a number of them. I chose to be low key in terms of my sexuality even though within the directives of the system, discrimination on the basis of race, creed, sex, and sexual orientation was forbidden.

The work was challenging and rewarding. At times, I would cover chapel if a priest couldn't make it for the morning Mass. I would lead a liturgy of the Word, with prayer, scripture, and a brief homily. Over the years, I was able to provide comfort and support to a wide variety of patients. The two most difficult units to work in were the NICU and PICU which treated babies and pediatrics. There were amazing recoveries but also profound losses. As much as possible, I also worked on the psychiatric unit, feeling an affinity with the patients.

Although we were a Catholic hospital system, we also had a Rabbi on staff and the Protestant chaplains outnumbered the Catholic. We approached those we served within their own context of spirituality and religious belief. In fact, it was against hospital regulations to attempt to sway someone to any particular faith tradition. I was fortunate to have both a Protestant background as well as being Catholic. I loved the old Presbyterian hymns I learned as a child, and, having taught myself to play the harmonica, would occasionally play an older patient a hymn. The music and memories often brought comfort.

Chaplains not only worked during regular workdays, we often were assigned to be on-call weekday nights and weekends. I would spend the night in the pastoral call room of the hospital I was covering. Working days, occasional nights, and weekends proved taxing.

Being able to share with Joo and having his support made the hard times easier. Seeing each other was difficult depending on my weekend work schedule. Joo had little interest in my faith and religious activities but had a strong sense of ethics. When he was with me in Richmond, he enjoyed just staying around the house and watching golf or tennis on TV. Being in a relationship, I had no interest in going out except occasionally with friends. One good friend, Sam, was great at getting a group of us together for a movie or dinner. He was involved in a church and did a lot of volunteer work.

Joo got a Master's in Business Administration from the University of Virginia and our life moved on. One day after six years he said that he might have a business related problem but was working on it. A short time later I could tell it was something serious. He shared with me that the small company he had formerly worked for was being investigated by the federal government. They were looking into his boss and another employee but not into him. Time passed and other employees were now examined including Joo. It turned out that Joo had been involved in white collar fraud under the tutelage of his boss who had promised him a green card if he cooperated. Joo had so wanted to stay with me and in the social freedom of the U.S. that he made the tradeoff.

The investigative process took a year from the initial hints to his trial. I was at the trial as were other friends of ours who were character witnesses. Joo was sentenced to thirty-six months in prison to be followed by immediate deportation to Korea. He could never return to the United States.

His prison was located in the middle of Pennsylvania mountains. It only held those convicted of felonies who would be deported immediately upon the completion of their sentence. Inmates were from different populations including Haitian, Dominican, Korean, Salvadorian, Mexican, Indian.

I drove him up to the prison through the Pennsylvania hills to a small road just off a two lane highway. There was a small sign, easy to miss. We only had a minute before the officers came for him. I will never forget his terrified look as they led him away.

Joo called me every day for the next three years and we'd speak for a few minutes. I was able to visit him once a month. Making the seven hour drive usually on a Thursday, I'd see him Friday morning and return Friday afternoon. We had to sit a certain distance from each other with a table between us. We ate from vending machines. Prisoners were allowed to have their own money and I would send some of Joo's to him every month through the administration. Normally I would stay for three hours, and Joo would ask me about my life.

An important aspect of his experience was group support and protection. At different times there were up to fourteen other Korean guys in the prison. They relied on each other socially and for safety. It was never known that Joo was gay. One of the jobs he had was as prison librarian. He organized the library and signed the books in and out. He was a veracious reader and covered about a book every three days, over three hundred and fifty in the three years of his imprisonment. I was able to see him for the last time one month before he was deported. He would not be able to visit any English-speaking country due to intelligence sharing.

Joo's first year back in Korea was very difficult and he mostly stayed in his mother's home and read and watched TV. His prison record could not be known. He found a good job through a former boss. He worked killer hours with little sleep but was able to support himself and

move forward. The other area of concern was marriage. His mother, relatives, and old school chums were incessantly attempting to set him up with blind dates. It was oppressive at the beginning but over time cooled down. Knowing of his sexuality was not an option.
Once Joo was back in Korea we kept in touch weekly using the internet and phone calls. He was one of my best friends and I valued his input as we shared about our lives.

I was sixty-three when I first went to a financial planner to consider retirement. It wasn't until the next year that I found an advisor I liked. After looking over the information I sent her, Sue asked me, "So, do you want to retire tomorrow?" I was amazed. The previous two planners I consulted recommended working until seventy or seventy-two. I told her I'd like to retire at sixty-five.

While saving money towards retirement, I continued to meet with Sue to fine-tune the plan. I believed I had a choice of staying in Richmond, moving outside the country, or doing both. I remained unsure which option to choose and simply continued working.

On my 65th birthday, the hospital administration gave me a lovely retirement party and a number of my colleagues spoke of our time together. There was a long table set with cakes, cookies, beverages. The pastoral care staff and a cross section of hospital employees were present. I was delighted that friends from custodial services and the phone bank were included. The Vice President of Mission, Paul, gave a lovely farewell with significant positive comment.

A sense of freedom and relief continued until I discovered that my department had changed my official retirement date from December 1, 2013, back to November 26, the day of the retirement party. It had been December 1 to insure immediate eligibility with Medicare and supplemental medical coverage. So, for my first month of retirement, I couldn't even drive my car for fear of an accident.

The good news was that I had already bought several cases of good cheap wine from Trader Joe's. No need to do that shopping. A couple of glasses and my anxiety over lack of insurance flowed away. I felt free… no midnight pages, no overnights at the hospital, no filling in shifts for other chaplains. Occasionally catching a Netflix movie but reading novels mostly. I was set.

Once the medical coverage came through, things were fine. I went back to doing the usual evening activities and caught up with friends. Desiring more companionship, I went to several bars but didn't meet anyone. My intentions were mixed. I was committed to Joo in prison but knew I might never be with him again due to his immediate deportation following his release.

 Not going in to work every day was a significant adjustment. I got up late and had no pressing obligations or daily social activities. When it started to get dark, I'd raid my kitchen pantry for a bottle of red wine and be set up for reading and journaling. Wine helped me deal with a growing sense of loneliness. I believed that the strong and deep friendships with my chaplain colleagues would continue and did not anticipate how dependent they were on work proximity. I missed the daily life with colleagues and friends. Not having work opportunities to care for others left a vacuum.

There were few chances to meet guys through activities. I met Joo through Match.com so I thought I would try that approach by corresponding and making friends. After some poor responses, one night there was a brief piece of poetry waiting. What beautiful writing and it was original. Something about a sparrow having gotten lost in a storm and looking for its home. It really touched me. I knew just how that felt. The author's picture was small and partially shaded. I could only imagine how attractive he was.

Writing back, I acknowledged the beauty of the poem, and said how nice it was to meet someone of culture. The response was humble and interested. We continued our correspondence for several months. The writer, Drew, was from South Carolina. The distance didn't matter, we were connecting. My spirits elevated. I'd found a special friend. I focused on my writing and communicated my deep feelings to Drew. As his gentle poetry flowed, I knew I'd found a country flower and wanted to see it in bloom.

At last, an opportunity popped up. There was going to be a big gay event in Richmond and Drew said he could get a ride with a friend. Wow, finally. I felt ready to meet and build on our relationship. I envisioned him in my bedroom, stroking each other and whispering gentle phrases back and forth. We would meet at my house on Saturday morning and go down to the weekend event.

The minutes of waiting were agony. At last appeared a short fellow sauntering down the sidewalk. Running back into the house, I tried to slow my breathing. The doorbell rang. Taking one last breath, I slowly opened the front door. Oh my God, the guy was really…. Ugly. Although he was supposed to be in his thirties, he was balding. His teeth were very large, and he had a birthmark on his head that reminded me of Gorbachev. I looked into those pale watery eyes and thought, "I can't even kiss this guy".

My etiquette took over and with a big smile I opened the glass door. In came my intended, bursting with joy. I hadn't really planned anything, believing chemistry would take care of itself. I thought fast and said,

"I wonder if you'd help me with something". "Sure". "This old TV needs to go in the shed out back", "Sure".

Turning my back, I led Drew into the small rental part of the house. We each took a side of the big old TV. Backing down the stairs, I opened the back door. In my surprise, I had forgotten about Coco, my cat, who never was allowed outside. She dashed out. I screamed,

Figure 29 Coco

"Let go, Let go" and dropped my end of the TV to go after Coco. The TV crashed out of Drew's hands onto the floor. I chased after Coco. She had not gone far in the new environment.

"Coco, Coco" she moved a little, I moved a little. Coco moved a little bit more, and I moved a lot more. Grabbing her fiercely, I raced back into the house.

Drew looked shaken. We continued with the chore not knowing if the TV would work after the fall. Deciding it was best to get out of the house, I suggested we go downtown to the event. A variety of booths were scattered around the park area. I wanted to visit various friends but didn't want to introduce Drew to them. I felt embarrassed, I'd alerted them that my new boyfriend was coming for the weekend. I bit the bullet and went around to some booths with Drew.

How could this fiasco be backpedaled. I told Drew I needed to do some volunteer work at a couple of booths and got away for a couple of hours. I felt cheap and superficial not being able to get beyond the physical, but there it was. When we were back together, a group of friends said they were going out to a hamburger joint. I said strongly we'd go along too. We sat beside each other, but I focused on the others.

When the meal was over, I told Drew,

"I'm sorry but I am tied up for the evening. If you like, I can take you to my house and your friend can pick you up there."

"That would work fine for me David," so we headed home. When Drew's friend arrived,

"It was fun meeting you Drew, have a good trip home."

"Thanks David, I hope you enjoy the rest of your weekend."

And he was gone. I thought to myself, "I will never trust the Internet again!"

Considering all our correspondence, I decided it would be gracious of me to write to Drew. I wrote saying I had enjoyed meeting him but that he wasn't what I was looking for. In response, Drew responded that quite honestly, I wasn't what he was looking for either. I was shocked, hurt, and surprised. I couldn't imagine how it was possible Drew didn't want me.

Another way I thought I could fill my retirement hours was to invite my friend Jim down from Philadelphia to visit. We both had been in the theatre and often shared favorite stories such as when I was in summer stock on a showboat on the Mississippi. I played Elwood, the lead in *Harvey,* with only seven days to learn the part while concurrently rehearsing *Wait Until Dark.*

Opening night, I felt overwhelmed, but the show must go on. In the first act there was a scene in which Elwood sat at a table and was joined by another character. He was to ask Elwood a couple of questions. We started the scene, and all seemed well but in the middle of the scene, the the actor looked at me with glazed eyes and whispered, "What's my line?" then frantically, "What's my line?" I, who had spent night and day learning my own lines, had no idea. I got up, said, "It was nice seeing you," and exited stage right.

Jim and I decided to go to the musical *Into the Woods* and were excited to see it. After a show, we usually went to a bar to compare notes about lighting, scenery, voice production, acting. It was great fun. At intermission we got a couple of drinks and observed who else was in attendance. I liked sitting in the first tier close which gave a broad view of the stage as well as of the audience.

Show done, we headed to one of the small gay bars in town. I always hated the noise level in bars but a few drinks helped me tolerate it. We sat at the bar and went to town. Jim said,

"The lead's voice had a distracting vibrato and the scenery was a little much for that stage." I said,

"Lighting was slow in transitioning. One of the leads was stiff." Drinks flowing and criticism built until we headed home.

I felt a little groggy in the morning, but coffee helped. We decided to go out for breakfast. I usually had high fiber cereal at home but Jim expressed less than no interest. We showered and prepared to meet the day. Coco fed, we headed out the door. I unlocked the car and got in. Starting up the car, I looked to my side mirror. It wasn't there. "What the…?" I was stunned. "What has someone done to my mirror?" Jim looked at me perplexed and said, "Don't you remember, you drove into a fence last night and the mirror broke off". It wasn't until later that I learned the term "blackout drunk."

BABES

Once Jim left, I was alright for a couple weeks with my quiet evenings. I then wanted more but didn't want to go far. I discovered I liked Babes, a local lesbian bar on Cary Street, less than a ten-minute walk from home. I enjoyed the friendly atmosphere with some of the regulars and the on-going banter. It felt comfortable to occupy a bar stool right next to Al, a retired postal worker and Sam a car mechanic.

They both lived close by and most every night would walk over to Babes. After several hours in the bar, they would go home to their wives. After my first visit, Joyce, the bartender, knew me and my choice of wine.

One night, a guy was sitting on my stool. Al signaled and whispered that the guy, Mark, was new and a little bit down. He and Sam were trying to make him feel at home. I went down one stool and sat on his other side. I was immediately interested. Mark had a slight build, curly brown hair, and an early time-worn face.

"My name's David. How you doing?" Mark turned slowly and with sad eyes said,

"I guess I'm ok." I felt for him right away.

"Well, you've come to the right place. The guys are friendly and the bartenders excellent."

"I haven't been here before… but felt like a drink."

It was clear to me that Mark had several drinks before he arrived. I prided myself on being a good listener. I didn't always remember what was said but enjoyed playing the part. Mark went on,

"Thank God it's Friday…TGIF. Work isn't going so good."

"I'm sorry…what do you do?"

"Well, what I really like doing is playing the guitar and singing but work in a grocery store."

"That can be tough."

"Yeah, it really can."

"Let me buy you a drink… I bet it will help you feel better."

"OK man, that's nice of you."

Feeling generous by this time, I ordered a round for my regular guys and whatever Mark was having. Joyce said to Mark,

"Another Tequila Sunrise?"

"Oh yeah, I want to feel real good when the sun rises man… uh, I mean woman."

Joyce shook her head slightly as she turned to make the drink. She had a pretty face, strong arms, and a long ponytail. When she returned with his drink, Mark tried to take her hand. It didn't work.

We kept talking. Mark shared that he and his girlfriend were having problems. I thought…Girlfriend? What's up with this guy? He seems gay, he's in a lesbian bar, and he's talking to a gay man about his girlfriend. But then I thought, Wait a minute, what's up with me? I'm in a lesbian bar attracted to a straight guy, talking with him about his girlfriend. I made to go, but Mark said,

"Please don't go. I'm really enjoying being with you. You are such a nice guy."

I just couldn't tear myself away after that. Mark said he wanted to play me a song he'd written. What the heck. I was feeling very good and warm and thought who knows. I paid for the five rounds and escorted Mark out the door. We walked about half a block and sat on a bench. Mark got his guitar out. I noticed he had slim delicate fingers as he began to strum. Mark sang with a gentle tenor voice. The lyrics were saying I love you and I miss you.

I got tears in my eyes, took Mark's hand, and said how beautiful it was. Mark looked at me and said,

"You know, my girlfriend and I have talked about being bi-sexual." I couldn't take it anymore. I grabbed Mark, kissed him on the mouth, and started pulling him home down Cary Street.

"Wait a minute", Mark yelled but I was hauling him, yelling,

"Come on, you're coming home with me. You're bi-sexual, It's ok, I want you".

Mark put up a fight but I was stronger. I dragged him along the sidewalk. Mark broke away and I went after him. I was not going to let this guy go. It had been so long, I needed to have him. I put Mark in a bear hug in the middle of Cary Street. Cars were passing, honking, I didn't care. Mark started to cry and say,

"Please, please, let me go. I don't want to be with you. Jill and I were just talking, Please let me go".

Finally the fear and panic in his voice reached me, and I released him.

The next couple of evenings, I went looking for Mark to apologize. I realized the following morning how forceful, even violent I'd been. On the second day I found him on the patio of a café across from *Babes*. He looked frightened when he saw me. I started to apologize but he and his friend jumped up and ran into the café. I bit my cheek and went into *Babes*. Joyce, the bartender, told me what she observed and heard about what happened two nights before. She advised me to stay away from *Babes* for a while.

I was hurt. I had tried to apologize. It just didn't feel fair to be treated this way. I decided I'd show them and stayed home for a while. I went back to my wine, my reading, and quiet evenings with Coco. After a few glasses I'd mellow. But then with more time, the desire to be with people arose. I shunned *Babes* and went downtown to a bar with a restaurant section. It had a real mix of gay men, but the atmosphere didn't seem that friendly. After a few hours of hanging out I'd feel more comfortable and strike up conversations.

One night I overstayed and barely made it home. I got up in the middle of the night to go to the bathroom. On the way back I slipped on the oriental rug and fell onto the pointed edge of my night stand. My right side hurt but I crawled back into bed. In the morning, I suffered a terrible headache and pain in my side. I pulled up my t-shirt to see a bloody gash. I didn't want to deal with stitches and several days later a big area of my side and hip were black, blue, and green around the gash. It was impressive, and feeling proud, I took a couple selfies of it. It began to heal.

Two weeks later it looked much better. Deciding to go out, I visited the same bar but had a better time. Making it home I crawled into bed.

Middle of the night I went to the bathroom. Coming back, I slipped on the same rug, went down on the night stand again. This time I also hit my head on the floor. In the morning, proud of my survivor skills, I took selfies of this new gash. It never occurred to me that there might be a connection between my injuries and my alcohol consumption.

Alone a great deal of the time, I spent quiet days and evenings of wine and reading. One night I decided to go to the gay Italian cooking class held monthly at St. Mark's church. It was a small event to show how well some in the group knew cuisine and how to prepare it. Everyone paid $20 and brought a bottle of wine. Most in the group were interested in the preparation and were able to ask informed questions. I, on the other hand, knew nothing about cooking but enjoyed the camaraderie and opportunity to sample various wines. This particular night had a fine variety of wines to compliment the hors d'oeuvres. The long table was set for fifteen with good china, flower arrangements, silverware and two candelabras. The setting was the specialty of one member who spent hours planning and arranging.

My good friend Sam was the chef of the month. He took his preparations and presentation very seriously. The final product was my only interest. The dinner went well with ample cuisine and flowing wine. I left the gathering in high spirits and headed home. As I came into my neighborhood, I got an urge to just do something more, something different than just going home.

I stumbled but didn't fall. Grabbing the door, I propelled myself into *Babes* once again. There was a cover and fortunately the door keepers didn't know me. A crowd had gathered for performers' night, a drag queen special. I hoped Sandy would be on. At another performance I'd found him especially attractive. The other drag queens were usually large and overdone. Sandy was small, energetic, and athletic. I headed to the bar and got my glass of red. Boy, was it good going down. I could feel my excitement growing.

The first drag show I ever saw was in the late 60's in New York City. Featured was a Diana Ross performing "Ain't No Mountain High Enough." She was terrific. I found it mesmerizing. It was one of the first times I went home with a guy. Brut cologne stayed a favorite of mine since that night. For spring break, I visited my parents. All was fine until I started having itchy eyebrows. I asked my mom if she could see anything. She got out her magnifying glass and examined me. Scabies, oh my god, and my mother discovering them. Fortunately, she was low key about it.

I still found drag shows entertaining. I'd costumed in drag several times when I was younger. One time a Thai friend who live in my apartment building took charge of me for a Halloween presentation. Outfit, make-up, jewelry, hair. I was a wonder. There was a picture taken of me looking delicately up at the camera with limpid eyes.

Anyway, *Babes* was packed. I made my way to find a table, jostling here and there. Along the fringe of the rough wood dance floor, tall tables were featured with tall bar stools. No tables were empty so I felt entitled to join a couple at a table. I could charm them if need be. They ignored me. I turned my focus to the room. In one corner the drag queens were condensed into a curtained dressing area. First an arm stuck out, then a leg, then a head shouting for a drink. The crowd was mixed, straight couples, gay couples, lesbian couples, lesbians with straight friends, gays with lesbian friends, some groupings were unidentifiable.

I signaled a waitress and got my next wine. What a great place, nothing like it. The music, already painful, was raised several more decibels. The MC, a roughhewed queen with gravel voice, welcomed and introduced the first performer. I needed a quick drink to handle her. Overflowing her green bustier, she stomped from table to table, glowering, cajoling but flattering the handsome in the crowd. The next one out was better put together but confused her lip-synced words… her mouth went one way, and the words went another. The crowd responded with sympathy, cruelty, and delight.

JAKE

Time for a second bathroom break. I headed for it and grabbed another glass of red on the way back. As I settled back onto my bar stool, looking sideways I noticed an attractive guy sitting by himself enjoying a tall beer. God, where had my eyes been. This guy was by himself. Shoulder-length black hair, chiseled face and he was still alone. He did seem to be enjoying the show, laughing, singing some of the words. Maybe he wanted to be alone. Another drink would make the decision.

By now Joyce was up. Oh could she dance, run, jump, seduce. Money leaped into her special waistband. As lovely as she was, my eyes were on the dude still alone. I just had to say something, so I leaned over, "Hi, my name is David". Not too creative but at least a beginning. The guy smiled at me and yelled, "My name is Jake". Boy was he cute, nice warm smile, put his hand out even, and we shook. Good handshake. We watched the next several performances, commenting as they went. I moved over and bought a couple more rounds to be hospitable. I had not been with anyone since Joo went to prison three years before. Now I wanted to change that. I said,

"You know, I don't know if you'd be interested, but I live in the neighborhood."

"Really? Are you asking me over?"

"Well, if you want, it's been a long time for me".

"It's been a long time for me too, I've been in jail".

"Oh, that's interesting".

He's really cute and he seems to like me. And what a relief, because of Joo, we have something in common.

"Well, I've been visiting my partner in prison for the last three years, in Pennsylvania."

By this time, the lights at *Babes* seemed to dim. I took hold of Jake's hand for a moment and then said, "Let's go." I felt groggy but thought I'd be better outside. I decided I could drive the few blocks home and Jake would follow me in his truck.

Fumbling and dropping the keys to my house, we got in and Jake followed me to the bathroom. We took turns then headed to the bedroom. I kept the lights off. The shadowed street light through the window gave a sense of mystery as our naked bodies slammed together. We both performed well and fell into a deep sleep.

With the dawn I began to regain consciousness. I realized what I had done and rolled over to view Jake. I was struck wide awake. Jake was still handsome but in the middle of his throat was a large tattoo of a Swastika. The nightmare had begun.

One of the first things Jake said was,

"You can't let anyone know we had sex. I was in jail for six months and had to act straight. I'm out on parole, if word ever got back to the guys, I'd really be screwed." We sat quietly in the living room with our coffee.

"I really like you," Jake said.

I could now see other tattoos on Jake's chest. I swallowed, and said,

"I like you too". He walked around examining the objets d'art, the carpets, and art on the walls. He appeared pleased with himself. Meantime I was trying to figure him out. He seemed like a nice gentle guy. When the sex was included, he was hot.

We decided on breakfast in one of the finer greasy spoons Cary Street offered. Sitting across from him, I struggled with the swastika. After breakfast Jake said he'd be back in touch. I felt a connection and my sense of loneliness dissipated a little.

That evening I was having my normal wine hour(s) when the doorbell rang. I opened the wooden door and on the other side of the glass door was Jake. I thought it would be days before he showed up again. I opened the door with a little trepidation.

"Yeah, you know I really like you and we had a good time and I thought why not come over and hang out". In he came in. I had beer in the fridge and offered. His eyes lit up and he went with me to the kitchen.

He suggested that we watch TV. I almost never watched TV but agreed. A series of raucous game shows continued as the wine and beer flowed. We sat on the settee holding hands as the volume washed over me. Finally, the insipid media circus was enough and to get a break I initiated making out. This turned into something more and the evening was finished by 9:30pm when Jake left.

Getting up the next morning, I saw his truck out front, without him in it. My anxiety kicked in. I wondered what was going on. I heard some noise in the backyard, looked, and there was Jake with gardening tools, trying to get my lawn mower started. It felt like too much too soon but there he was. He explained how he could help around the place, and I would pay him. There was no question in his suggestion. I felt caught and agreed.

The morning after that, Jake was out front washing my car. I really, really, didn't want my good African American neighbors to see this guy with a swastika in the middle of his neck. I asked Jake to put a shirt around it or something. From a distance, my car looked bright and clean. But later, the sponge Jake used must have had metal in. There were broad scratches over much of the car.

In my weekly conversation with my brother Neal, I mentioned my predicament. Neal became rapidly concerned. He said it sounded like a potentially bad situation. He cautioned me and questioned how much I was drinking.

Jake wanted me to go with him to his apartment. I drove over and parked. At least three guys lived in the apartment, all on parole. I met a Rick and his girlfriend Nancy but we didn't stay long. We headed to a pharmacy where Jake said he wanted to get something. When we got there he explained that he needed a certain type of medicine to help purify urine of any traces of marijuana use. He said he wasn't smoking it now but he had been before he went to jail. He had a urine test coming up in a few days and just wanted to make sure. Said he needed me to buy it for him. I felt funny about it but went ahead.

Two nights later, Jake showed up needing a ride. He said he couldn't use his father's truck and it was important. I started feeling overwhelmed and said I needed a glass first. We had a couple of drinks, fast sex and off we went.

We picked up his friend Rick and Nancy and headed to downtown Richmond. Rick explained that his sister had some money for him and they were going to pick it up. I found myself in an area of town I didn't know existed. We ended up in a cul de sac surrounded by grey apartment buildings. It was poorly lit. Jake said he was going with Rick to get the money. As soon as they were about 100 feet away, a guy appeared and some sort of discussion went on.

It felt wrong. I said to Nancy in the back seat that they weren't seeing Rick's sister, they were negotiating. It made me angry thinking that I may have been used to do something illegal. When they got back, I yelled at Jake for using me. He acted shocked and assured me that Rick's sister had given the money to the guy for them, and that was all. He looked hurt at being suspected of doing something illegal, after all, he was on parole.

I spoke with Neal again who said it sounded like Jake was using drugs as well as using me. By this time, I really wanted Jake to go and suggested that we not see each other for a few days. Jake was opposed to this idea. He told me that he now loved me and that when love wasn't returned it really made him angry, and he sometimes got violent. I was trapped in a cycle of fear and threat.

I had a four-day program as a volunteer chaplain coming up. It was a retreat for local Richmond residents who had AIDS or were HIV positive. It would take me away from Richmond and Jake. I could explain that due to confidentiality, the retreat could not be visited. It would give me the chance to get away, out of my own head, and help others.

How the hell had this started with Jake. I remembered that drunken night, ten days before at Babes. When I spoke to Jake and brought him home, I had been smashed, so drunk that I didn't even see the Swastika until it was too late. Maybe my brother was right, maybe I did have a problem with alcohol.

I poured a glass of wine to help consider this possibility. In preparation for the retreat, I perused the retreat calendar and saw that for the first time in twenty years, there were going to be two recovery meetings offered to the participants. I decided I would attend them. I was now handling Jake with kid gloves, careful not to anger him. Would I be able to present the retreat in such a way that he would accept my absence?

Next time with him I explained the situation with the retreat, that I was on staff as a volunteer chaplain and had to be there. He seemed to understand. But when I dropped him off the day before leaving, Jake seemed unsure and I had to explain all over again. Grudgingly, Jake exited my car and unbeknownst to either of us, my life. The retreat was a positive and reassuring experience. I was able to support and give counsel to the group. I also attended the two recovery meetings. When I returned home from the retreat, I didn't respond to Jake's texts. After four days the texts stopped. He must have turned his sights on another prospect.

BEGINNING RECOVERY

Until Jake happened, I never even considered that alcohol might be a problem for me. My life seemed so normal with it since the time I was eighteen at Georgetown. I was now sixty-five. Did it really make sense to question it. But the situation with Jake shook me. I took a good look at what had caused me to pick him up. I was alone, lonely, and drunk. I continued with him for almost ten days, initially drawn in and then inebriated to manage the stress. I was blatantly used without realizing it. It was clear to me that without the alcohol none of this would have happened. I concluded I might need some program to help me. I didn't know anyone who'd ever done one. The timing of the retreat felt like a miracle. I had escaped Jake and gone to my first two recovery meetings.

 A few days after the retreat, I attended my first regular meeting. It was a men's meeting held in a church basement past the University of Richmond. Having no experience, I thought it was the way meetings usually went. The meeting was loud, boisterous, friendly, supportive, with male humor and strong hugs. It was great. I then went to a meeting the next night held in another church basement. It was a Twelve Step meeting led by two elderly long term recovery members. There was a great difference in the energy and how it was conducted. It felt very civilized, too civilized. One of the suggestions made was that a newcomer go to 90 meetings in 90 days. I managed 87 in 90 days.

One challenge for me was that in the four meetings I regularly attended, no member ever made reference to being gay or in relationship. I knew there were gay guys present. Other types of relationships were shared about. It felt like there was a silent agreement that it wasn't ok to share about that part of my life. I also had trouble connecting with others after the meetings. As soon as a meeting ended, people would go into little groups, and I couldn't push myself to join. I was aware that both of these issues were partially due to my own fear and concern about not fitting in. A fear that had plagued my life.

Early on I got a good sponsor. During my first two weeks, I observed him interacting with a student and liked the sense I got of him. Although he was a Marine Sargeant, he was open and supportive of me as we went through the Twelve Steps. I located two gay meetings and included them in my regular weekly attendance.

Just stopping drinking did not mean that all of my life issues had disappeared. I heard an expression that stopping was only ten percent of the solution. The other ninety percent was changing habits, thinking, self-centered orientation, and more. It was necessary to work through the Twelve Steps to be able to make the changes.

I went back to my quiet evenings reading on the couch, but now with Coco and Coke. What a relief. I would finish reading one book and go immediately into another to have my mind occupied. I visualize a story and fantasize about what was coming. I preferred this approach over movies and tv where everything was provided. I loved John Grisham novels with the suspense, surprises, and the hope that good can win out. I bought a lovely Persian designed journal and started writing.

These activities worked for a time, but then decided it made sense to hit the Internet again. I wanted to see who was out there. I would not get hooked this time. There were lots of older guys, called bears, looking for young guys who needed an authority figure. Plus, there were young guys looking for the same. Disappointment after disappointment but then a message came through. A guy named Johnathan, handsome, bleached, ruddy cheeks, blue eyes. He had a gentle soft smile as he looked up into the camera. He was looking right at me, a fire was lit, I was hooked and wrote,

"Thanks for your message, you seem like a nice guy. What do you do?"

"I work as a waiter but really want to get into film."
"You look like you'd do well!"

"Thanks, it's a tough go but it helps to have friends' support".

"Well, I have a feeling that I'd like to be your friend."

It didn't take long and I was fantasizing how great it would be to have a chance to spend time with Johnathan. My weekly phone conversation with Neal was due. I knew Neal might be skeptical, as he tended to be about these things, but this time I felt sure. Neal listened patiently and then,

"So where does Johnathan live?"

"Ahhhh." I stalled as I realized that I wasn't sure. I knew Johnathan had grown up in Kansas so,

"Yeah, well, Kansas, but he's a really nice guy". I didn't want Neal to know I wasn't sure. Next text I asked Johnathan where he was located.

"Yeah, well actually I'm living in London. I didn't want to tell you too soon. I was afraid you might cut me off".

I took a deep breath, exhaled and decided that this didn't have to stop me.

"I wouldn't cut you off. I really like you. I feel that we have something real going here," I responded.

"I'm really happy then."

That night, I relaxed on the couch with a warm feeling that felt something like love. I could fly to London. I had the time, the money, even miles saved up on American Airlines. Why not meet Johnathan? What was to stop me from spending a week in London going to West End shows and being with Jonathan when he wasn't working. Johnathan said he liked the idea and I began to make flight plans. Meantime Johnathan told me,

"Right now I don't have my own place. I'm a little short on cash, when you get here, I think you'll need to stay in a hotel. I'm really really sorry." Not wanting him to be upset about it, I said,

"That's fine, don't worry, I can afford it."

When Neal heard of these developments, he carefully expressed caution.

"David, you don't know this guy, I know you're feeling something for him. I hate to say it, but it's possible he might plan to take advantage of you." This pissed me off,

"Neal, it's been a long time since you've been with someone, you just don't remember what it feels like. Where's your sense of adventure?"

"Well what if this guy Jonathan isn't really what he seems to you? He could even be dangerous".

I blew Neal off and continued making travel plans. Noticing that Johnathan's look varied considerably from frame to frame, I requested more pictures. Then came an e-mail suggesting that instead of my going to London, why not have him come to Richmond and just move in with me. I could show him around and help him get a job.

Starting to wonder, I spent another evening on the couch. What to do? I felt sure that Johnathan was the one and London would allow us to get to know each other. It did feel a little bit like a mail order bride situation. I was hesitant to call Neal but felt it might help.

Neal, with stark clarity, pointed out that without even having met the guy, I would be turning my home and my life over to a stranger. He reiterated that I still didn't know what Jonathan looked like. "Don't forget how Drew looked in person."

Back on the couch that evening with Coco and Coke, I looked through the pictures again. I wrote to Johnathan that his coming to Richmond was probably wasn't a good idea. He sounded hurt and betrayed in his next communication. He then capitulated and said it would still be ok for me to visit him in London. But by this point, my zeal for the project had died.

My solo life in Richmond continued. I tried for years to find a Catholic parish where I felt welcomed and could be open about myself. I did find one church and became active in it. I joined the Knights of Columbus, a fraternal organization that contributed to and supported the good works of the church. I was welcomed but also felt a certain distance from older members.

I then became involved with an Episcopal church that was welcoming to gay men and women. A number of gay couples were active in the congregation. I found another Episcopal church which I also liked and began going there. The priest was compelling in his preaching and focused on social justice. They offered an inquiry class for those interested in becoming members and I went for several months out of curiosity. It would be two months before joining was possible. At this point I felt I must make the decision concerning moving.

I learned from my financial advisor that I didn't have sufficient income to live in Richmond for six months and then spend the other six months abroad. I was afraid I wouldn't be willing to make a change later. At this point in Richmond, I only had a few close friends. I had concerns about my financial viability if I remained long-term in the United States.

A former boyfriend, who had worked as a contractor in the Yucatan, Mexico, spoke highly of Merida, the capital city. I had visited Merida over two previous summers and attended two Spanish language schools in the process. I liked Merida and considered it a possibility. As tended to be my nature, procrastination kept me from the final decision until six weeks before the day I left.

I had to sell my house, sell my car, and donate to charity or give to family all my furniture, rugs, clothing, artwork, everything. My niece was a major help and encourager in the organizing and disposition of my possessions. We took a picture of me in the middle of seventeen large garbage bags of clothes to donate. I stayed in a motel for the last two nights of my time in Richmond. My niece's husband took me to the airport early in the morning. I shipped two small boxes of books. I flew south of the border with a total of five suitcases and little Coco in her carryon case.

EARLY MÉRIDA

My first mistake upon arrival was losing the immigration document given me upon entering the Merida airport. I needed the document to finalize my status as permanent resident within thirty days. I was striving to keep track of five suitcases, Coco, passport, and papers while struggling to communicate in Spanish. I was already exhausted from the last-minute selling of my car and finding an airport motel.

I arranged to meet the house rental agent when I arrived downtown. Giving the address to the cab driver, I sank into the seat, closed my eyes, and concentrated on my breathing. I arrived at the rental and the agent ushered me into a grand foyer with a living room off to the side. He walked around showing me the house, pool, and *casita* small house for guests. I was amazed and chagrined by what I had done. The house was enormous, much more than I required. With a large pool and grounds, it was more like a palace, and I was tied down to it for two months.

I went about setting myself up. The bed in the master bedroom was king-size, extravagant for me. I unpacked and oriented myself. The kitchen was grand, and I found a large bottle of spring water. I didn't know how it operated. Finally, through experimentation and flooding the kitchen floor, I realized it had an electric pump to bring the water up.

On the first night, I was so tired I brushed my teeth using tap water and drank from the tap to quench my thirst. I repeated this in the morning. I had an appointment at a Spanish language school and left to introduce myself and get started. I liked the school and the friendliness of the director, the assistant, and the two teachers I would work with. Scheduled for three hours in the morning and two in the afternoon, it would be intense.

First thing on the second day, it struck, Montezuma's revenge. What my mother in Egypt called Gippy Tummy. And it struck and it struck. The diarrhea lasted seven days. The school assistant kindly got me special medicine.

I had no sense of where I was in Merida. Since I was a child, I had an extraordinary inability to know the cardinal directions, or remember a route, or know which direction to turn after leaving a place. Because of this, for several weeks I limited myself to the Spanish school via Uber. I also needed to find the English-speaking recovery meetings held twice a week. I got the address online and went. As it was early July, there were only three attendees. It was a start. For the rest of the evenings and weekends, I stayed in, prepared simple meals or ordered out, and watched movies on Netflix.

The first two months were, without my full awareness, extremely stressful. I had not yet connected with a skilled psychiatrist. Coco did provide some comfort as well as responsibility outside of myself. I was making progress in the intensive Spanish. I spoke with the other students but didn't feel a bond with any of them.

The pressure of loneliness built. Hyper energy slowly infiltrated my mind and body. I wondered how I could meet someone. There seemed few options. I broke my resistance and turned to the internet. At first I tried the dating scene but lacked computer agility and rapidly gave it up. One restless night, I came across ads for escorts. Lots of them, cute and sexy. At first, casual looking was enough. Then, I was unable to stop. After a couple days the search had taken over my evenings. Screen after screen of their resumes and pictures. I feared they would think me wealthy with the opulent house, swimming pool, and guest rooms. Yet one night my hand went for the phone.

The first escort, *scort* in Spanish slang, that I called was available. I made an appointment for the next evening. Juan said 300 pesos. I had no idea what might be reasonable. When Juan arrived at the door, he was tall, thin, with an unattractive face. He did not at all resemble his internet shot. I had no idea what to do so I kissed him and went into the pool. I loved the sensation of skinny dipping since my time at Lake Mohonk. Now I enjoyed it more than I was enjoying Juan. When we reached the bedroom and our bodies were actually close, I was overcome by the scent of a sacren baby powder. I had to repeatedly turn my nose away from him. When we were clothed, I paid him. I experienced a wave of relief as the large wooden door closed and Juan was on the other side. The uncomfortable jarring experience was not something I wished to repeat. Better the fantasy than the reality.

Within two days, my energy level had risen again. My desire for companionship overwhelmed me. I returned to the internet. This time I chose Esteban who looked smaller and cuter. In his picture he exhibited a lengthy tattoo of a snake wrapped around his torso. Esteban arrived wearing a cute little cap and carrying a night bag.

As we entered the pool, I knew this was it. Love at first sight and first touch. The guy was a turn on, but I could not turn myself on. I wanted Esteban to spend the night but he had to leave. It had been such a sensuous experience I thought he might not be interested in the money, but Esteban graciously accepted the 500 pesos negotiated upfront.

Later, thru What's App, we set a rendezvous for the next evening.

 I started getting excited early. I watched the clock and counted the minutes. Esteban did not appear. A message came saying not to worry. He was running a little late, but was now leaving the house. I asked were his house was. Progreso, an hour's bus ride away. Esteban finally showed up around 10pm. I was learning about Mexican time. It was lovely at last to see him. Resentment fled. Another moving night through Esteban's advanced skills, yet, incomplete. He was gone by midnight with 500 pesos in his pocket.

Esteban mentioned that he would be in town at a club if I wanted to see him on Saturday night. I had no idea what a Mexican club might be like but longed to be with him. At 10pm, I arrived by taxi and was invited in. It was a small mansion with pillars and hanging plants. There was a young man at the front desk, who invited me to sit.

Esteban was phoned. He appeared with short shorts and a muscle T shirt. The T shirt revealed more skin than cloth. We sat in a gardened patio. Gentle rock music was played. A couple of large rooms could be seen, one draped like a tent. We sipped our drinks. I with a Pepsi, and a good-looking Rum and Coke for Esteban. Several men passed through and turned into different rooms.

The doorbell rang and a number of older men came through. Their destination was the tented room. Esteban said there was going to be a show at 11pm, if I wanted to see it. I was afraid he might be in the show and did not want to see other men goggle or touch him. I said "No". We were escorted into a room. It was small, lightly decorated, with an unmade bed. Esteban and I made the bed and freshened the room. He came to me rubbing his body all over me. I had the strongest desire to take him. I was unable, no matter what he did. When I left the club, I had the sense Esteban was gliding away to make his tent performance.

 I needed to change rental houses. My contract was running out and I didn't want to pay so much for another month. After a week of stressful searching, the agent found a cheaper house but still oversized and overpriced as I learned later. It wasn't hard to pack my five suitcases and get Coco in her carryon.

Remaining mad for Esteban, our next meeting was set. At the appointed time, he called to say he was stuck in Progreso and the bus didn't run late enough. I quickly figured that I could take an Uber for the forty-five minute ride to the beach and pick him up. An hour later, I arrived in the town square. I tried calling Esteban a few times. The call wouldn't go through. In a frantic state, I asked the driver to just keep going around the square. Esteban did appear carrying his bag and looking bedraggled. He had been sleeping on a bench. I was delighted just to sit in the back seat holding his hand for the midnight ride back to Merida.

Figure 30 Home

I anxiously hunted for a house to purchase. I located two main options. The one I chose was a twenty-minute walk to *Plaza Grande,* the park at the historic center of town. The house needed only two weeks of work.

Still at the rental, I was touched by Esteban's domesticity as he helped make breakfast. We sat at the heavy wooden dining table acting like a regular couple even though renumeration remaideded part of our caring.

With great excitement I told Esteban that I would be buying a house, and we could live in it together. I would help him get a job in Merida. He was silent for a few moments before he said he liked the idea. I was deeply moved and we went on to plan for him to come the following weekend to celebrate his birthday. In my elated state, I carried forward with plans to incorporate Esteban into my life. I had already spoken to him concerning the importance of commitment in relationship, how being timely was a responsibility, and how cultural differences could be worked on. I just knew he was in full agreement. Although our verbal interactions were limited, love would cover the gaps.

Esteban was due to arrive at 6pm on Friday for our special weekend. He didn't show. I waited for half an hour and then sent a note. I wrote again, and then again. I called but there was no answer. I became increasingly angry but also concerned that something had happened to him. I never heard from Esteban again. I eventually realized that he had put me on a no contact lock on his phone. I was hurt, angry, puzzled. Later, I found some gallows humor in the fact that I must have been overwhelming for a prostitute to turn down the amount of money he was collecting from me.

I got a recovery sponsor and was working with her. She tried to warn me concerning the gay life in Merida, especially related to escorts. I couldn't hear it, I had been in love. After a couple of weeks, I began to see how much I tried to control Esteban. I never asked him what he wanted. I felt embarrassed that I had gone so far for what turned out to be simple lust.

A year later, I was walking down Calle 60 and a guy pulling a small suitcase on rollers, crossed in front of me. Something felt familiar about him. I noticed that he was rather thin with bad complexion. I kept walking then stopped. It was Esteban. I turned around. We were about four hundred feet apart. He had also turned around. I gave a little wave. He waved back. I turned to walk away then decided to turn back. He was gone. As I continued on, I smiled to myself realizing I had felt some dark pleasure that his complexion was bad and he was thin and less attractive.

Once Esteban was gone, my physical desire increased. I took to the internet obsessively, night after night, hiring guys that appeared attractive on the screen. But after my Iphone was stolen by one, I had to slow down. I felt desperate with no outlet.

I found out about a club/discotheque called Blue. I was feeling lots of energy one night remembering my disco twenties and I decided to go to the club. It was in an elegant old mansion with a central dance floor bordered by large wooden booths. I was shown to a booth which opened right onto the dance floor. Soon I was joined across the table by an attractive man who started asking me questions. He also asked if I'd order him a drink, which I did. This continued and suddenly three more thirsty men joined our table.

Meantime, a variety of shows were on. Some single men danced alone then with several drag-queen performers. The drinks were flying. After several hours, I was told that for a price there were special rooms upstairs for more privacy. My energy was so high at this point I thought what the heck. I was expecting just one guy but they all joined in and with them came their drink orders.

At 2am I was having trouble focusing. There was a lot of warm skin for me and cool alcohol for them. I left at 3am, exhausted but miraculously alcohol free. The next morning as I struggled to recover, I found crumpled receipts in my pant's pocket. During the night I had authorized various credit card charges. Through blood shot eyes I was horrified to discover receipts totaling over $1,600.

With a sponsor, I was able to move forward in my recovery. I had been given the name of one psychiatrist who I saw several times, but did not feel he was diagnosing me properly. I was fortunate to then find an excellent psychiatrist skilled in medication management as well as in counseling. Over a number of weeks, I moved away from compulsion and desperation.

I focused on furnishing my new home. The process took five months to complete. The house was best described as a small colonial in the Hermita section of Centro Merida. I had it painted a colonial mustard with white trim and kept the white angel over the doorway.

The house was divided into two small buildings. The first building held the dining room, living room, washroom, and a bathroom. The back door led to the patio. The outside kitchen was off the patio, enclosed by sliding windows and fine wood cabinets.

The second building was beyond the patio, a villa in appearance, and one entered through a hefty wooden door. There was a bedroom and small study separated by a bathroom.

The study windows were my delight. They opened onto a verdant garden. Narrow, at two feet wide, the garden was filled with palm trees, large green leafy plants, a large flowering bush, and an aggressive bougainvillea. Hummingbirds, their wings sounding like small children clapping, frequented the blossoms as well as butterflies and other winged creatures. The rain and sun were most generous in supplying the garden with its needs.

After six months, I felt the need for spiritual support beyond the recovery program. I experienced emptiness in my life. I heard about an

English-speaking Catholic Mass held in a chapel which was part of the cathedral on *Plaza Grande*. The chapel was a small space with a small congregation. Several good musicians, part of the congregation, had formed a choir with a pianist. After several weeks, I was invited by fellow worshipers to breakfast following Mass. There was no regular priest. We never knew who would show up to preside. Some of the priests were good, some were passable, and some gave unprepared and unappealing homilies.

After a couple of months, I noticed that one member of the choir, Peter, would rush out before the end of Mass. I asked and was told he sang at another church as well. I spoke to him, and he said it had a fine priest and invited me to come one Sunday morning.

What I found was a small church, St. Luke's, with few congregants. The priest had a dynamic personality and a compelling message. He focused on the intrinsic dignity of each human being. He also spoke of the historic reasons and conditions which led to injustice, classism, and various forms of discrimination. The challenge for me was that St. Luke's was an Episcopal church, and I was looking for Roman Catholic. Knowing the priest had been a Roman Catholic priest for twenty-five years, made it more comfortable.

I attended both for a while but then began going only to St. Luke's. The people were friendly. A service in Spanish followed the English service. The hymns in English and Spanish were familiar to me. There was hospitality between services with coffee and cookies. It was a much longer walk but felt healthy. I recognized some members of the recovery community who attended. I became an unofficial member of St. Luke's by attending services every week.

I continued with my life of recovery and St. Luke's. Several months later I went down Calle 61 on the way home. I enjoyed passing the small gay bar and disco, Rincon Maya Rush, four blocks off Plaza Grande. I had been in the lower bar once sharing the space with two intoxicated patrons. I liked knowing there was some sort of gay presence in my world.

As I was passing the entrance a white T-shirted guy was entering. He motioned for me to join him. I hesitated but said to myself, "What the heck," and proceeded in. He introduced himself as Juanito. Behind the bar was Maria, a middle aged woman with a slightly caved in mouth. I asked for a Pepsi Light and was informed that they only had alcohol. They sent me across the street for soda. When I returned, Juanito made a point of saying he had his own apartment in a good neighborhood.

He was attractive in a rough way, teeth slightly dark, taking every opportunity to demonstrate his muscles and the large Greek tattoo on his left bicept. It didn't seem to be from any Greek alphabet that I knew. Juanito said he was thirsty and asked me to get him a drink. Maria first checked with me and then his whiskey and water appeared.

During the forty-five minute chat, Juanito's glass was refilled three times. As part of my story, I told of being in recovery. Both Juanito and Maria were supportive. They thought no alcohol meant no hard liquor but of course didn't include beer or wine. The concept of complete abstinence for three and a half years seemed to overwhelm Juanito. Maria said she thought it was a great thing to do and sat on a chair beside us.

Juanito said he worked upstairs as a dancer and gave several demonstrations. There was no question about his physical attractiveness. He made it clear that he really wanted me to see him perform. He worked four nights a week and there were twelve dancers in all. I said I loved to disco. The fact that I was retired and lived alone in my own house shocked them. Julia lived with her five children. After the first ten minutes, Juanito asked for my phone number for What's App. By the end of the time said he was ready to visit me in my home. I put a damper on that idea. I was not clear concerning his commercial endeavors. It was the longest conversation in Spanish I'd had.

I finished my Pepsi Light and paid for all the drinks. I hugged Maria and gave her a kiss on the cheek. Following a passionate hug from Juanito, I began walking home down my street, Calle 66. Halfway home I heard a beautiful hymn emanating from a church. I stopped and asked if I could listen. I was escorted up to the second floor and into the sanctuary.

A small choir was rehearsing. The minister left the piano and came over. Here I was, a foreigner with very short hair, pale skin, white pants and colored shirt appearing in his sacred space. He was cordial and invited me to sit and listen. He mentioned the 11am Sunday service.

After twenty minutes, I left with a small bow and hand on my heart as Dad used to do in Egypt.

The next Saturday, I went to an evening Spanish language Mass at the main church in Santiago *colonia* district. There was a good children's choir and the priest was young and good looking. After church I decided to take Juanito up on his offer to see him perform. This meant I had to wait at home until 11:00pm to walk over. Three hours to fill. I called Neal and kept him on the line for forty-five minutes. I napped, meditated, prepared, and left.

The well-formed bouncer, Daniel, gave a lovely smile as he welcomed me. After paying the door charge, I climbed the stairs and was welcomed by security. The sliding door allowed me into a small narrow room, filled with older men, some younger guys, and the dancers with pert chests and rounded posteriors. The noise level was unbearable. Fortunately, I brought earplugs. A bar waiter set me up at a tiny table with a small metal chair. I could barely see the stage.

I ordered a virgin *cuba libre* Coke with lime. I finally thought I saw Juanito as he half nakedly danced for a table of older men. He then quietly appeared bigger than life out of the omnipresent artifical fog. I found myself sitting with Juanito's muscled body leaning over me. A moment of quick friendliness and he was on stage. Juanito just couldn't get the rhythm right. His practiced moves didn't flow. Stripping off his negligible T-shirt, sweaty arms pointing and hairless chest heaving, he occasionally gave a sweet smile when he heard his name called. The crowd seemed unimpressed as he left the stage.

He rejoined the older group to dance and drink beer. His return to me was affectionate, followed by intimate dance moves and the consumption of a large pitcher of whisky sour. Juanito kissed my cheeks and made gestures of removing his shirt, but I gently stopped him each time. I made it clear I did not want sex, only to be friends. He said oh yes that he liked me as a friend as his second pitcher arrived. I had tried to get the waiter's attention to limit it to a glass, but my bar skills were rusty.

One dancer was phenomenal, at least part of him was. Perfect chest muscles, washboard stomach, strong thighs, great rhythm, excellent dance moves, and a face of tanned ice, frozen and perfectly chiseled. At no point during his performance did he give any facial expression as his body gyrated beneath him. He remained so when he finished. Neither looking left nor right he strode through the crowd of admiring faces.

Around 1am I needed to go home. I paid the bill of 1,000 pesos ($56). My share being 80 pesos for three cokes with lime. Juanito suddenly kissed me on the lips and was adamant that we should get together soon.

After walking two blocks heading home up Calle 66, I felt the presence of someone behind me. At first I let it go, but then I thought it safer to check. An unattractive man from the club was behind me. His Spanish was challenging as it exited inebriated lips. He said he was heading to another bar. As we walked one more block, the guy mumbled something with the word *cobra* in it. I didn't understand and waved goodbye. The next morning, I looked *cobra* up on Google, "to charge". Did he mean that he charged or that the bar charged?

Juanito wrote to me on What's App with, "*Hola, como estas?*" Hi how are you twice, followed by "Why don't you answer me?" Later came a gym shot holding his cell in front of his face. Later yet a question asking was I upset with him, accompanied by a crying face emoji. I decided after a couple of hours to write back with the truth, or most of it, in a form that might get through.

"I am not upset with you, you are very nice, good looking, with an admirable body. It's my problem, an atmosphere with alcohol is not good for me. Depending, a restaurant, bar, or disco can be a dangerous place for me. Also, it's true that I can no longer pay more for alcohol. It's an action that goes against my conscience and I know that it is not good for others. I am very sorry Juanito, but this is the situation. Thank you for understanding, God bless you my friend"

I believed I had covered all the bases for a friendly departure. I was wrong. His response shot back,

"Don't be upset. When you want, it would be fine for you to invite me out to eat in another place, let's do it. You're a very nice guy, my esteemed friend, I like you a lot, it's good when you're with me", followed by an emoji with two hearts for eyes.
My response,

"Let us see friend, I need time to think and thank you."

In return, another gym shot.

"It's fine, take care friend."

I felt I had treated Juanito not only to alcohol, but to a degree of kindness and respect. I didn't think he got much of that in his life.

CHALLENGES

I moved on with my life of friends, recovery, church, and writing. A few months later I wasn't feeling well. I had a painful sore throat, headache, cough and my voice sounded strange. I managed for several days and then decided to seek help. The friendly, abundant assistant at the internist's office was able to squeeze me in. The doctor had an excellent reputation and spoke fluent English. His office was always crowded. As per custom in Mexico, after arriving on time I waited an hour or more. I complimented the assistant on her new hair style and stood for twenty minutes until a seat opened.

When it was my turn, I went in, was greeted, and efficiently questioned. My pulse and blood pressure were taken and throat examined. "Hmmm, it looks like you have thrush", he said. I blanched. My only knowledge of thrush was from decades earlier when I was an AIDS volunteer and the friend I was working with had thrush. My doctor prescribed two oral medications and a third to be injected in the Emergency Room.

I was already taking three psychotropic medications for my bipolar disorder as well as meds for blood pressure, thyroid, etc. I duly added the new regimen onto the old. I looked up thrush and was greatly relieved to read that it was fairly common and did not require a deadly origin. I began to feel better until I didn't. I thought I just needed to stick it out. I continued with the two regimens. I was aware that something was wrong following my regular psychiatric appointment on a Thursday. I didn't remember much except that my psychiatrist would be gone until Monday. I went home and tried to make something to eat. I had trouble swallowing and just went to bed.

By Friday I was having trouble keeping my balance. A recovery friend took me to the internist. I was encouraged and told to check in on Monday. I went home and to bed. I woke in the middle of the night to go to the bathroom. I couldn't move. The edge of the bed seemed far away. My muscles didn't respond. I kept at it and finally reached the edge, but the room had changed. There were tapestries floating in the air at the bottom of the bed. I reached out to touch one and it wasn't there.

I discovered a new bureau by the side of my bed. I placed my hand on it to steady myself and crashed to the floor. It wasn't there either. I decided I had to escape to the bathroom. I got into a crouching position on the floor and attempted to rise. I fell backwards and hit my head. I kept trying, each time banging my head on the cement floor. Using all my strength, I crawled to the toilet and pulled myself up. When I finished, I re-entered my bedroom. It had become a different room.

This room had floating veils also but the patterns were different and there was no bed. I figured if I could get to a wall, I might be able to crawl around the room and find the bed. I started out. I crawled with one hand rubbing against the wall so as not to lose it. This led me to an unknown doorway. I thought, "Maybe this is where my bed went". I crawled through and after a few feet hit a dead end. I crawled back out. I tried to stand but again hit my head on the floor. Finally, I found a bed and with great effort pushed all my weight forward to reach the top of it. Laying half on and half off, I rested.

The nightmare continued for two and a half days. I found new corridors and entered cavernous spaces. I passed through several mansions while overcoming beings who wished me harm. Towards the morning of the third day there was a moment of lucidity. I found my phone and made a call. A recovery friend arrived and took me to my psychiatrist. After hearing and observing me, I was instructed to stop all medications immediately. Within less than twenty-four hours I found myself almost normal.

The addition of the three new medications on top of my psych meds had confused me. As a result, I had unknowingly doubled my lithium dose causing lithium poisoning. A new trial period started to determine an acceptable replacement for the lithium. The lithium had been my mainstay for a number of years.

I decided to try dating again. I felt I had learned something about the process and could managed it better. Through Grinder the dating app, I met a guy named Hector who was tall, slim, and with smooth skin. He had a handsome face and seemed sensitive, gentle, and liked reading. We came to my house for pizza and a movie. We kissed a little bit. We wrote to each other that Friday about how we both enjoyed the time together.

I wrote the next day and didn't hear back for four days. I was beginning to give up, but my friend Lee encouraged me to be patient. He said it sounded promising from what I'd said. Hector finally wrote saying he had problems with his cell phone but could now get email on it. He also asked about Coco, which touched me. I decided that Hector was a good person for me to draw close to. I invited him to go to the symphony with me the next Sunday.

 Hector said that he had been to the symphony once, long ago. It was an activity that I wanted to share with someone special. It was a fine experience that we both enjoyed. Afterwards we came back to my house to have something to drink. We ended up in the bedroom half naked. I was very taken with him, enjoying his black hair and smooth skin. After a while, I noticed that he made no effort to respond in kind. He just lay there. This disturbed me, I wanted some reciprocity. He needed to go and said he would write. We had no further correspondence.

As I thought about him later, I realized that I had been impatient. I didn't take cultural aspects into consideration. I hadn't allowed us to get to know each other better before precipitously moving on.

Another challenge in terms of dating was money. In the US, I would be considered middle class, but in Mexico I appeared wealthy to some. This gap could affect dating. In most cases I would have more financial resources to offer. I needed to understand how generous to be. Too much generosity and I could be used or slip into using it for control. My goal was to find a balance by sharing equally in decision-making.

I asked myself what motivated me to seek a relationship. Was it a fear of dying alone, was it wanting a guarantee that I would be cared for, was it the sweetness of someone concerned I might trip on the sidewalk?

Neal said he thought writing was my salvation. I needed to focus on what I had in my life, rather than what I didn't have. Objectively I felt fortunate. As part of appreciating my life, I decided to print out all my manuscript written to date to gain a sense of the overall picture. Also, I was hoping to garner some further direction. I wanted the satisfaction of physically holding my life story. "Look," I could say to myself, "Look at all you've done!" This reminded me of my mother, needing strong signs and symbols of progress, meanwhile it was my father who did the work.

As I approached seventy, I found myself thinking about my body. It was shifting and I needed to acknowledge the reality. In the past I thought of my body as an object to be used to attract, to seduce, to be ever youthful, to exercise and keep in fine shape. My body had been more of an objector tool than as an integral part of me. I remembered one time in my early thirties when, with a friend in New York, I rebelled against my body. I was wearing a tight striped red and blue t-shirt. I got so frustrated with my obsession of youth that I screamed and tore the t-shirt off.

As I continued to consider my aging body, I thought, "This body is going to be seventy. It is my reality." I looked closely in my closet mirror and took it in. I was not thrilled but strove for acceptance. I did feel gratitude that it had held up so well. Keeping my body attractive had been a top priority. I wanted to change and focus elsewhere. I wanted to embrace and love my body as it was. I needed my age to grow on me.

Months passed; I was feeling on top of the world. All aspects of my life seemed to be going very well including resources, house, pets, recovery, church, friends. Every day I made a gratitude list as part of my morning prayer. And yet, there was one thing missing. I didn't have a partner to share all the goodness with. Indeed, I had no prospects. But then came a simple thought, "Don't I have the right to have someone special?"

And that idea started a cycle. How could I connect with someone since there were so few venues in Merida for gay men to meet. The answer kept coming up, the Grinder app. I sent a WhatsApp to my friend Reggie saying I wanted to have a coffee with him. I hoped to gain some wisdom from his dating experience.

For three months, I, with my psychiatrist's coordination, slowly reduced and then stopped my daily Prozac. I stayed on the Wellbutrin and Olanzapine. I stopped Prozac so I could regain sexual energy and expression. This in hopes of a relationship. I ended the Prozac on November 20. It was like an early 70th birthday present six days early. The other present being a trip to Paris in April.

I met with my friend Reggie at *Café Punto del Cielo* A bit of Sky, a nice café across from *Plaza Grande*. He shared with me his skill and experience with the Grinder application. I made a promise to myself that I would start dating with a meeting for coffee, followed by a dinner date, then some type of activity. All of this taking place before any affection kicked in.

On the following Saturday, I used Grinder and made a date for 2pm Sunday. After being involved that morning in church for four and a half hours, I arrived on time but the guy didn't show. I decided I'd give him thirty minutes. I was about to head home when I wrote to another guy, Ernesto, who had sent a "Hi" to me. I asked him for a photo. It came through, cute guy. He offered to be at the café at 3:10pm. I thought "What's to lose" and agreed. He arrived with a great smile. As we began speaking, I spilled my coffee. Without hesitation he raced over to the counter and brought back some napkins and cleaned it up. I was impressed.

We talked some, then just on impulse I asked if he wanted to see my house. He hesitated for a minute, and then agreed. I told him it was close. I had planned to walk but as we hit the street I became afraid we might run out of topics. I got us a cab. At home I showed him around. Importantly he liked Coco. Then we went to the patio to meet Victoria.

I invited him to see the rest of the house. When we got to the bedroom we were like magnets drawn to each other. Immediately deep kissing and hugging. He felt wonderful. Soon on the bed, rubbing through clothes, then shirts off. He had perfect smooth skin. I was amazed at our passionate compatibility. By the end, I was very sweaty but how fine it was lying together.

Throughout the time I had left Victoria outside and she was most distressed. Crying, scratching, banging, non-stop. I think it was the first time I had ever ignored her. My heart and body parts had been involved elsewhere. Ernesto and I showered together, washing each other gently then toweling down. His loveliness and compelling smile stopped my breath at times.

Meanwhile, I was scheduled to meet my good friend Pablo at the cathedral for our usual Sunday outing to *Plaza Patio* for back massages, Chinese food, and a movie. Originally our time was for 4pm, then he moved it to 5. It was so fun walking with Ernesto. He was gently protective at street corners. We met Pablo at the restaurant *Los Trompos*. Our conversation was mostly in Spanish, and I tried to keep it going. Pablo was somewhat quiet in social situations but had excellent English. Ernesto was quiet but communicated to me with small movements as we sat side by side.

Figure 31 Victoria

How fine it was to be with someone. It had happened so fast. I had transgressed the principle of getting to know the guy first, but this seemed so right. Ernesto came from a middle-class family. His father was an engineer, and the family had two cars.

Initially, there was some delight. We sent texts back and forth, experimented sexually, and dined out. But delight turned into obsession. I felt addicted. Ernesto was constantly on my mind. At times I was fearful and other times thrilled. I realized the relationship was not healthy when I went out to dinner with two close friends. Ernesto was to join us. He was late, then very late. I spent the time texting and trying to call him, to the exclusion of my friends. It was behavior that I would normally never do. I could not stop myself. When he showed up, he needed money and said he couldn't stay. Later, I was chagrined by my behavior as my friends told me they were concerned about me.

It took me six weeks to finally put the whole picture together. The picture included Ernesto's heavy drinking and lack of responsibility in honoring commitments.

I had spent more than $500 on him and realized I had no emotional attachment left. It had been a whirlwind that blew out. I told him I needed a break. He was resistant but finally agreed.

My hypersexual energy continued. I moved into one-night stands thru Grinder. I was caught up in the abundance of available men. One of them came under the auspices of wanting to learning English. After one was gone, I would immediately be texting to make a date for the next. It was a madness that had to stop.

I needed to relax. There was an advertisement on Grinder for a massage therapist, non-sexual. I thought this was what I needed. What was the worst thing that could happen? A lousy massage? I planned for him to come over. At 7pm he arrived at my door. We talked a little and he told me that a warm cup of herbal tea would help relax me. I found chamomile and apple. He said the chamomile would do the trick.

I heated the water and brought him to my bedroom. He had a little bag with him which I assumed held massage lotions. I removed my exterior clothing and retained my briefs. He started to rub my back. After a few minutes he reminded me to have more tea. I did so and relaxed more.

Next thing I knew I was waking up and it was morning. I was dizzy and disoriented. I had no idea what was wrong with me. I stumbled to the bathroom and became more conscious. And then I remembered, I had been getting a massage, and… What had happened? I sat on my bed to collect myself. I went to put my watch on, and it wasn't in its usual place on the nightstand. That was strange. Then I thought maybe I had put it with my other watches in the nightstand drawer. I opened the drawer, and my watch collection was gone. I had been robbed.

I looked at my bedroom wardrobe and noticed one of the doors was slightly ajar. I went over and opened the door. The small drawer was pulled out. My passport was gone. I was now trembling with outrage. I went into the study at first thinking there was nothing to take there. I opened the desk flap and remembered the rings I had collected for fifty years. Slowly I opened the drawer, all gone. This included my father's high school graduation ring.

Breathing heavily, I went into the other part of my home. Things appeared normal until I turned around and the television connected to the wall was gone, leaving the naked arm support. It was all too much, too much to take in. I sat on the couch trying to think. I went to the bedroom to get my cell phone. It was gone. I went back to the front of the house to get my back up cell. It was gone too. I used the landline to call my friend Lee. I was still unclear in my thinking. Lee grabbed Reggie and they came over to support me.

The masseur had all night to go meticulously through both parts of my house and storage. Months later I was still discovering losses: family silver, $700.00, glasses. I ended up calling the experience, "The tale of the massage larcenist."

I was grateful. I could have been raped and murdered. This experience dramatically ended any further sexual compulsion. In working with my recovery sponsor, I made a commitment to not engage in any intimate activity for a year.

Two weeks later I became depressed. I had been feeling low and then on a Sunday slept for sixteen hours, only going to the bathroom twice and letting Victoria out. The next day, Monday, I slept for twelve hours. I did not know what was going on. The following day I had an epiphany. It crossed my mind that I had been reading lots of stories concerning the Trump policy of separating migrant children from their parents at the U.S./Mexican border. I realized that unknowingly, this reality had taken me back to my experience as a 7-year-old when my mother abandoned me in boarding school.

When I shared this with my recovery sponsor, John, he at once agreed with my thinking saying it made perfect sense. He said it offered me the opportunity to work on my emotional sobriety. But first, I needed to focus on myself in a loving compassionate way. He suggested I write a letter to myself as my father and share my experience with him. Then, I could write back to myself as my father having read the letter. I took three days to go through the process. At the end of the three days, I was coming back into balance.

I did not want to go to church for the Mexican Independence Day fiesta. It was called *Grito de Delores*, Cry of Sorrows. But I felt I should at least make a symbolic appearance and support the Spanish speaking church community. I waited for the rain to stop. It had been raining in the evenings for three days. The night before, I took an Uber home from a small dinner party. The trip felt as if we were riding a gondola through the canals of Venice. The driver had never seen such waves.

Around 8:30pm, I got ready. I decided I would wear a bright red *gayabera* dress shirt. I added a large, loud, multicolored Mexican *sombrero*. I had bought it for fun at our church bazaar. Attempting to leave my house, I kept forgetting things and was throughly frustrated by the time I got in the Uber.

Boldly I entered the courtyard of the church, *sombrero* carefully angled. As my gaze swept the groups at the tables, I saw that not one man was wearing any sort of festive costume. I was alone in my folly. There were only two other *extranjeros* foreigners present who left right after I arrived. I felt foolish and out of place. I was like the fool at a banquet. I became angry with myself for coming.

So, I was angry, hungry, embarrassed, and feeling alone. Even after five and a half years in recovery, I had missed the clues. This set of feelings was the perfect combination for desperately wanting a drink. And there it was, a half jug of red wine, my drink of choice, five feet from me on the food service table. My eyes latched onto it. I looked around again to see if I could join a table. I just didn't feel confident enough with my Spanish. The music played, the voices rose and fell and I fled in my conspicuous hat. It kept the rain from my head but not from my heart. I remembered a line from the French writer Verlaine, *"Il pleure dans mon coeur, comme il pleut sur la ville.* It weeps in my heart, like it rains on the town." A vision of my drinking days in France rose up.

As I waited in the rain for an Uber, I realized the situation had created the perfect storm. The thought of a drink came again as I entered my home. But no physical impulse stirred to bring thought into action. Instead, I went to see if Oso, the resident black and white neighborhood cat, was safe from the rain. He yelled at me loudly and I took him some food and petted him. For a moment I felt more connected to Oso than I did with those at the party. I went back home and gave my own ailing Coco a lot of attention.

I had experienced the erosive sensation of standing out, not fitting in, and having no support. Chances were excellent that everyone in the group had come to the fiesta with someone else. How much easier to show up as a couple, a family, or with friends. I had felt slapped in the face with the sensation that I was alone and didn't belong.

I found it ironic that the night before, at a small dinner party, I felt so appreciated and included. Anita, elder sister of the hostess, had sent me an e-mail in the morning saying how much she'd enjoyed me and that I was very interesting. It was the two of us who had taken the Uber gondola as I translated the driver's political opinions for her.

I thought about my emotional compulsion to fit into any cultural or linguistic setting. It had driven my behavior throughout my life starting in my childhood. An urgent desire to fit in had been running from Egypt, to New York, to Illinois, to Japan, to France, to Central America, to being gay, to being Catholic, to Mexico. I had never accepted that it is the natural order of things that people form groupings with their own and that often I was not one of them. The drive to overcome the separateness haunted me. I was not willing to embrace the fullness of just being me. Learning more to accept who I was would have been a great gift to come out of the fiesta experience.

MY SEVENTIETH YEAR

On the cusp of my seventieth birthday, with lots of energy and thought, I was happy planning my party with Miguel's help. It was only the second social gathering in my home.

Bringing together the different parts of my Merida life was my goal. Expected were a mixed crowd consisting of Mexicans, *extranjeros* foreigners, gay, straight, religious, non-religious, low income and high income. I remembered the party I gave in my condominium on 16th Street, NW in Washington. How exciting the combination of people was.

I asked the caterers to plan on fifty. I invited a little over forty but wished to be prepared for *parejas* partners, and other guests. Miguel helped rearrange some of the furniture by moving the patio alabaster table and chairs into my bedroom, the bed to the corner, the end-tables back-to-back, and using the bottom of the bed as a couch. I opened the bedroom door so there could be flow throughout the house. I bought nine more pillows for the two couches and the bed. I thought they looked great, black, red, and patterned. I had a strong sense that there would be lots of food left over for doggie bags. The caterers, the Capi family, Antonio, Guisel, and son Miguel, were lovely.

My birthday celebration was a hit and much appreciated. It ended up with thirty-seven guests and five staff. At first the crowd started small in the living room and just expanded with more guests. I encouraged new ones to move out into the patio. As the patio got crowded, the guests were escorted into the guest room/study, and then into my bedroom. The highlight was the disco dancing in the living room with strobe lights. Lee said he thought it was the best party he had ever been to. The time flew for me.

The next day I was sitting on a park bench between my friends Lee and Bill. Both of whom were older than I and had boyfriends in their late 20s. Both of their guys were attractive. I knew there were issues related to money, health, and family. I also knew that there was caring and affection.

I was working to accept that I might not have a partner to share my life with. Lee pointed out that I had Miguel and Pablo as good friends. That was true. They were important to me.

I thought a key might be the difference between boyfriend and partner. In my thinking, the idea of partner came with expectations of forever and must live together. If I could allow myself to embrace the concept of boyfriend, then I thought the relationship might be committed but less demanding. I also might be better able to handle emotional attachment if I were working daily with a value-focused schedule incorporating prayer, my language study, recovery, and writing.

I asked myself what I would do with the attainment of seventy years. I prayed for clarity, desire, and the will to move forward as God intended for me. I had the desire to write yet so much resistance also.

I pondered the purpose of my writing. Was it to encourage insight on the part of a reader that could then be transmuted into generosity of spirit. Was it to share my experience of the presence and encouragement of God's spirit within us. I wanted to inform, entertain, challenge, instill hope. Was it possible that I might do so? Did I have the will, courage, and stamina to continue to reveal my life?

The past so easily sprang up within me. One afternoon as I was walking Victoria to *Hermita Parque* Hermita Park, there was a group of teenage students about a quarter block in front of me but on the other side of the street. They were walking away and laughing. My instant response was fear and to prepare to defend myself. Here it was, fifty-five years later, accompanied by my strong Victoria, and yet fear from my early years struck. I was taken back to the darkness of boarding school and the persecution I suffered.

I was reading, in translation, the *Autobiography of Andre Gide*, written in 1924. It took place mostly in Paris. This reading represented a step in the direction of increasing my cultural and literary awareness of France. I was focusing on writers of gay material, such as Andre Gide, Marcel Proust, Rambeoux, Baudelaire, Verlaine. I read them when I was a young man before entering the gay world. I remember being fascinated. Compared to current literature, they had a most genteel way of handling, "The love which dare not say its name."

I found with Gide, humor and vast descriptions of places and situations. This was the style of the times. But I moved through the detailed descriptions with alacrity. Gide showed great self-awareness as a young man. He was a prodigy in music, literature, languages, religion, and in describing his young, pure loves. Like me, he had early sexual experimentation which was discovered. His family looked for a cure. At one point while sobbing and sobbing, he cried out, "I am not like others, I do not belong!"

I realized it was a year since I might have died. In other words, being drugged by the massage larcenist. Making a vow to not engage in an intimate involvement for a year, gave me time to process. That year was ending. I believed and hoped I had come to a new place. I wished to never again plunge into the loss of power and control.

I wished to have a dedicated writing practice. I wondered if I were too comfortable and lacking in the compulsion of a starving artist. Then asked, may I not have a good life yet be creative?

In July I had written every day for thirty days. It was not an explicit commitment, but rather a daily drive. I wished for that same call to be upon me again. I wanted to be as faithful to my writing as I was to my morning prayer time, feeding Victoria and Coco, and taking my medications. Discipline was a habit in these other areas and could be applied to writing. I realized that with each of these activities I had a clear understanding of what was involved and of the outcome. With writing the outcome was unknown.

I started to write. I ran to make coffee – *un cafecito* a small coffee. I felt I couldn't write without it. What fun, I really loved the stuff. I was thinking it's the coffee that makes the writer. What did that say about me who only chose Nestles' Clasico instant coffee.

I re-read some material and knew that I must be willing to accept rejection. I believed the most important quality of writing was honesty, a willingness to reveal one's authentic self. I was striving to live this in my life, and it needed to be true in my writing as well. I was sure that other writers struggled with this issue as well.

I wanted to write my life story because I believed it was possible to gain some peace, some wholeness, from living through a difficult childhood, an addicted adulthood, and a sober retirement. That in later years, we could come to understand, accept, and appreciate ourselves. That we could choose to evolve. And I believed that God offered us help every step of the way, whether we knew it and acknowledged it or not.

I retrieved my Baroque covered notebook written in Paris. It held the pen from Les Deux Magots café in Paris. Hemingway frequented Les Deux Magots, as well as Gertrude Stein, Alice B. Toklas, and F. Scott Fitzgerald. What fun. I also had a small cup and saucer from the Café de Flore. It was also very popular with the artist poet writer elite of the time.

I finished reading a novel by John Grisham, *The Rooster Bar*. What a lousy representation of his work. The plot, hard to determine, was weak. I kept waiting for something significant to happen. It was like crumbs falling from a small cake. It was most unsatisfactory in comparison to his usual meaningful work. I hoped he used a ghost writer.

The on-going involvement in my church was essential to my life. I continued my hospitality duty and making reading assignments. I also prepared a homily and preached. It took me three weeks to prepare, do the biblical research, use personal material, and develop a structure. I practiced a lot. From the video, the delivery seemed natural and fluid. I got positive feedback from the congregation. The video recording was hard to hear. My siblings in the States expressed pride even though they really could not hear the video. I did notice that they showed absolutely no interest in the content.

I found myself noticing, allowing myself to notice, guys more readily but felt no draw. One early morning returning home with Victoria, I passed a narrow doorway with a guy leaning, backlit, beautiful, and sensuous. I considered him an angel with a blessing reminding me in the moment that I could simply appreciate.

A wonderful aspect to the second part of the year was the number of fine women who moved to Merida and joined their long-term recovery to our meetings.

The last two times I saw my psychiatrist, he asked me how I was feeling sexually. I realized I had thought little about it. To be available for intimacy, it was necessary to come off the Cymbalta and Prozac. Because of the depression, I had needed to add these to my regular regimen. It took several months to get off them.

My friendship with Miguel continued. He proved a dedicated friend even though he now had a girlfriend, Angela. He moved from his parents' home to his own apartment. My other good Mexican friend, Pablo, and I continued to see each other once every three weeks. At times I struggled to find our commonality, but we did enjoy each other's company as we went to the plaza for back massages, dinner and possibly a movie.

EARLY PANDEMIC

During the early days of the Covid pandemic, it was hard to write, to be motivated. All my thoughts not focused on Covid were quickly brought around to the virus. The worldwide pandemic was the grey envelope covering all else. The virus interrupted any cogent thought patterns, logical planning, or lifesaving solutions. It was the grand inquisitor that all had to pass by. I recalled the first stages of the AIDS pandemic in 1982.

At the beginning there was simply a short article in the Washington Post picked up from The New York Times of May 11, 1982. It mentioned a new disease that was disproportionally affecting gay men in New York City. There were no known similar cases in Washington. But it spread, and spread, and spread. The cause was undetermined, with no known cure. Gradually rumors circulated of the illness of various friends and acquaintances.

I had my hair cut in the salon of a flamboyant gay couple. They were a hoot as we would say. The next time I went, only one of them was there. His partner was not feeling well. Next cut the partner was in the hospital. Next cut he was dead. And the shop closed. The remaining partner wasn't feeling well.

We lived in fear for two years not knowing how GRID (Gay Related Immune Deficiency) was contracted. Fear, fear, fear was everywhere. We did not know at the beginning that we could give a death sentence to a guy if we slept with him. How cruel to, in an act of love, give death. We did not know.

In the new pandemic, it seemed that we could give death by our mere presence. The recent word was that the virus might be airborne, not just spread by droplets and surfaces.

I was trying to decide when I needed to isolate myself completely. I would only leave the house to walk Victoria. Lee was determined to still go to Plaza Grande for coffee in the mornings. I feared the possible nearness of others in the park.

I contacted Gonzalo, my contractor, for the installation of a potable water filtration system in the kitchen. That way I would not be dependent on water delivery. I felt I could then isolate. The good news was that our Tuesday and Thursday recovery meetings might be available on the Zoom app. The St. Luke's services could also be on Zoom if Padre José figured it out. How painful for this extraordinary man to see his creation shut down. I hoped it was only temporary. There was also the difficult dilemma of whether to go to the church's mission in the south of Merida. The visits offered sustenance and spiritual support, but in so doing might bring the virus.

I had trouble concentrating and doing anything I considered

productive. I hadn't done any writing in a few weeks. I finished reading a book, took an hour's nap, and sat down to write. I noticed my emails. That was the end of the writing.

"We are the World; We are the Children" video was forwarded to me. I sent it on to fifteen others. It was good and heartwarming to share it. I cooked for myself for the first time in years. I fried two eggs. They were fine. With concern, I saw only two loaves of bread left in the freezer. I wondered how I could manage grocery shopping.

I arranged to give a month's wages to the woman who cleaned my house. I feared for her and her children and prayed for them and all the others at risk. I walked in the street to my friend Lee's and hung out. He was six feet away across a table with two fans running. His renters, Johnny and Joe, were upstairs on the balcony.

My friend Sister Elizabeth from Philadelphia wrote concerning her nursing work with infected patients. She was in a horrendous situation. Even her emergency care doctor was on a ventilator. She was such a fine person, and we really connected during the Spiritual Exercises retreat. I sent her a supportive note. Miguel was going to visit me. I wanted to sit on the patio to be safe. He hated the heat and would sweat. I hoped he would understand the need.

Communicating with my psychiatrist, I informed him I was making contact through Zoom with my recovery community. In terms of St. Luke's, I said we were using a chat line on What's App. Letting him know Miguel was in touch with me, I also mentioned I had a supply of medications for three months. I said I rarely went out and suggested he and I use face time on our phones. I told him it seemed ironic that just at the point of dating, I had no thoughts of making new social contacts.

I had a phone conversation with Miguel. He thought his mother may have been exposed when she visited the hospital to see his sister and her new baby. We decided to wait for a week to see if he would visit me.

Neal sent me a link to know the exact moment-to-moment status of the virus throughout the world. He and I were far apart on this. I was only interested in what was happening locally. For me, the less negative information the better, lest more fear kick in.

I had a call from Joo in Korea. His ongoing friendship was a great gift. I worried that his boyfriend was not careful at all. He said of himself that he loved the current situation, the isolation, that he was a perfect homebody. Joo said he had honed that skill in his three years of prison. I thought it would be hard when he returned to an office environment.

I sent a poem to Neal. His response to the poem was, "Has some good elements in it…. Edit like crazy." My challenge was that my poems came naturally and quickly. Also, my poems communicated what I wanted them to. For me to take the hatchet to them seemed like gutting their naturalness and inspiration.

Neal also said he remembered some good poems I had written in the past. However, he did not like my recent poems. He said that when he returned to Florida, he would look up the old poems he had in his journal. I remembered a period when I was suffering in love over Don in Washington. I would wake up in the middle of the night with poetry pouring through my mind. I was hyper-manic during that period. I found it curious that Neal remembered liking them even though some had a religious aspect.

I sent my poem "Lord of Life" to my friend Jane in California. She wrote back that I was a mystic. She named some of the great mystics of the church. I wrote back that being a mystic did not resound with me, but I did feel that my poetry came thru me.

LORD OF LIFE

Lord of Life, we reach out to you this night
Our vision dims, we lose our sight
Take us Lord, refresh us by thy might
That we may rejoice once again,
And be present to your light.

Words and darkness bring us fear
We forget to trust, forget to peer
Into that Word who for us was born
To bring us to you, that we may be shorn
Of our darkest secrets and thus reborn.

My shopping was now done by a service. I would leave the groceries they brought in the foyer for three days which was the length of time the virus lasted on plastic. On cardboard it lasted twenty-four hours.

For months it was only Padre José, Wendy, Patricia, and me in person at St. Luke's. To be safe, I did not receive communion. One of the things I was doing was working on my poetry. I wrote three poems over a few day's time. I also decided to read another classic, *Kidnapped*.

I received an email from Sister Elizabeth with a photo of the masterpiece of Jesus raising Lazarus that we had seen in the art museum near Wernersville while on retreat. How amazing that she remembered and then found the photo in her camera. I wrote back that being in my senior years, I didn't know which was more impressive, that she remembered to find it, or that she could find it.

I practiced on grandpa's harmonica for my concert on Lee's patio. It would be the last time I would see Johnny and Joe. They were leaving the rental space upstairs at Lee's. We had a fun time together. I enjoyed Johnny and knew Joe less well. Johnny was sophisticated in a gentle way with a corny sense of humor. We sat in our assigned seats more than six feet apart with the two fans running. Drinking coffee, we joked and laughed. I played hymns. The highlight was, "Mine Eyes have seen the Glory." "Red River Valley" was their sendoff.

I assumed I was safe by keeping distant from others during my walks. There were so few pedestrians and vehicles on the streets. The walking helped me feel that life was normal. My average step count was low. In the past, leaving Lee's I would swerve off Calle 66 and go to Bisquets Obrigon café or to Las Vigas restaurant. How I missed them.

I wrote to my dear long-term friend Jane. She was taken with a poem I sent her, "Hijacked." She put it on her bed stand.

HIJACKED

Is it happening again just when
All was well how was I to tell
I would have to mend, one more time.

Lurking in the dark, getting ready to bark
My fear rose up, Must I take this cup

My gear box dropped,
My emotions popped
Thrown over the wheel
Such a rotten deal

Waiting for shadows to flush
Five weeks seems too much
I could burn out by then,
But if not, When

Too much time on my bed
Tears can't be shed
Like a barren garden
I beg for pardon

To make it plain, I am desperate to gain
A foothold on the normal

It was hard to keep track of the days. And now Coco was ill again. She threw up in the living room. How sad I was. Checking her bowl, she still had a lot of food. I gave her some petting. I had to trust God to see me through. She was so precious and had been a part of my life for fifteen years. I celebrated my sixth recovery anniversary and Victoria's third Birthday. I thanked God that Victoria was so young. I knew that sometime soon, we would lose Coco. I found her a great example of a survivor with spirit. She was a joy and an amazement every day.

EASTER

I took a photo of part of my house with the bougainvillea and the moon above it. I decided to use it as an Easter card. I sent out thirty to recovery friends, church friends, family. The first service at St. Luke's was long yet there were twenty-five on Zoom. I assisted in all three services. My experience of a spiritual buildup to Passion Week and Easter was followed by a letdown.

Walking to Lee's was good. I stayed clear of the few other pedestrians. I walked mostly in the street. Lee gave me a cup of coffee and we waited for Padre José. He came a few minutes late wearing shorts and sandals. At first it was sharing, but at some point, he repeated the essence of his Easter sermon. He also spoke in detail about the Jesuits and Ignatian spirituality. I shared about my former partner Joe as an influence in my becoming Catholic. José said that I was now Episcopal. I responded, "I am with you, but my formation is so deeply Roman Catholic and Ignatian that I am probably both."

My nephew Bren sent a couple of pictures on messaging of two of his daughters playing drums and guitar. I wrote back that it looked like his house might sound like my neighborhood. Across the street there was an extended family with two boys, young and unskilled. One was practicing the drums, and the other straining out notes on the trumpet. They did this on their aunt's patio, it was like having an involuntary outdoor concert next door. They only played occasionally, and I became accustomed to it. I was grateful for the signs of life.

The corona virus continued to dampen my desire to be creative. My energy and attention went to basic survival. This applied to money, food, batteries, lights. I had my list of groceries which I added to often, just to make sure. But then again, nothing was sure.

Because I had been keeping distant from others, I wasn't wearing a mask while walking one morning. All was well until I hit a pocket of people. I was slow in the uptake and passed a guy in a red shirt and cheap mask. He was four feet from me. I turned my head away from him but got a whiff of his cologne. I thought, "if his cologne can get to me, and if he is contagious, the virus can get to me as well." When I got home, I went rapidly to the bathroom and washed for twenty seconds.

I prayed and cried about my precious Coco. She stopped coming out to yell for her food in the morning. She would only show up once Victoria's walk was over. She ate but was so thin. It was not easy finding the balance of her having enjoyment but not pain. She was such a precious little girl.

Working with my fine local vet, for months I tried to find a healing path for her. She had both gastritis and a liver duct problem. I attempted various foods to entice her to eat. What she loved most, chicken, was harmful. We tried good high protein food which sustained her for two weeks, but then her eating decreased noticeably. I started adding Purina kitten chow which she loved, but was also bad for her condition.

I again wanted to cry when she walked away from me. Her hip bones were razor thin and her hind legs indented from lack of muscle. In the living room, she attempted to jump up onto her favorite table. She didn't make it and fell backwards. When I told my brother Neal about her fall, I almost broke down, my voice catching in my throat. Neal was most sympathetic and supportive.

Coco scared me so. I yearned for her to improve. Her attitude was still positive. One morning she sat in the sun at the screen door. Her attention was riveted on something I couldn't see. Her little head jerked this way and that, following the invisible to me movement of a tiny creature. It lifted my spirit and all was well.

Then I couldn't find her, and she didn't respond to my call. I found her lying in the bathroom behind the shower curtain, still, still, very still. I thought she had stopped breathing. Then I saw some small abdominal movement.

Usually when I called her to give her affection, she would run away at first and I would chase her down. The time came when she walked slowly away from me. I could pick her up without a chase. She was light as a feather. I sat on the couch, holding her like a baby, her little paws wrapped around my arm. Holding her close to my chest, I gently stroked her naked belly, softly speaking her name the whole time. She lay still, purring and staying with me for as long as I was willing.

I did so want Coco to come back to her vital self, dashing across the living room when she had a good kitty box visit. Leaping up on the couch to do the absolute no no of sharpening her claws. If only she ate a lot, and vomited a little, I would have been thrilled.

I wept, feeling the pending loss of my precious little one who had been my companion for fifteen years. She was part of the life that Joo and I shared; she carried the name that he gave her. It would be hard for him when the time came. Miguel was very fond of her also and cared for her daily during my recent travels. A week ago, I was looking forward to more years of shared life with her. That hope dissipated, and I strove to prepare myself. I visited the vet and picked up more of her anti-gastritis pills to crush and put in the nutrient gel I placed on her paws to be licked off.

I had a lot of 'what ifs' in terms of my care for Coco. I bore the guilt of having decreased the amount of my affection when Victoria came into our lives. It was Miguel who pointed this truth out to me. Realizing this helped me refocus on Coco. Losing her would be the third time of letting go of one so special to me. I wanted to focus on gratitude for our shared life. In terms of my Mexican life, I am not sure I would have withstood the vast loneliness of my first months in Merida without Coco and the need to care for her. I prayed for the courage to offer her up when it was time.

Coco was suffering, and so the time had come. We made our last visit to the vet. He injected her and placed her on the floor. She was dying as she tried to come to me. It was like a knife stabbing my heart. I placed her in my lap. When she stopped moving, I let out a cry and keened and keened for her. The vet was truly kind and understanding. I walked home alone.

I went to the vet to pick up Coco's ashes. He gave me an attractive dark metal box with the ashes of Coco and a certificate. What a fine man. We had to be physically close while working with Victoria. I washed my arms and hands extensively upon returning home. I left the box with ashes in the foyer for three days. I had some fine communications with Jane about CoCo's passing. What a dear friend, we shared similar sensibilities about creatures and spirituality.

I listened to the last hour of a tape by Fr. Richard Rohr speaking on contemplative prayer, speaking of the false self and the real self. So clear, deep, and meaningful. I felt to do centering prayer was crucial to deepening my true self in God. I was terrible at it. I nodded out significantly about every three minutes. However, I knew that what was important was to dedicate myself to it and allow God to be in charge.

I missed Coco so much. I kept looking for her at the screen door. I missed her looking at me and crying for my attention or for her food, depending on the time. We were in such a pattern. I didn't write for several weeks. It seemed the details of my life were not as important.

Using What's App, I started sending out a short daily greeting in Spanish to several recovery and church friends. The first one said, *"Buenos Dias, necesitamos solomente tres cosas, Fe, Café, y Amor"* Good Morning, we only need three things: Faith, Coffee, and Love, with a picture of a cup of coffee.

A friend, Arturo, responded to *Buenos Dias* by asking if anyone was staying in my spare bedroom. I knew he was in a bad living situation. It took me a few minutes of fantasy before responding. I had two responses. One was concern and sympathy about his unhealthy living situation. The other response was sexual. Fortunately, I knew that he would be a recipe for disaster, a warning of the power and seductiveness of my sexual energy. I responded that I only had my bedroom and the study where I spent most of my time.

I continued listening to "The Universal Christ" CD by Fr. Rohr and found it profound in expressing the essence of Christian theology grounded in Scripture and the Franciscan way. One aspect that gave me comfort was Rohr's universal approach to all of creation. He himself experienced Christ in his fifteen-year-old black lab. It touched my heart as I applied it to Coco. My ongoing connection with her was grounded in the biblical promise of a new heaven and a new earth. It also drew me closer to Victoria in her sweetness and appreciation of affection. I enjoyed lying on the couch in the study with Victoria sprawled over my leg asleep as I listened to the CD.

I worked on my centering prayer meditation. I remembered other practices of meditation in my earlier life including Zen, mindfulness, and chanting a mantra. With centering prayer, I tried Fr. Thomas Keating's image of sitting on the bank of a river and, as a thought came, putting it in a little boat and sending it down the river. Also, I used the word 'light' as my sacred word to return to when a thought came up. I noticed I did not nod out as much.

My practice of not watching any TV or movies and focusing on reading continued. I finished *Great Sea Battles* of the mid/late 16th century. The slaughter did not appeal to me, but the sea action did. I remembered reading years before Patrick O'Brien's *Master and Commander*, and the twenty other novels in that series. They were full of personal relationships, ocean voyages, challenges, intrigues. I decided to go into my e-book library and looked up *Master and Commander*. I was hoping I had forgotten enough of the twenty-one novels to reread them.

I stayed away from the living room for two weeks; it was where Coco spent her last days. I then decided to have dinner there with Victoria beside me. It was sad. I kept seeing the absence of Coco and mourned loudly with some keening. Victoria was confused but joined in briefly. In my sharing with friends about the loss of Coco, I received many remarks and notes of understanding and support. I did want this suffering to serve a purpose, to deepen my sensitivity to the suffering of others.

Walking a very enthusiastic Victoria was a consolation from the loss of Coco. I prepared by putting on my red cap, getting the poop bag ready, then always having to go back to the refrigerator to get the cat food. As part of our walk, I fed a black and white street cat. I called him "Oso" which meant bear in Spanish. He survived a car accident and was hale and hardy.

It was then Victoria's turn to prepare. This involved her eventually sitting after jumping all over me when I picked up the leash and yelled "Sit" numerous times. As I strove to attach the leash clip, Victoria moved vigorously. Once connected, I opened the iron door followed by the iron gate but had to keep her inside as I crossed the street and fed Oso. Victoria cried like a baby at this impediment to her walk.

Being directionally challenged, I favored the same route to Hermita park which fronted La Hermita church. I read that it was good for the brain to vary patterns, so I tried crossing the street in a different place each time. Did not last. Also, I normally wore my watch on my left wrist and changed it to the right one. It kept returning to my left wrist.

Straining the leash, Victoria was always anxious to get to the park. The park was small but with enough grassy spots and trees to keep Victoria's interest. Our goal was to pee in the park and poop on the street where it was easier to pick up. Peeing would seem the easier task. Not true. To urinate, Victoria required a runway. She would go straight for a number of feet, then make circles, and finally crouch down for her business. If any new smell drew her attention, the takeoff was postponed.

One day while early in the park, an orange and white cat came streaking towards Victoria and then veered away. We were both surprised. Victoria took chase and I had no choice. The cat took a couple passes and then disappeared into some shrubbery which hid a large disposal unit. This was not standard cat behavior. The next day, this display was repeated and became a regular pattern. The orange and white warrior had no fear of Victoria and would come right up below her nose then streak away. I was already feeding Oso so I decided to bring a baggie with cat food for this one too. After several months, a second orange and white cat appeared. But it was as sedate as the first was bold.

There was a city gardener responsible for the upkeep of the park who I always greeted. One morning he was watching me with the two orange and white cats and told me they were brothers with the first one named Hugo and the second Paco. I thought they were females because there was no other sign. It was now a little tricky. I was used to calling them girls and Victoria and Coco were girls. It was tough to adjust. Oso was not so hard in that he was prominently indicated.

I also learned that they lived in the private walled park attached to the church. Its large wooden gates at the bottom were about three inches above the ground. Hugo and Paco squeezed back and forth. During fiestas, they sometimes disappeared for days. I would miss them and was delighted when Hugo again streaked by and sharpened his claws on a tree root as Victoria smelled his tail.

Some men slept in the gazebo of the park or on the benches. Several of them made their living collecting used plastic bottles. The park often had trash on the ground or in receptacles. The gentlemen would find items of worth in them. One morning I noticed a fellow sitting on a bench surrounded by four large bags filled with plastic bottles. I greeted and gave him something. He said his name was Miguel, thanked me, and was there the next day. Miguel was from a small town outside Merida. He was friendly and gregarious. He liked Victoria and we enjoyed the play between the animals.

PANDEMIC CONTINUES

For months I had little desire to write. Instead, I found Covid was encouraging me to connect with friends who had been important earlier in my life. I tried to call Johanna in New York. She had been a dear friend in the late 70's. Johanna answered the phone and was thrilled to hear my voice. She shared about her daughter. She said her daughter may lose her house. Johanna was living there as well as her granddaughter and two babies.

Johanna then went full force into the state of the union, presenting conspiracy theories as realities. She spoke of Bill Gates, 5-G, and another conspiracy about the Covid virus. I was shocked, it was as if she had slapped my face. I cut her off after a bit, saying I wanted to hear about her sons. She switched gears. A year earlier Freddie was in a bar fight. He broke some ribs and then stopped drinking. He was currently playing the organ for Mass in a local Catholic chapel. John was being wonderfully generous to desperate friends. Johanna and her partner had joined the Catholic Church. They were doing the rosary, the scapula, and being very faithful.

I said I needed to go. I could not stand for her to return to the conspiracies. Once she was into a movement, she was relentless. We left it that she would contact me. She never did. Talking to her was painful. She was the one person I felt had loved me unconditionally since I was twenty-nine. I always got so much support from her. I found it ironic that we met in a group that many would have called a cult. Later we did Ken Keyes *Handbook to Higher Consciousness* which could be called a sect. And now she was back in a context that felt cultish to me.

I was delighted to see a plastic collector in the park whom I hadn't seen in a long time. He was the one whose dog got hit by a car. He hadn't gotten another dog. He remembered Victoria's name. I was so concerned with safety that I neglected to talk with him very much.

I started wearing one of the N-95 medical masks from China. Earlier I went around a corner and almost banged into a guy walking his dog. I felt vulnerable from the incident. I thought the N-95 would be better than the two other types I had. It was harder to breathe in, so it must have had a better seal.

I spoke to Joo in Korea. He encouraged me to write. I did have a sense of a vast umbrella, not of rainbow colors, but dull and grey with no promise of life-giving rain, no breaking through of the sun, no canopy of stars, just hanging, close overhead, drooping in places and unchanging. Life was again like being at sea as Patrick O'Brien described, a constant loss of time and place.

My sponsor sent me a recovery document, "How to stay spiritually fit in a pandemic." It was helpful to have a checklist of what needed to be accomplished in a day. It set a direction and actions to be taken at different times. It gave a comfortable routine with plenty of time for reading.

I picked up the Patrick O'Brian naval series. After eight years, I found them new and fresh. They were intelligent, relational, suspenseful, imaginative, and complex.

I did not want to put effort into anything. I felt like a C minus student, just hanging on, with no desire, no effort to excel, to achieve. In the virus's continuing shadow, all else seemed insignificant. I was living in a shadowland, bereft of passion, intelligence, and creativity. The virus was a great vampire sucking life out of people, society, the world, out of me.

A painful consequence of the virus was I had to drop the dream of traveling to Europe. I needed to change travel arrangements and postpone the Cambridge University's three-week writing seminar for a year. I wrote to the Z Hotel Soho in London and postponed. I rescheduled Cambridge. I was doing this in the living hope that it would be possible the next year. I wrote to the Familia Hotel in Paris. I negotiated with Aeromexico to transfer flights to the next year.

The heavy rain caused Victoria's water bowl and food bowl to overflow. The bougainvillea was weighed down with water and one of the large branches was beaten down and partially broken. I couldn't get my iPad to go on-line. I wrote to Mary, my sponsor, and she was kind enough to come over. What a treat. She was able to get me back online. I had my usual tiredness but not as bad. Took an early nap and then read and enjoyed it. The windows open, it was cooler and looked like more rain.

I was striving to fast using the principles of The Fast Diet by Dr. Michael Mosley. For seven years I had followed this diet, and it kept me healthy and slim. Twice a week my diet was fiber cereal at 1pm, then half of a high protein/high fiber bar at 3:30pm. This was followed by dinner consisted of two hardboiled eggs, 2 pieces of toast with butter, and V-8 juice. I would practice this twice a week.

In a family communication, Neal shared that he was not sleeping well. My nephew Brendan wondered if it might be free floating anxiety related to the pandemic. I thought it was a good term. I pondered if it contributed to my feeling tired several times a day and needing to nap.

It was a regular day except Victoria was sitting right beside me and just staring at me. Then she got excited and started jumping on me. I went out to throw the plastic ice cream cone for her. Down the walkway it went. She watched, and I went to retrieve the cone. She looked interested, so I tossed it again… and I fetched it again. There was something wrong with this picture.

Miguel called to check in, wanting to make sure all was well. It was always so refreshing and uplifting to have even the shortest conversation with him. I felt low again although I was taking short naps, and an hour-long meditation/nap. I had so little live interaction with people. It was hard to help others out, as well as work on developing myself.

I walked to Lee's to be with him, Greg, and Filipe. What fun we had. They seemed like a healthy couple. I wondered at first, but each time I was with them my positive feeling was reinforced. Greg left for the States and Filipe would follow two weeks later. They expressed concern about reentry into Mexico due to the pandemic.

ORDINATION

I had kept constant in my attendance and involvement in church functions throughout the difficult years. This included setting up the patio for social activities, arranging for scripture readers, giving several homilies, and serving on the Vestry Committee which guided the church. Once the pandemic hit, I continued attending via Zoom. Later, when the church was permitted to have a small number of congregants, I attended.

I received a note from our priest, Padre José, saying he would like to meet with me. We met by video call. In the call, he offered me ordination in October as a Permanent Deacon for St. Luke's. Some of the basic functions would be setting up for hospitality, setting the altar, processing in, assisting at the altar, reading the gospel, giving homilies, and covering for him when he was away. The services I would lead would be communion without consecration, in other words, a Liturgy of the Word.

I asked for some time to consider. I was drawn to the possibility but also had concerns about the safety aspect wondering if others were taking the virus as seriously as I was. As I considered, it seemed possible the diaconate might fulfill the spiritual trajectory of my life. Serving as a deacon would be intellectually and spiritually stimulating. I would be doing service which I was not currently doing. Being a deacon might provide an organizing spiritual principle for my life, as well as a sense of identity which I had not had since being a hospital chaplain.

I wrote to Father José about my concerns, and we had a positive discussion. He addressed each concern. I became more comfortable with the idea. Others also would be ordained in October, several as priests and another deacon. We would have some classes, but he felt with all my theological training and life experience, I would be well set. He thanked me for the service I had already given to the church.

I spoke with my recovery sponsor about my fears and concerns. I wondered if the responsibility might be overwhelming. I also feared for my physical safety due to the virus. I was able to get some objective reaction to my fear of being overwhelmed by the position. I also spent time discussing it with my spiritual director from my former Jesuit retreat center. She was very encouraging and excited for me. She emphasized that it would be essential for me to be grounded in a strong spiritual life. She said on-going spiritual direction was a part of that process. I was happy and relieved that she and I would be able to continue spiritual direction through Zoom. This ongoing support felt like another confirmation of my moving forward.

Another step I took was to join a weekly telephone prayer group coming out of Washington, DC. Centering prayer, an ancient monastic meditation renewed by Fr. Thomas Keating, was the focus. The group turned out to be ten elderly women who had been in the practice for many years. What fine spiritual support I found.

The process moved forward. I focused on reading materials drawn from the Roman Catholic tradition. I understood the role of deacon was fundamentally the same in the Roman Catholic and Episcopal traditions. From reading, I felt the depth of spiritual growth offered by the diaconate and wanted to be open to it.

A meeting was set up at church for those to be ordained by the bishop. I was assured that Covid safety measures would be taken. The day came and it was pouring rain when I left home. The streets were flooded. I persevered and arrived soaked up to my knees. In the church patio, tables were set at a distance from each other. Fr. José led us through issues and the process we would be experiencing. All seemed well organized and promising.

Then came time for dinner. Pizza arrived to be shared. Everyone gathered at one table, right beside each other, talking and eating. I was horrified. It seemed completely unsafe. It was too risky to join in, so I left. As I thought about it later that night, I decided I could not continue the process. There would be several more meals and activities before the ordination. They would follow this same pattern. I was sad and demoralized. I was losing that which I felt would add great meaning to my life.

DEPRESSION

Several months passed as I strove to keep my life going under the loss of the diaconate ordination and the cloud of the pandemic. My well-being began to falter. Gradually, over three weeks, I felt myself slipping into a depressive state. In consultation with my psychiatrist, I doubled my Prozac. We then added Cymbalta a week and a half later. After several weeks I thought the Prozac was starting to kick in. I waited for the Cymbalta. It could be up to four weeks for it to take effect.

I managed survival basics with a two-hour nap in the morning or afternoon. My life seemed like a ship in rough seas that could not find its way to safe harbor. I did not feel I could manage human interaction. I was not in touch with recovery or church friends, nor could I do any writing. I wanted to support Fr. José by attending the Zoom services but just could not make myself.

Both Miguel and Joo again encouraged me to do some writing to help deal with the depression. They were such wonderful and concerned friends. I would get fearful if I wrote a What's App to Miguel first thing in the morning and he didn't respond quickly. Fear came so easily. A poem came to me:

Wretched Foe

Fear, what a wretched foe
Planting dark seeds in the garden of my heart
A natural feeling, Hard to know at first
Dark blossoms gradually expressing
Overshadowing the light
Denying life to the gentle good
If watered, growing rapacious
Calling out to each other,
Claiming a majority that can push through,
Cajole, intimidate, deny,
What can withstand this black weed

Light persists in its effort to grow love,
 care, kindness at the core
It instructs to uplift and strengthen
A laugh is instrumental in encouraging
A gentle touch
A kind word
The dark blossom is confounded by such
It is burnt by this light
It takes a recess to reload
But finds its poison has boiled away
And an alien sound, music, has entered the garden

Heavy rain fell for two nights. It was as if heaven was doing my weeping for me. When I went out to walk Victoria, the street was so flooded, it again looked like Venice. Wearing my knee-high rubber boots, we went around the block the other way to get to the park. Hugo, the park kitty, was there and glad to see us. He cried a lot at first and then did his running around Victoria.

I got an email from my friend Jane of the Salvadorian mission. She thanked me for the "Good Things of the Week" program from CNN that I forwarded to her regularly. She was waiting to find out when she would go to Georgetown in DC for the vaccine. She had thrown a marvelous 50th Birthday party for me at her home. What great memories of a dear and wonderful friend.

The depression lasted and lasted. I continued to feel I was barely able to survive. I fixed the simplest food, took Victoria for a brief walk, went to a few Zoom meetings, and occasionally did Zoom church. I read a little and watched HBO, "Game of Thrones." Watching the series was a saving grace when I couldn't read.

I didn't feel better, but I was trying to write. I had my noble beast with me, thank God. Victoria provided me with responsibility, humor, and affection. I still felt a strong draw to sleep. My eyes were so often heavy, feeling pulled down.

Taking action was one solution. Writing was one form of action. Doing simple chores was another. In terms of writing, I was again dwelling in a shadowland.

Lost

I seem to have lost my way
Nothing seems to pay
No energy for the day
One moment driven by internal force
Fully functioning and creative of course
Then nothing seems to matter,
Just the pitter patter of the rain

Having stripped my gears
I reach out to my peers
But can they help, none are seers
Can I make it plain
This empty space inside
I so want to hide

But my gear shift is shot
I feel so caught, must this be my lot
How to explain,
My past comes to haunt me

Can I let it be
Blindfold my instincts of panic and doubt
For I really don't know what it's all about

I focused on cooking for myself. I made a new soup using canned beans, a little can of salsa, cans of vegetables, corn, olives, and onions. Enough was made for three meals. My sponsor who died, John, would have been proud. He said cooking was a way of taking care of oneself. What a lovely human being he was. He died the way I think he would have wanted, on the stage of a recovery program where he was presenting.

I had my usual tiredness but not as bad. I took an early nap for an hour. I was reading and enjoying it. The windows were open. It was cooler and looked like it would rain more. Miguel called to check in. He wanted to make sure I was OK. His call was uplifting.

I finished book three and just started book four of the *Master and Commander* series (eighteen to go). Miguel and I tried to use video for our calls, but his internet connection was not good. It was important for me to have frequent on-going contact with him. Angela, his wife, was starting back to work doing nails and haircuts. She said she would be as careful as possible concerning Covid. Her family and Miguel's family had both been Covid free. I told Miguel I would add her to my prayer list.

Heavy rains made Victoria act out. She was jumping and barking. She was unhappy with everything. I tried holding her, talking to her, playing with her. Running her through the house to tire her out didn't work. I feared the rain would build up and I wouldn't be able to walk her at all. I was also concerned about being able to feed Hugo the park kitty, and the other little cats I fed.

As the weeklong rain cut back, I began coming out of the depression. As I started to feel better, I got a sense of how bad it really had been. I could not appreciate how debilitating the depression was until I was escaping it.

JUAN

The pandemic began easing its death grip. The air in town seemed clearer. The sun seemed brighter. I was no longer alone on the sidewalk. Over the course of the two years the pandemic reigned, I had developed social anxiety. With the help of treatment, I pushed myself to re-activate relations with recovery friends and church friends.

I made an appointment with a recovery friend. It was near San Juan Park, close to my home. I was not familiar with the restaurant she suggested but was excited to find a new place nearby. It only took me about ten minutes to reach the restaurant. I got a seat looking out a window onto the street and was brought a menu. The next thing I knew my friend was walking down the sidewalk past my window. I couldn't call out, so I went running to grab her.

As I rounded the corner I ran into a man. It turned out to be Juan, whom I had known as a waiter for seven years. At that moment, we decided to exchange contact information. I took down his WhatsApp number. I continued to the right restaurant where my friend was and had a nice lunch. When I arrived home, I thought about Juan. He was the final guy I had thought I had potential with. After a couple of days, I wrote to him. We decided to meet on a Monday evening. By Sunday, he had written to say he had to work on Monday, could we set another time. We made it for the following Monday.

Meantime, feeling a lack of personal contact in general, I decided that I should cancel my current commitments on Mondays and Thursdays and start going to the live recovery meetings. Three days before Monday, I realized that I had both a recovery meeting and Juan at the same time. I decided the meeting was more important. I contacted Juan and cancelled.

The next day, I thought about how I was older, the lack of commonality, that he didn't speak English and I with limited Spanish. A similar situation three years earlier led to disaster. I realized it was the darkness in my past calling to me, striving to pull me back into chaos. I saw I did not have to return to it. My recovery had brought me to end this long painful chapter of my life.

ORDINATION ANEW

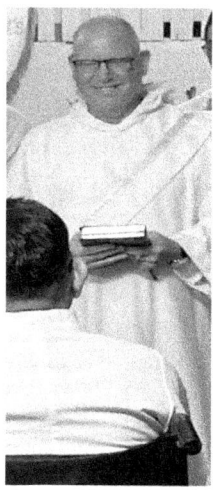

Figure 32 Ordination

There was a notable change at church. The result was a new opportunity for my diaconate ordination. I feared it might fall through again. The possibility had felt so right before. The giving of service to the poor community in the south of Merida felt like a calling. I remembered my earlier excitement and desire. I remembered my father and my grandfather going out into the villages to minister. Maybe it would be possible. I had to be patient and live in the unknown.

The official pandemic strictures eased. Mask requirements relaxed. Plans moved on for the bishop to come and perform the ordinations. I prepared myself as best I could. The day came, we lay at the feet of the bishop and received ordination. The church expressed delight for this new ministry. It was a time of mystery and gratitude. I thanked God for the journey I had been on. I was open to the grace of seeing what more God had planned for me.

Following the desolation and depression of the Pandemic, my life began anew. I found a little kitty I named Alex. For weeks he was living across the street from me under a car. I finally decided to adopt him by grabbing him and chucking him into the foyer. It was a challenge at first for Victoria, but they became good buddies. They hung out together when I was away from the house.

I traveled to England and France. While in England I attended the summer adult education program at Cambridge University. I found it excellent to be with other international students and imbibe in the many presentations and cultural activities. These included giving a Shakespeare sonnet in one class. It was delightful to be upon the stage again. In Paris I returned to my practice of visiting historic sites and churches.

In terms of my faith life, I was able to serve as deacon in both St. Luke's and the mission of Buen Pastor. Giving the Gospel in Spanish at the mission was a special opportunity. How good it was to be in service to the fine adults and children of Buen Pastor.

In my recovery life, for the first time, I took on the role of sponsor to help a new member navigate the beginning of the 12 Steps. There was some good learning in it for me. I also returned to the United States to visit my brothers, my nephew, and his family. It was so good to be with them and share our experiences of the last years.

In terms of this book, by grace, I ran into a neighbor two houses down who said she was not only a writer, but also an editor. She was willing to look at my manuscript and gave me excellent guidance and encouragement. She subsequently suggested the fine publisher of this book who turned out to be her brother. I am most grateful to the communities I am a part of, to dear friends, and to my family, brothers Neal and Paul, and nephew Brendan.

I Yearn for Thee.

I yearn for Thee and trust in Thee
Save me from the foolishness of my own design
My mind strives to put it together
To make sense of it all.
But the only sense is to live as fully as I can
In this day, in these circumstances,
Loving and caring for others as well as for myself.

As the eagle soars towards heaven
So, I yearn to be in the flow of your Spirit
Lifted by your love and compassion
Enthralled by the wonder of your creation

Release me oh God of my myopic vision
Bathe me in the font of your Grace
Which encircles all the earth
That I may know the fullness of your call
And grow in sharing you with all.